The Which? Guide to Counselling and Therapy

About the authors

Mike Brookes is a registered mental nurse and counsellor currently employed as a practice nurse and practice manager within Islington Primary Care Trust, North London. He has previously worked for psychiatric rehabilitation services and as a GP liaison nurse in substance misuse.

Dr Shamil Wanigaratne is consultant clinical psychologist at the South London and Maudsley NHS Trust and is head of clinical psychology of the Trust's addictions division. He is also honorary senior lecturer at the Institute of Psychiatry, Kings College. He has worked as a clinical psychologist in a number of NHS settings and in private practice.

Acknowledgements

A lot of very knowledgeable people have helped in the preparation of this guide. The authors and publishers would especially like to thank Dr Chris Barker, Cath Brookes, Padmal De Silva, Dr Tim Fox, Kathy Fried, Joanna Hanes, Dr Robert Hill, Dr Luke Mitchison, Dr Bill Mitchell, Dr Anula Nikapota, Dr Nancy Pistrang, Gerry Rebuck, Sue Salas, Greg Scott, Jane Scott, Dimitri Sklavounos, Ramona Sterling and Heather Wilson.

Helen Barnett, Sue Freeman and Wendy Garlick at Consumers' Association also contributed to the book.

We are indebted to Robinson Books for permission to reproduce from David Smail's *The Nature of Unhappiness* the 'Possible availability of powers and resources' diagram in Chapter 1.

Dr Chris Barker, Dr Nancy Pistrang and Dr David A. Shapiro kindly gave us permission to reproduce the 'Opinions about psychological problems' questionnaire and key.

The authors would also like to thank the many people with whom they have worked over the years, both clients and colleagues.

The Which? Guide to Counselling and Therapy

Mike Brookes and Shamil Wanigaratne

CONSUMERS' ASSOCIATION

Which? Books are commissioned and researched by
Consumers' Association and published by
Which? Ltd, 2 Marylebone Road, London NW1 4DF
Email address: books@which.net

Distributed by The Penguin Group:
Penguin Books Ltd, 80 Strand, London WC2R 0RL

First edition May 2003

Copyright © 2003 Which? Ltd

British Library Cataloguing in Publication Data
A catalogue record for this book is available from the British Library

ISBN 0 85202 923 3

For a full list of *Which?* books, please write to Which? Books, Castlemead, Gascoyne Way,
Hertford X, SG14 1LH or access our website at www.which.net

Editorial and production: Joanna Bregosz, Liz Hornby, Nithya Rae, Barbara Toft
Original cover concept by Sarah Harmer
Cover photograph: Peter Cade/getty images

Typeset by Saxon Graphics Ltd, Derby
Printed and bound by Creative Print and Design, Wales

Contents

Foreword   7

Introduction   9

Questions to answer before beginning counselling   12

1   Why see a counsellor or therapist?   13

2   The different schools of thought   38

3   Formats for talking treatments and where to go for help   65

4   Mental health services in the NHS   92

5   Common concerns and practical considerations   112

6   Do counselling and therapy work?   138

7   Preparing for your first session   148

8   Troubleshooting   156

9   Safeguards: legal and ethical matters   182

10   Specialist areas of counselling and therapy   197

11   Talking treatments, culture and difference   208

12   Non-talking treatments   221

Appendix I: Clinical diagnosis of psychological problems   237

Appendix II: Opinions about psychological problems:
Questionnaires   245

Appendix III: Opinions about psychological problems:
Key to interpreting results   251

Resources★   257

Index   277

★ An asterisk next to the name of an organisation in the text indicates that the address or website can be found in this section.

Foreword

Whenever I am asked if therapy or counselling is a good thing, the best answer I can muster is that therapy is a bit like marriage.

If you find the right partner then marriage is indeed a wonderful thing, and one of the best decisions you will ever make in your life. But with the wrong spouse, marriage can be an absolute nightmare and will seriously impair your mental health.

Similarly, with therapy, if you discover a talented therapist then the treatment will undoubtedly be a useful enterprise on which to embark. But with a counsellor who doesn't know what he or she is doing, the scientific evidence is that therapy could make you worse off than if you did not go in for it at all.

One of my many criticisms of the world of therapy is that it has done little to educate consumers and assist clients in finding a good clinician, and that it has provided lamentably impoverished advice on what kinds of therapy might be best for particular problems. Worse, little guidance is available on what alternatives to therapy there might be and when to stop therapy.

This last point is vital because although many are suspicious of the side-effects of medication, they forget that therapy has side-effects and adverse reactions as well. Just as it is possible to get addicted to pills so it is possible to become overly dependent on a counsellor.

This worrying lack of information is at last beginning to change with the publication of this important book.

The authors, who are professionals in counselling, have taken a subject which generates manifold opposing passions, and dispassionately dissected the issues in a way that is understandable to anyone, within or outside the field. The book is therefore a welcome addition to the distinguished tradition of Which?, of a balanced and fair approach that has the interests of the consumer at heart.

That Which? Books has entered this arena can only be brilliant news for consumers. For unlike any other goods or service a person might purchase, finding a good therapist or therapy remains one of the thorniest consumer challenges. This is partly because it is practically impossible to obtain a personal recommendation, given the taboo and stigma that still unfairly surrounds mental health issues.

Also, like marriage, it's difficult to shop around first.

But now, at last, the solution is in your hands.

Dr Raj Persaud MSc MPhil MRCPsych
Consultant Psychiatrist and Senior Lecturer
The Maudsley Hospital and Institute of Psychiatry, London
Author of *Staying Sane: How to Make Your Mind Work for You*

Introduction

More people than ever recognise that talking has a lot of potential as a means of dealing with personal problems; not surprisingly, interest in the subject of counselling and therapy has grown remarkably in the UK today. In some ways this is a return to more traditional beliefs, because in the past it was common to deal with distress by taking your troubles to religious representatives or other learned people within the community. But it would seem that changes in Western society during the twentieth century resulted in these older methods being largely abandoned.

However, the renewed enthusiasm for the 'talking treatments' approach to problems has come at a time when there has also been a relative loss of faith in the medical and other care professions. We no longer believe that doctors, nurses and other professionals are incapable of making serious mistakes, or that these people are somehow above the everyday human weaknesses and faults shared by the rest of society. This means that although people may be more likely to opt for discussion with a skilled practitioner as a way of managing their personal and emotional difficulties, they are also likely to be wary of the process. They will not be inclined to accept blindly whatever they are told about their problems or about the process of counselling and therapy itself. In other words, people are now very keen to know what they are getting into when they go to see a practitioner of talking treatments, and usually have a lot of questions to ask about what is involved.

The idea for this guide came from the authors' experience of clients asking precisely these kinds of questions. The difficulty of giving 'sound-bite' answers led them to wish that there was a good information pack that they could give to people. There is no shortage of books on therapy and counselling written for and by professionals, but there is relatively little out there that tries to answer from a British perspective most of the key questions potential users may have. This book seeks to help fill this gap.

The most common questions clients ask about counselling and therapy are:

- do I need therapy?
- what is the best therapy for me?
- how do I prepare for a session and what should I anticipate?
- I've been seeing a therapist for a while, but he (or she) hasn't explained anything – how do I find out more?

The Which? Guide to Counselling and Therapy attempts to answer all these and more. It begins by looking at how we can, and usually do, resolve stress-related problems by using support mechanisms within our families and communities. However, sometimes these resources are not sufficient, and people may find it more helpful talking to a counsellor or therapist. Counselling can deal with a range of issues, from day-to-day concerns, to more serious, long-term psychological problems.

To help you decide whether you need to go to a counsellor for help and which type of counselling is best suited for you, the book discusses (in Chapters 2 to 4) the different approaches to counselling, the theories behind them, the formats they use and what types of conditions they are considered most appropriate for. Working through the questionnaire in Appendix II and using the key in Appendix III can also help you choose the therapy that is best suited for you. The book also tells you how you can access such help and even how to prepare for your first meeting with a therapist.

Two chapters (5 and 8) are devoted to addressing concerns you may have about the process or the therapist, and Chapter 9 tells you what your rights as a client of counselling are. If you are a parent or guardian of a child who needs counselling or if you have an addiction of some sort, Chapter 10 will point you in the right direction, as it deals with specialist areas of counselling and therapy. Chapter 11 covers cultural differences and how to find the best type of practitioner for you, and Chapter 12 looks at more alternatives to counselling.

This book has two overriding aims. The first is to help make people aware of the potential pitfalls of seeking out a practitioner of talking treatments. Although many professional organisations in the UK provide guidelines on training and working practices in the field of counselling and therapy, membership of these bodies and adherence to those guidelines is not at this time compulsory. This means that you might be unfortunate enough to meet a practitioner who has not met any recognised standard of training or achieved any real measure of skill, and whose work is not reviewed or overseen by anyone of competent status. Although you should be able to trust staff employed by big organisations such as the NHS and social services, it is wise never to take a practitioner's abilities for granted. Legislation is being considered by the UK government to provide for the compulsory regulation of the counselling and psychotherapy professions. Until this becomes law, this guide will help to show you what questions to ask to guarantee that the practitioner that you are seeing is capable, ethical and knowledgeable about the work that he or she is doing.

Second, the book seeks to help people to get the most from engaging in an episode of counselling or therapy. Reading this guide should make you more confident about the process of seeking out support, and more able to obtain what you need from the many choices that are available to you.

Questions to answer before beginning counselling or therapy

Points to consider	Refer to
Do you have a problem that warrants help?	Chapter 1
What are the alternatives to talking treatments?	Chapters 1 &12
What talking approaches are available for your problem?	Chapters 2 & 3
What evidence is there that a particular approach might help?	Chapter 6
How do you go about getting counselling or therapy?	Chapter 3
What talking treatments can you get from the NHS?	Chapters 3 & 4
What are the costs of private therapy?	Chapter 3
What happens at the first session?	Chapter 7
What are the most common pitfalls and problems?	Chapters 5 & 8
How do you evaluate whether counselling is helping you?	Chapters 7 & 8
What safeguards are in place?	Chapter 9
What kind of specialist help is available?	Chapter 10
Do talking treatments take account of cultural differences?	Chapter 11

Chapter 1

Why see a counsellor or therapist?

The world we live in grows more complex every day. Western countries have undergone massive economic and technological development in the last century, and although this has improved life for many people, it has also increased the pressure on them. Psychological pressure, or stress, can arise from trying to be successful or keeping up with others, or by feeling left out.

Pressures of modern life

Despite the fact that the UK is believed to be the fourth richest country in the world, a significant proportion of the British population still lives below the United Nations' poverty level. Even for people above the poverty level, life is often a struggle to get by in a world that seems dominated by material goods and the sense of the advantages of wealth. This experience is sometimes called disenfranchisement or social exclusion. Stress arising out of lack of money often contributes to personal problems and in some cases gives rise to a state of 'learnt helplessness', in which we feel that it is impossible to make positive changes because the cards are stacked too heavily against us.

These days we seem to believe that people should be strong, confident, happy, attractive, sexually fulfilled, have settled families, and be working towards achieving their full potential. If we do not meet these aims – many of which are to do with money and belongings – we experience stress because we have not fulfilled our expectations of ourselves. In some parts of the UK, entire communities are in this state, because two or three generations have experienced unemployment – may never have worked – and have never been able to achieve any of the goals demanded by this kind of thinking.

There are many ways to re-evaluate your life and counteract the pressure from society and the media to chase what may be an illusion of happiness. Professional counselling and therapy are not the only means of examining your situation and changing your life. Self-help is available in the form of books and audio and computer products, some of which are excellent; or you may find the help you need by talking to an untrained but sympathetic person. Some of these options are discussed later in this chapter. In addition, Chapter 12 explores other alternatives such as art therapy. At the end of the book you will find a Resources section with further information on a range of resources including self-help manuals, website addresses, and specialist organisations focusing on specific problems.

Stressful events, and your resources

Stress, in the form of life events, affects everyone at some time. We can't avoid bad things happening to us, and we will react to these events with sadness, confusion, rage, or perhaps enter a state of shock and feel utterly miserable. These are all normal emotional responses. They are not necessarily 'psychological problems' or symptoms of 'mental illness'.

The resources you have (the positive things going on in your life, as illustrated in the diagram of your 'power map') will determine how you cope with the pain of negative life events. How you cope can also be affected by other factors such as childhood experiences, and, of course, by any support you receive.

In the 'power map' model, resources equal the power to manage distress. If we imagine this as a cake, the more slices of the cake you have, the more power you possess and the more you are protected from developing psychological problems.

Your resources fall into four main areas.

- **Material** resources such as having money, having a job, being literate and well educated, and having your own space to live in.
- **Personal** resources such as intelligence, confidence, and the insight (deep personal knowledge) that comes from understanding the past. The term 'embodiment' is used to describe physical attributes like strength, good looks and good

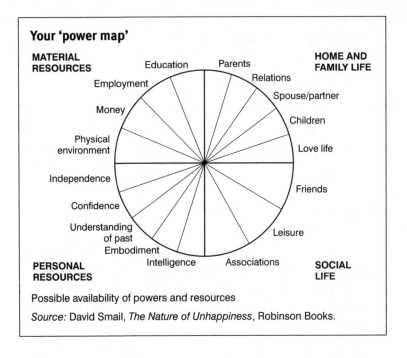

Your 'power map'

MATERIAL RESOURCES

HOME AND FAMILY LIFE

Education

Parents

Employment

Relations

Money

Spouse/partner

Physical environment

Children

Independence

Love life

Confidence

Friends

Understanding of past

Leisure

Embodiment

Intelligence

Associations

PERSONAL RESOURCES

SOCIAL LIFE

Possible availability of powers and resources

Source: David Smail, *The Nature of Unhappiness*, Robinson Books.

health. Having ambition and motivation – the desire to improve oneself – is also seen as a personal resource.

- **Home and family** resources include parents, a partner and a love life, children and relatives.
- **Social life**, as a resource, includes having friends, having hobbies and leisure activities, and belonging to clubs, societies and associations.

Having more slices of the cake can cushion you from the effects of stress and may contribute to the feeling of well-being that we call happiness. Perhaps in specific cultures or sections of society these resources would be defined differently or be arranged in different orders of importance. But in any event, making an assessment of what slices of your personal cake are missing can help you to take steps to fill in the gaps.

Counselling and therapy could help you to identify the gaps clearly and work towards obtaining what's missing, but there are other ways of doing this, too. With good resources and support, your experience of distress should be reduced over time and you should begin to feel and act as you did before the stressful event that caused it. This does not necessarily mean that all negative emotions will be wiped out, but it does mean that your experience of negative emotions will be sufficiently reduced for you to get by and overcome the worst effects of the stress.

These issues do not affect only adults, but can easily relate to children and adolescents as well. Further information about working with young people can be found in Chapter 10, but this entire guide should be seen as relevant to people of all ages.

What are the effects of stress?

It is not easy to find a satisfactory umbrella term for the different ways we may feel when faced with major stresses. Whatever the language used – terms such as human misery, psychological distress, despair, psychic pain, psychological and psychiatric symptoms – we are talking about emotional, psychological and spiritual experiences that can be seen as reactions to what is broadly termed 'stress'.

We all experience distress in everyday life. Continuous distress arising from a life event, or from other causes such as the absence of resources and support, may result in some individuals developing more marked psychological reactions which, if not tackled early on, may become more serious. Sometimes these chronic problems result in people finding that they cannot function in their role in society, and this is often referred to as a breakdown; such more extreme problems are discussed in Chapter 4. Often the way to avoid this is to recognise when we are in pain, and ask for the assistance that we need.

The effects of stress can take many forms, both physical and mental, and can include any or all of the following symptoms:

- headaches
- tiredness and sleeplessness
- inability to concentrate
- reduced appetite
- irritability
- sexual problems or lack of sexual interest
- palpitations
- panic attacks

- stomach disturbances
- loss of confidence
- reduced resistance to physical illness.

When to look for help

Different people have different thresholds for managing their personal difficulties. In Western society it is often thought of as admirable to be silent and uncomplaining; admitting that you are in need and are finding it difficult or even impossible to manage your daily life can be seen as a sign of weakness. In many ways this belief is simply wrong, and we might deal much better with our own problems and those of other people if we were more willing to accept that everyone suffers from stress, disappointments and loss. This guide promotes the idea that asking for support is a good thing, and that 'talking treatments' such as counselling and psychotherapy are a useful (perhaps essential) tool in the modern world. Definitions of counselling and psychotherapy are introduced towards the end of this chapter.

There are, however, other approaches that you may want to consider before starting to look for a professional approach to talking over your problems.

Alternatives to counselling and psychotherapy

Friends and family

Most people, when distressed, will talk to a friend, partner, member of their family, or colleague. Research has shown that having at least one confiding relationship tends to protect your mental health and is a major factor in determining whether you are at risk of developing greater psychological problems.

Sometimes, however, the source of distress or the nature of the problem means you do not want to discuss it with your family or friends. This can give rise to a situation where you have to 'bottle things up' and try to deal with it yourself. Increasingly, and for various reasons, people find themselves isolated and lacking close, confiding friendships or relationships. This is especially the case when they have moved away from home for employment reasons. Making friends or developing what is called a 'support network' is not always easy in unfamiliar places, particularly big cities. Isolated individuals often have no option but to bottle up their feelings when distressed, so they become vulnerable to worse problems and may later have to seek professional help.

Clergy

One way of getting support if you do not have family or close friends is to make use of what can be broadly termed 'pastoral care'. Depending on your religion or preference, finding a church, mosque, synagogue or temple near you and asking to talk to the vicar, priest or imam is an option open to you. Christian pastoral care is available almost anywhere in the UK, although the presence of other religious support may depend on the area you live in. A member of the clergy will always be pleased to talk to you and advise if professional help is needed. This resource is often not used by the public, perhaps because people are afraid of being judged or fear attempts at religious conversion. In smaller communities such as rural parishes, people may be reluctant to seek help from local clergy because they are well known to them, and they worry about confidentiality. In such situations, the solution may be to seek help from a priest or a member of the clergy from a neighbouring area.

Community leaders and elders

In some communities, including those of some ethnic minorities, there may be community leaders or elders that people can go to for advice and guidance. Approaching these people may be preferable to consulting a religious representative. But talking to someone in his or her own community may, equally, be the last thing a person wants to do when experiencing difficulties, because of the possible loss of face.

Self-help groups and organisations

Self-help groups and self-help organisations have experienced a huge increase in both popularity and number since the 1970s. This is clearly a response to a need in our modern society. Alcoholics Anonymous (AA) was one of the first, and is probably the best known, of the self-help groups. In the USA there are many self-help groups based on the AA model that address a variety of problems and issues, and some of these groups also function in the UK. Self-help organisations and groups can offer support around personal issues like sexuality, anxiety, bereavement and other difficulties. For many people, assistance from self-help groups and organisations is not only an alternative to therapy, but may be the only help they need to overcome a particular difficulty.

Telephone helplines

When in distress or in need of guidance, the need to talk can be overpowering. An anonymous listener at the other end of a phone can be an ideal solution. The Samaritans are probably the best-known telephone helpline in the world, and many people owe their life to this organisation. Most self-help agencies also run telephone helplines with experienced staff or volunteers available to provide invaluable help for callers. They also act as a resource for information on how to obtain further assistance.

Self-help manuals

Many people wish to search for the information which will help them make positive changes in their lives. Self-help publications have become a first step for many individuals in getting the advice they need, and a good self-help manual is often seen as adequate to overcome difficulties. There are hundreds of self-help manuals available in shops and on the Internet, and the Resources section lists a few. Before contemplating counselling or therapy it is a good idea to explore self-help in this form, which is also known as 'bibliotherapy'.

But there are also limitations to this approach. Many manuals are broad and general in their coverage and may not be specific to the problems you are having. Getting hold of a publication that deals with your specific problems may require several trips to bookshops and buying a lot of books.

Self-help cassettes and CDs

There are many self-help audio tapes and CDs on the market. These products are not only helpful for those who have reading difficulties but have many advantages including the chance to follow instructions and act out exercises (as with relaxation tapes). The voice of the therapist on a tape can become a familiar calming and inspirational influence. These products can also be listened to anywhere, for example when driving a car or sitting on a train or plane, and this makes them particularly versatile and user-friendly.

Self-help CD-ROMs

New computer technology has enabled another interactive form of self-help for psychological problems – CD-ROMs. This medium is particularly useful in delivering structured interventions, by getting you to follow a step-by-step programme from a therapist. The CD-ROM enables you to follow the programme at your own pace and has the capacity to give you limited feedback when you are making progress. This kind of reinforcement of your actions gives the medium an advantage over self-help manuals and tapes. Two good examples are the CD-ROM entitled *Restoring the Balance* produced by the Mental Health Foundation* for those with mild to moderate anxiety and depression, and the CD-ROM called *Beating the Blues* produced by the Institute of Psychiatry* for those with depression. Information about other products can be found on some of the websites listed at the end of this book in the Resources section.

The Internet

The Internet offers a world of help to its users. Health and mental health websites contain cutting-edge information that you can access in a matter of seconds. If information is power, then having access to the Internet is very empowering indeed: type a key word into a search engine, and you may well find the necessary help to overcome a wide range of difficulties. Some useful UK website addresses are included at the end of this book. Increasingly, a lot of information is produced specifically for the Internet, leaving non-Internet users at a real disadvantage.

Using the Net makes it easier for people to obtain not only self-help manuals but also individualised help. This could be in the form of individualised manuals compiled for you based on your responses to an assessment questionnaire, or even real-time consultations with a clinician. This is referred to as 'e-therapy'. Do not trust all the information you find on the Internet, however, since much of it is inaccurate. A selection of well-researched and reputable websites is listed at the end of this book.

Other alternatives

Other approaches to managing personal problems include the use of medication, complementary remedies, body work such as massage and aromatherapy, religious and spiritual ways of promoting healing, and what are sometimes termed self-improvement activities. Your own beliefs and attitudes will probably determine which of these seem useful and which would not work for you, but these other treatments are significant additions to the ever-growing 'menu' available to us. They will be considered in more detail in Chapter 12.

Identifying the problem

If you have tried any of the above approaches and still feel distressed and unhappy, it may be time to consider whether a talking treatment is the right approach for you. Sometimes the key to whether counselling or therapy will help is indicated by a combination of the nature of the problem you are experiencing and your general beliefs as to what will lead to positive change.

Examples of problems

A A 16-year-old boy feels very pressured by forthcoming examinations, and is finding it difficult to sleep. His appetite has disappeared, and he has been avoiding friends for the last two weeks. His exams will be over in around a month's time.

B A woman of 83 has recently lost her husband of more than 50 years, following a long illness. She says she is unable to cope with housework and other practical issues alone, and is often tearful and despairing about the future.

C A 51-year-old man is made redundant after 20 years at the same firm and believes that he is now unemployable. His relationship with his wife is suffering because, as he admits, he is continuously angry and dismissive of other people's problems.

D A woman of 46 finds herself in increasing trouble: she is drinking heavily most evenings and has mounting debts because so much of her income is spent on alcohol. Her partner has told her to 'get her life together' or he will leave her.

E A 33-year-old man has been wanting to settle down into a long-term relationship but finds himself scared to commit to any of the several girlfriends that he has had in the last five years. He relates this to an unsettled childhood, and has a similar difficulty in maintaining interest in career or leisure interests, seeming to need the excitement of new challenges at regular intervals. He doesn't know how to reconcile his conflicting desires for long-term commitment and regular change.

F A woman aged 42 has recently become divorced from her third husband, and is primary carer for four children aged between 6 and 17. She believes that she has sabotaged all of these relationships and is stuck in a cycle of emotional pain that she sees as eerily similar to that of her own mother, who twice married abusive men and was emotionally distant from her own children.

G A 37-year-old man is diagnosed with an inoperable brain tumour, and has been told he has, at most, a year to live. He is devastated at the thought that he will not see his two young daughters grow up and that none of his plans for the future will now be realised.

H A woman aged 19 is sexually assaulted by a neighbour and, after pressing charges which lead to the assailant being sentenced to a long term in prison, she continues to feel vulnerable and panicky, and partly blames herself for what happened.

I A 27-year-old man who has always known that he was adopted decides that he wants to find out about his birth parents. When he finally locates his mother, he feels totally rejected when he is told that she has no interest in further contact with him because he was a mistake that she has worked very hard to forget.

J A 22-year-old woman who has previously had romantic and sexual feelings only for men now believes that she is a lesbian, and is frightened that her family, friends and religious community will reject her. The situation leads her to consider whether this means she has to redefine her aims in life.

All these situations have a basic similarity in that they concern an individual in pain, feeling confused and wanting this to change. But otherwise they are very different: some of the problems encountered are short lived, whereas others relate to behaviours or events that have lasted over many years. Some are in response to a specific event, and some have no clear or identified cause. A few are likely to change simply by the passage of time, but most appear likely to continue unless they are made to go away. Most deal with situations that can be worked with and changed, but some are the result of situations that are inevitable or beyond repair. And some seem 'worse' than others, although it is easy to see how any of these situations could be very difficult to live through.

Human experience does not lend itself to broad generalisations, because we are all unique, and we live in unique situations and lead unique lives. Consequently, it is hardly surprising that our emotional and psychological responses vary enormously, even when different individuals are faced with similar stresses or traumatic events. However, simply saying that each of us is different, so that we can't really talk about 'common' problems or 'typical' situations, is not much help. We have to find some way of communicating about the kinds of difficulties we may encounter and what we can do about them. This doesn't mean that the issue of difference has gone away – in fact, the ways in which one person, social grouping or culture may differ from others is referred to repeatedly in the following chapters.

Ways of identifying the problem

There are at least five possible ways of looking at, and understanding, psychological problems:

- by making a diagnosis
- by identifying behaviour patterns
- by looking at psychological development
- by identifying a traumatic event
- by identifying 'spiritual' concerns.

Examples A to J above can be used to illustrate these five approaches.

1 Diagnosis

A diagnosis is a medical assessment of a problem and the giving of a useful label to that problem that tells us something about it. The problem may be a disease with a clear cause, course, and signs and symptoms to be observed, as in measles or 'flu; or it may be less specific and open to a number of different interpretations, as with a rash or a headache. Most people's psychological difficulties can be diagnosed under one of two main types:

- **depression** – a state of unhappiness associated with low energy, low self-esteem and self-worth, the belief that things are unlikely to improve soon (if at all), and perhaps tearfulness and slowed-down mental and physical responses

23

- **anxiety** – where the person feels 'on edge' all the time, tends to panic, has increasingly negative expectations of life, has obsessive or repetitive thoughts, suffers from poor sleep, and has racing or over-stimulated mind.

These problems are also frequently encountered together, with alternating or combined symptoms, in what is usually referred to as *agitated depression*. We are all likely to experience these feelings at some time in our lives. Other diagnoses are used to describe common psychological problems: for instance, 'phobia' or 'obsessive compulsive disorder', which are explained in more detail in Chapter 4. Of the scenarios listed above, Example A is a clear example of anxiety, and Example B of depression; several others could be said also to fit these definitions in a broad sense.

Many practitioners of counselling and therapy do not accept that feeling sad or agitated, however severely, is a type of illness, and prefer to see these experiences as a normal – although deeply distressing – part of human existence (indeed, of human development). In other words, the problem may need to be addressed and an attempt made to drive it away, but this does not mean that there is anything 'wrong' with the sufferer, just that the person is in need of support and of having his or her feelings acknowledged. This is a very credible position to take, although it is fair to say that even if depression and anxiety are not illnesses themselves, they can certainly lead to illness and dysfunction. Prolonged lack of sleep, poor appetite and constant worry can eventually become life-threatening if unchecked.

Although it is certainly not the only way to look at personal difficulties, diagnosis is very important in the healthcare system of the UK, not least because shorthand labels like 'depression' and 'anxiety' save time and make it easier to talk about problems. 'Depression' is much quicker to say than the lengthier definition given above. But it is important to remember that a diagnosis is only a label, not a solution for the problems to which it refers, and sometimes these labels are not very clear or very specific. Diagnostic terms will be used on many occasions in this guide, because they happen to be the most popular kind of labels used in the UK today to describe personal problems.

More on diagnosis can be found in Appendix I.

2 Behaviour

Another approach is to look at difficulties as being outwardly visible, because they lead to strange or exaggerated or problematic behaviours. Examples C and D might be seen in this way, where uncontrolled anger and excessive drinking have become the source of significant complications on a daily basis, both for the individuals themselves and for the people around them. Often the behaviour itself is unremarkable – losing one's temper or having a drink are acceptable in most cultures, and do not in themselves indicate any real issues to be resolved. But the degree of distress caused and the sense of being out of control that a person may experience are the signs that support is needed. A means of changing behaviour must be found if the resulting feelings of unhappiness, or painful consequences, are to be avoided in the long term.

Sometimes behaviours are best understood as lifestyle issues, and just how serious a problem they are can be assessed by looking at how central a place they have within our daily routines. Alcohol use is a good example of this: if too much of our time and energy is being devoted to worrying about where the next drink is coming from, so that most of the important aspects of our lives – such as work, leisure and relationships – are suffering, it would seem clear that the behaviour has reached a crisis level. This can be true for a lot of otherwise normal activities like eating, sex, gambling, and even going to the gym or the shops. Any problematic behaviour that is becoming part of our regular lifestyle can be seen as an outward expression of inner troubles that may require some attention to make them go away.

3 Psychological development

Another, and in some ways more complex, way of understanding our personal issues is to see our common mistakes and flaws as signs of being psychologically 'stuck' in some process or at some point in the past. Examples E and F above are situations where individuals link their present experience to things that have previously happened to them and wonder what this says about them, or how the pattern can be changed. Looked at from a slightly different angle, the consequences of these events could be said to have become aspects of their personalities. A particular worry or tendency may start out as only an annoyance; but if it persists over months or years, it can almost turn into a part of who we are, even though it is very probably unwelcome and not something with which we are comfortable. If we also come to hate this part of our personality, we may be doubly stuck in a cycle of negativity, hating who we are and hating ourselves because we cannot change it.

'Personality' is actually a very difficult thing to define adequately. It is the sum total of all the things that make us into a unique individual: our physical and mental qualities, our memories, our beliefs and attitudes, our skills and personal strengths, and a great deal more besides. Many psychologists believe that personality is formed by processes of development that we undergo from birth (or even before birth, when we are still in the womb). Passing through these processes is a learning curve that gives us the tools we need to interpret life and other people. By this logic, a particularly difficult experience at any stage of our development can lead to 'incomplete' passage through that stage, and leave us trapped or at least troubled by the issues concerned. It certainly makes sense that what happens to us as children or young adults can have many consequences in later life, because it is in those early years that we are learning who we are and how to deal with the things that happen to us. We are also observing how other people behave and perhaps deciding if they will be role models for us, giving us an example of how we should conduct ourselves. And it is fair to say that long-standing problems that develop in this way are likely to require some real working at before they will go away.

4 Trauma

Just as past events can be a cause of ongoing pain or distress, so too can a recent event. Examples G and H above are examples of a specific trigger leading to huge suffering and confusion. Often this is made worse by the all-too-understandable desire to somehow rewrite history and 'undo' the circumstances in which one finds oneself, or to discover an explanation for what has happened that makes it seem less destructive or terrifying. The concept of 'post-traumatic stress disorder' has entered public consciousness because of the frequency with which the media and health professionals use the term. But whether one chooses to see trauma as a very distinct and specific diagnosis, or instead as a fairly loose and general label that describes a wide range of experiences, is perhaps unimportant.

It is obvious that people have undergone sudden and devastating responses to painful events since the dawn of humanity, not just since this term became popular.

The need to somehow deal with a new reality, however unfair or tragic it may seem to the individual concerned, is also referred to as an *adjustment reaction*. Sometimes, depending on the circumstances, these adjustments cannot be made easily – they may not even be possible at all. In such cases, the effects can become long term, moving well beyond the traumatic occurrence itself and becoming a lasting issue for the individual affected. In this respect, the boundary between trauma and personality-shaping events, as described in section 3 above, is not always clear. In situations such as Example G, where the trigger is the sudden knowledge of an incurable illness, the idea of long-term adjustment is irrelevant; but this only means that the struggle to find answers is more urgent and perhaps even more important. The individual can choose to deny or ignore this knowledge, but he or she cannot choose to deal with it later. We do not always have the time we may need to look for the answers we want.

5 Spiritual beliefs

The word 'spiritual', in our society, has come to be largely associated with religion. In the field of counselling and psychotherapy, however, it usually has a broader meaning. Spiritual concerns could be matters of identity or our feelings about the larger issues – the meaning of life and personal existence – whether or not these involve specific religious beliefs. Examples I and J above are not primarily concerned with issues of faith, although organised religion may certainly shape the way in which the people described deal with their situations. But they are examples of problems that relate to self-definition, our place within the scheme of things and how we fit in with the people who are important to us. As such, these cases could be seen as being as much about philosophical questions as about practical worries. This does not mean that they are somehow removed from daily experience: these examples are very much concerned with what is happening in the here-and-now. But they also relate to bigger and more basic concerns for the people involved, and are not only about the present moment.

The decisions we make about who we are and what we believe, and the way in which we deal with the reactions of other people to the conclusions that we reach, are of huge importance. We can find either major stress or (just as importantly) real peace of mind at the end of this process. This being so, we will often need help in living through these highly personal debates and emerging on the other side with the ability to celebrate ourselves and our decisions. Counselling and therapy can be a very useful means of finding a context for these periods of internal struggle and the opportunities for growth that they bring.

Summary

The following table summarises the five different models listed above for looking at personal problems. They are not, by any means, the only perspectives available; there are other ways of understanding human experience, and so differences of opinion about what causes suffering are possible. Most of the cases described in Examples A to J can be explained from several of these perspectives and, arguably, from all of them. It should be emphasised that these

Five ways of looking at our experiences

	Cause of problem	Evidence	Likely solution
Diagnosis	Unwanted and distressing feelings, e.g. depression	Signs and symptoms	Extinguish signs and symptoms
Behaviour	Destructive consequences of daily routines, e.g. excessive drinking	Repetitive actions	Change behaviours
Psychological development	Past events, especially in early life, e.g. separation anxiety	Life patterns and recurring situations	Break patterns and change situation
Trauma	Recent events, e.g. assault	Struggle to accept or understand events	Gain greater understanding and put events into acceptable context
Spiritual beliefs	Unanswered questions about major personal beliefs, e.g. sexual identity	Inability to define the meaning or purpose of one's situation	Consider beliefs and find greater awareness of self and situation

ideas do not have to be in competition with each other. They may be complementary or parallel, existing quite comfortably side-by-side. Only the most dogmatic person would insist that any one model is always the best way to look at a given problem or set of problems. The counselling and therapy world contains many different viewpoints, and it is usually up to the individual seeking help to decide what ideas make the most sense to them, and so what kind of help they should seek. To help you in this decision, Chapters 2 and 3 examine different types of therapy, and Chapter 6 and Appendix I give some guidance on the effectiveness of different therapies for different kinds of problem.

Levels of distress

One final but useful guide when seeking counselling or therapy is to consider the level at which the problem seems to be located. This is summarised in the following table.

Locating distress

Level of problem	Likely consequences	Examples
Surface	Short-lived stress or disturbance	Pressure at work, ending a relationship, financial worries
Deeper	Periodic or ongoing problems in an area or areas of daily life	Negative family relationships, trouble with managing anger, regular low mood
Core	Constant and chronic pain or suffering that relates to critical unresolved issues	Permanent self-esteem issues, long-lasting addictions, inability to form relationships

Sometimes we may mistakenly see 'surface' problems as being less worthy of attention than deeper issues, and think we will be able to manage them quickly and without help. Although this may be the case, this assumption could be a serious mistake because it confuses level with intensity. All the examples of surface problems above can lead to suicide (and have done so), and so should most definitely not be taken lightly. On the other hand, core issues are often so familiar and so much a part of the individual that instead of leading to despair, they just give rise to a dull sense of resignation. The depth of an issue does not indicate its seriousness but is instead a sign of how complicated it is, and may be an indicator of what kind of change is to be looked for and what kind of help is needed. Sometimes a single rapid shift will rid us of a surface problem. Deeper and core issues may need more work, but they may also seem less like a crisis, and more like an area for personal growth. It is also worth pointing out that a surface issue that goes unattended can work its way deeper into us and very easily become a chronic problem. This is discussed in Chapter 4, when more will be said about the way that clear boundaries between personal problems and what we call 'mental illness' are often difficult to find.

Why treat psychological problems by talking?

So far, this chapter has gone some way to explaining the kinds of psychological problems people can experience. Chapter 4 and Appendix I examine types of problem in much more detail. But why is *talking* seen as a good way of dealing with these problems?

Talking is one of the most basic of human activities. We engage in talk for many different reasons: to share information, to obtain a response, to provide entertainment. It is a highly practical skill, and where absent because of disability or other circumstances, alternatives like sign language develop to fill the gap, because the need to communicate is pretty much universal. In our daily lives, a great deal is dependent on how we use words and what particular tone or manner we use to deliver them. Talking is the medium through which most of our achievements are planned, worked at, and realised.

Discussing a problem, and extending this to giving support and offering understanding through conversation, is probably as old as language itself. It is a much more recent idea for trained practitioners to use formal and consistent frameworks to identify, analyse and deal with personal difficulties. Probably the first significant attempt to create a means of explaining human behaviour and experience, and to apply this within an organised approach to conversation, dates back not much more than a century.

Of course, philosophy, religion and politics have existed for much longer than that, and have often been used as frameworks within which to seek answers and a way forward when in trouble. But we would probably not recognise even the most structured kinds of help from those sources as being the same as counselling and therapy as we understand them today. A talking therapy is not just talking with someone about a difficulty – that can be carried out by anyone, for better or worse. Neither is it someone using a personal agenda or belief system to explain what is wrong with someone else's life, and feeling smug and superior about doing so. To understand what it is, rather than what it is not, it is useful to know something of how the practice emerged.

A brief history

The nineteenth century was a time of great social and technological change within Western societies. Within the academic world, while religion continued to hold a very powerful position, there was also an increased sense of looking for concrete and 'provable' answers to the great questions of the day. For many people, it was no longer satisfactory to debate the meaning of life and the nature of human experience purely in terms of 'holy mystery' or abstract ideas. Instead there were attempts to look at the complicated questions of why people behaved in the way they did and how they developed intellectually and emotionally, and to provide answers that were scientific, rational, or that could in some way be proved by experimental methods.

Many theories dating from that time seem strange to us in the twenty-first century, based as they often were on social and political situations that no longer apply, and attitudes that no longer exist. But they are still significant because they laid the foundations for the first major figures in this field – people like Freud, Breuer and Jung.

From out of this desire to understand people from a different and more scientific perspective came another important idea. It became a common belief that a minority of people suffered, or were incapable of 'normal' functioning, because they had somehow deviated from the expected type of development described within these new theories, meaning that they managed their lives in ways harmful to themselves or others. If the particular nature of these deviations could be discovered, it might be possible to assist these troubled individuals in correcting the flaws in their characters or thinking.

And so along with the enthusiasm of a new science came the will and the energy to use its findings in an organised way to help other people.

Methods for achieving this began to emerge, all based upon the idea of meeting in a particular kind of setting, and using particular kinds of language and techniques of listening and talking to accomplish the task. Consequently, as far back as the first decade of the twentieth century, sessions of structured conversation between a practitioner and a client were taking place that are the clear forerunners of today's counselling and psychotherapy. These methods were the first steps in the development of psychoanalysis and analytical psychology; after more than a hundred years of experience and learning, they are still being practised today and continue to evolve. Chapter 2 examines this history in more detail.

What are counselling and therapy?

A discussion with a friend, colleague or priest is not the same as a session with a counsellor or therapist. A great deal of the confusion underlying this whole area may be because of the more recent preference for the term 'counsellor' to mean any kind of individual who offers support and works towards solutions with a person who has a problem. We are bombarded with counsellors these days: there are mortgage counsellors, fashion counsellors, debt counsellors and many other people who use the word to describe themselves. Almost anyone who talks with others as part of his or her job or role may refer to these conversations as 'counselling'. This is not only misleading to someone seeking help for a psychological problem, but it can be dangerous, in that it can lead to false expectations. Why has this particular word gained so wide a usage and so broad a meaning?

The use of the term 'counselling' within the care professions can partly be accounted for by a desire on the part of practitioners to distance themselves from the idea that they are providing 'psychotherapy' (the previously most commonly used generic label); this is because the word 'therapy' is used in the medical context, and a need for therapy might be thought to imply that someone is 'ill'. As shown above, using medical diagnosis is not the only way to look at personal problems, even if it is very popular. In the second half of the twentieth century, it was felt more and more that being unhappy or frustrated or wanting personal change was not the same as experiencing 'illness', and so, over time, the terminology began to change.

But in many ways 'counselling' was a poor choice as an alternative to 'psychotherapy' because to 'counsel' literally means to give advice and share wisdom. This is what debt counsellors do. But in the field of psychotherapy these are things that counsellors and therapists are usually advised *not* to do. In fact, the professional code of conduct of the British Association for Counselling and Psychotherapy★ goes so far as to state that counsellors do not generally give advice, and clearly implies that their relationship with a client is about offering the chance for discussion rather than the giving of instructions.

The practitioners described in this guide as 'counsellors' or 'therapists' are those who work from a clear and structured school of psychological and developmental thought, specifically towards relieving distress and/or aiming at positive change. While they should be skilled in their work, they are not experts who tell their clients what to do; nor are they merely advice workers handing out useful information, although that may be part of their overall role. In this guide, a 'counsellor' or 'therapist' is someone who is trained and/or highly experienced in his or her work, and the word 'counselling' is used to describe the work of such a professional.

This definition certainly does not intend to condemn the work or achievements of people who fall outside its scope, but it does draw a distinction between counselling as a professional discipline and, for instance, helpful opinions or emotional support given by friends or relatives. It also means that someone you talk to for financial advice or to improve your dress sense is not the type of counsellor that is being discussed in this guide.

Are counselling and psychotherapy the same thing?

This question is not easy to answer. In the sense that the description given above for 'counselling' could largely be used unchanged for 'psychotherapy', then yes, they mean the same thing. But many psychotherapists would deeply object to being called a counsellor (and vice versa). Different schools of counselling and therapy have strong opinions on their methods of working, and equally strong opinions on their professional titles and what these imply about their practice. Within the counselling and therapy world, the labels are considered highly significant. Exactly how significant they really are depends on a number of variables such as length of contact with the client, depth and breadth of therapy on offer, and the underlying philosophy.

It is impossible to summarise all of these differences easily, although Chapter 2 gives some guidance on the many kinds of talking treatments that are currently available. However, the different ways of working fall within the three main schools listed below, and there is some, though no absolute, link between these groupings and the labels used by practitioners.

- The first major school is the **psychodynamic approach**, and people working in this manner are usually called psychotherapists or psychoanalysts.
- The second major school is the **cognitive behavioural approach**, largely practised by clinical psychologists.
- The third is the **humanistic approach**, usually practised by counsellors.

Unfortunately, the above divisions are a generalisation, and by no means take account of the labels as used by all practitioners to describe their work. People may refer to themselves as a psycho-dynamic counsellor, for instance, or as a humanistic psychotherapist, or as a counselling psychologist. A counsellor may prefer cognitive behavioural techniques to the humanistic approach, and a psychologist could also be a qualified psychoanalyst. This overlap makes these terms almost redundant, and the current popularity of eclectic or integrative approaches (where different schools are combined to meet client needs) means that the boundaries are blurred even more.

The confusion over labels can be a major difficulty for the person who simply wants to find help with a problem. Fortunately, the quality of work done by a specific professional is not undermined by the often hotly contested debate over labelling. Some people do not really care what they are called, and may refer to themselves at times both as a counsellor and as a therapist. This may show a more pragmatic approach, but does not necessarily clarify the situation for the individual seeking help. It should also be acknowledged that some professional titles, such as 'psychologist' and 'psychoanalyst', should be used only by people who belong to the appropriate professional bodies within the UK. This is not yet the case for 'counsellors' or 'psychotherapists'. However, recent discussions in Parliament have been aimed at introducing legislation that will protect the public by making professional registration compulsory for all practitioners of talking treatments.

Poor definitions can give rise to a lot of confusion, and a person seeking help will want to be reassured that the practitioner is capable of doing the work required of him or her. Chapter 2 explains more about these different ways of working, and gives information about the ideas that underlie the main approaches to talking treatments. Chapter 9 examines the question of practitioners' training and competence to use these approaches.

This guide does not favour one way of working above others, and will uses the term 'practitioner' as a generic label for any professional giving structured psychological support to troubled individuals. However, it does make a distinction between professionals and lay people, and between practitioners, who are responsible and ethical in their work, and amateurs, who are not aware of (or ignore) safe boundaries, codes of conduct and organisational procedures. Similarly, the expression 'talking treatment' is often used in place of 'counselling' or 'therapy' because it is a convenient umbrella term.

The main aim in this guide is to give you the necessary information to decide what kind of practitioner is suitable for your needs, where to find that practitioner, and how to deal with the process of talking with someone over time and working towards a desired end. It does not promote the increasingly common belief that all kinds of counselling, therapy and analysis are basically the same. The school of therapy in which the practitioner has trained can have a big impact on the kind of support that you receive, so deciding exactly what kind of approach you want or need will be an important step when you choose to start a talking treatment. To help you make this decision, Chapter 2 discusses the different schools of thought behind much of counselling and therapy in the UK today.

Achieving personal insight

The process of engaging in therapy or counselling is usually one of gaining greater self-awareness or 'insight' so as to help us avoid further suffering or confusion, or difficult situations in the future. Of course, when we are in considerable pain it can be difficult, if not impossible, to stand back and assess our needs and see where our problems lie, how deep they are, and what the best way forward may be. How do we know whether we can benefit from a talking treatment, or whether it is what we really need at any given time?

Consider the opposing statements in the following table, and see which seems more appropriate to you. The table represents extremes, with little room for middle-of-the-road answers. Your personal beliefs will shape what most of these statements mean to you, and how they echo feelings and thoughts that you have experienced yourself, or not. Some of the expectations contained within these contrasting statements are not universal desires, and neither is the list meant to be exhaustive in any sense. There is almost no limit to the expectations that we choose to place on life, and so no limit to the disappointments we can feel. But the failure to find balance or an acceptable level of achievement in any of these respects (let alone all of them) may be an indicator that something is wrong.

Balance of my thoughts and feelings

I am fulfilled in my daily life	There is something missing in my existence
I feel calm and settled	I feel frustrated and anxious
I have successful relationships with other people	I feel isolated and lonely
I am enthusiastic and energetic	I am tired and not interested in anything
I manage stressful situations creatively	Stresses pile one on top of another
I feel in control of my life and can make things happen for me	I feel things happen to me whether I want them to or not
I have a sense of purpose	I don't know what to do with my life
I can make sense of the world around me	Nothing makes sense to me any more
I live for the future	I'm stuck in the past
I feel happy and settled	I hate my life

If several of your answers fall in the right-hand column, or even tend towards that column, then it is very possible that you would benefit from some form of talking treatment. Sharing your experience with another person (or persons) can be both helpful and empowering in working towards what you want to happen. It is up to you to determine whether:

- this means that you have a 'personal problem' or 'illness' or merely want to stop and think about where your life is going
- you require immediate help or want to think this through before you take any further steps
- whether you believe you **need** some help or merely **want** it.

We may give various reasons for seeking help. We may be experiencing pain, dissatisfaction, unhappiness, a sense of unease or even desperation for change. If we accept that the feelings are real (whether serious or minor, brief or lasting, clearly understood or a source of total bewilderment), then the best thing is to accept that we need to do something about it. This guide is intended to help find out what this 'something' may be.

Chapter 2

The different schools of thought

This chapter gives a brief introduction to some of the different theoretical approaches towards talking treatments that are commonly practised in the UK at present. The Resources section at the end of this guide gives details of sources of reliable information on other recognised ways of working not mentioned in this chapter. The aim here is to give an overview of the different schools of thought in counselling and therapy, what are the main ideas that underlie them, and how these ideas are used in practice (and in very contrasting ways).

As mentioned in Chapter 1, organised attempts at applying scientific thought to the management of personal problems date back to the late nineteenth century. Previous steps in this direction probably fall outside the definitions of what we would today recognise as formal counselling or therapy. As the study of psychology developed, so too did new ideas about its application to helping people in distress, and the current large number of therapeutic schools of thought is a reflection of an equal diversity of viewpoints within the field of psychology itself.

What is psychology?

Psychology is the study of the workings of the mind, and is mainly concerned with 'normal' functioning and processes, if 'normal' means the absence of problems. Probably 95 per cent of this field is devoted to everyday and routine functioning of the individual mind and not to what is more generally termed 'psychopathology' or 'abnormal' psychology – a situation in which the person is troubled, disturbed or unhappy. Psychology is often seen as a 'soft' science in which ideas are notoriously hard to prove or disprove, and foolproof experimental methods are generally lacking. This is in comparison to a 'hard' science like chemistry or physics, where clear facts are seen as being much easier to obtain, and the results of experiments are believed to provide indisputable proofs.

At its most basic level, psychology holds that:

- the individual human being has a mind
- this mind is aided by a memory and by processes of reasoning and the special senses of sight, taste, touch, smell and hearing
- some combination of life events and/or biological factors leads to the formation of a personality, or a mixture of qualities that make each person unique
- the individual uses these tools to successfully manage internal experiences (such as emotions and urges) and external experiences (such as physical behaviours and stimuli received from the outside world).

The specific nature of all of the above, and the relative importance assigned to any of these elements of the mind, varies considerably from one school of psychological thought to another.

The individual does not exist in a vacuum, of course. His or her daily experience is usually shaped by interaction with other people and agencies or institutions; sometimes these larger groups are themselves studied within the science of sociology.

What is sociology?

Sociology is also concerned with the analysis of human behaviour, but as applied to groups rather than single human beings. It looks at the ways in which people interact when they encounter each other. Its history is roughly comparable to that of psychology, being a discipline that really only began to gather major interest in the twentieth century, although political ideology prior to that time was often based around concepts and ideas that were closely linked to sociological concerns. It is related to *anthropology*, the study of cultures and societies which often takes an even wider view of human interaction than does sociology and which looks at the larger organisations and structures that humans create for themselves.

Sometimes the specific relationship between the mental functioning of individuals and the larger society in which they exist is called *social psychology*, which explicitly combines the ideas and interests of sociology and psychology.

The four main waves of historical development

The rapid expansion of psychology and sociology, in the late nineteenth and early twentieth centuries, led to the development of a distinct kind of thinking about the way in which people acquired significant personal problems. These ideas rapidly spread through the Western world. Later came counter-reactions to these ideas, and contrasting ways of looking at the same situations emerged. This complicated process of change has taken place over nearly a century and is still continuing today. But it can be simplified into four main 'waves': occasions when new and revolutionary ideas emerged, each with a particular scientific or philosophical basis. This section gives some explanation of each of these waves of new ideas; the following section gives specific examples of how they are represented within the world of counselling and therapy in the UK today.

1 Psychodynamic

For many people, the idea of therapy may bring to mind the name of the Austrian neurologist and founder of psychoanalysis, **Sigmund Freud** (1856–1939). Many of Freud's ideas, and much of his terminology, have passed into everyday language. This is perhaps surprising when you consider that for many years his work was heavily criticised, and he was deeply unpopular at the beginning of his career because many of his theories were considered obscene, bizarre and an affront to accepted ideas. What exactly was his achievement, and what did he say about human development and behaviour?

Fundamental to Freud's theories, and to the practice of psychoanalysis right up to today, is the concept of an *unconscious* level to the mind, which strives to express itself. Freud was not the first to suggest an unconscious, but he was the first to try to research its role in human emotions, behaviour and character, both in health and illness.

Freud initially attempted to find access to the unconscious world through the use of hypnosis. But he soon abandoned hypnosis in favour of the technique that is still used today, known as *free associ-ation*. Freud encouraged his patients (lying 'relaxed' on the famous couch) to tell him exactly what came into their mind, without censorship or dismissing it as irrelevant. As thought followed thought, and memory followed memory, Freud believed he was able painstakingly to arrive at the kernel of the individual's conflict – often some idea, memory or emotional event too painful or unac-ceptable to be allowed freely into conscious thought, and which had been *repressed* into the unconscious. Later, Freud wrote extensively on the way in which the unconscious expressed itself through illness, slips of the tongue, jokes and in dreams. He also described the bizarre and primitive rules that govern the unconscious world, and which give dreams their strange and uncanny quality.

Greatly influenced by the science of his era, Freud believed that, from birth, a person's unconscious mind would try to 'discharge' the tensions of his or her basic human drives, in order to gain freedom from tension, and obtain pleasurable satisfaction. Erotic and aggressive drives were present in infants and young children – first through *oral* satisfaction at the breast, and later through the *anal* phase (the satisfaction of eliminating bodily waste) and the *genital* phase. 'Fixation' at any of these stages – in other words, a halt in the progress of normal development – could show itself in various ways, for example as character traits or through illness. When first published, these ideas – which appeared to shatter preconceptions about the 'innocence' of children – were met by hostility, shock and deep scepticism. Equally shocking was Freud's idea that there is a universal psychological 'drama' which all of us have to resolve in the course of our normal development. This is the *Oedipus complex*, which describes the sexual longings of the child for the parent of the opposite sex, and the fantasised overthrow of the rival lover – the parent of the same sex.

Freud believed that the primitive drives of the unconscious rapidly came into stark collision with the strictures, rules and prohi-bitions that the infant and child acquired from parents, teachers and society. To avoid conflict, 'unacceptable' ideas and impulses were repressed from consciousness and from memory; but pressure from the unconscious to discharge these unacceptable thoughts remained. Freud called the part of the mind from which these prim-itive drives arose the *id*. He gave the name *superego* to the part of the mind that governed what should be censored, prohibited and driven back into the unconscious. Caught between the pressure from the unconscious to express itself and the censorship of the superego was the *ego*, which contained the conscious or known self.

The developing ego would try to deal with this conflict by means of *defence mechanisms*, of which repression (see above) was just one. (An example of repression would be not admitting to yourself that you are attracted to your best friend's partner, even though you find yourself dreaming of that person.) These defences enabled the individual to put conflicts and painful feelings 'out of mind'. A healthy method of doing this was to channel forbidden impulses into creative and positive activities (*sublimation*), which might be expressed in disguised forms in dreams; or in children, these impulses could be toned down to a non-sexual love of the child for both parents. But the 'damming up' of sexual or aggressive drives by rigid defences could also easily result in physical and psychological symptoms, causing anxiety and suffering for the individual, inhibiting his or her creativity and making it hard for him or her to build secure relationships.

While much of Freud's original legacy remains of fundamental importance, the body of work comprising psychoanalytic ideas has moved forward over subsequent decades, as understanding of this 'internal world' has deepened. There are now many different schools of thought which share these common origins but where the emphasis may have shifted; there are also theoretical differences and sometimes sharp divides. Despite such divisions, the different schools of thought that derived from Freud and **Carl Jung** (see below) all share the belief that the mind is organised around 'dynamic' (active) processes and structured around different levels of consciousness (awareness). This is why this overall category of therapy and counselling has come to be known as 'psychodynamic'.

There is another area of common ground that is crucial to the practice of all psychodynamic therapies. Freud recognised that during psychoanalysis individuals would, after a while, begin to attribute to the therapist thoughts and feelings that belonged, in reality, not to the therapist but to some other figure or figures in his or her life (often an important figure, such as the mother or father). In psychodynamic therapies, the feelings and ideas that the client attributes to the therapist represent a special type of relationship, called *transference*. At least as important are the feelings and ideas aroused in the therapist, which are called *countertransference*. Psychodynamic therapists believe that these transference-countertransference feelings represent and bring to life crucial relationships in the internal world of the client. Understanding these 'internal relationships' is central to the client's self-knowledge, particularly his or her emotional world and relationships with the world outside.

2 Behavioural

It was not always for reasons of good taste and social acceptability that critics questioned the basic ideas underlying the psychodynamic approach. As early as 1913, the American psychologist **John B. Watson** (1878–1958) attacked Freud's way of working on the grounds that it was unscientific, a form of 'armchair psychology'. Watson viewed psychoanalysis as the result of looking at human problems in an abstract fashion, relying less on what the subject told the analyst and more on the analyst's interpretation of what was said. In other words, he argued that when presented with the thoughts of a particular client, Freud would provide an explanation for those thoughts by sitting in an armchair after the client had left and coming up with some ingenious theory that explained the person's actions or emotional state.

Whether this caricatured and over-simplified view of psychoanalysis was fair criticism is very much open to question, but it is certainly true that the early methods used in psychodynamic therapy could not easily be researched or scientifically 'proven' as effective. It was possible to see whether the individual recovered or felt better after sessions with an analyst, but difficult to say with absolute certainty what had led to this improvement. (Chapter 6 says more on the problems of research into talking treatments and deciding what methods are the most effective.) The fact that many people agreed with Watson led to a wider reaction against Freud, and this opened the door to a completely new way of looking at things.

Watson simplified the model of psychological development to a much more basic framework. He argued that human actions were best understood by *stimulus-response analysis*, or the study of action leading to reaction. In some ways this was an extension of the work of **Ivan Pavlov** (1849–1936), a Russian scientist who was studying the effects of digestion in dogs when he made a fascinating but largely accidental discovery. Pieces of meat were fed to his test animals, which would begin to salivate when they knew they were about to be fed. Pavlov realised that the meat was a stimulus (action) and the salivation a response (reaction). He explored this further by ringing a bell before the meat was given to his dogs. Soon they began to salivate at the sound of the bell alone, because by a process of *association* they had learnt that the bell meant that food would soon arrive. Later the process was reversed, with the bell continuing to sound but no meat being offered, and after a while the dogs stopped salivating at the sound of the bell because they recognised that it no longer meant that any meat would be forthcoming. This process of acquiring and losing behaviours was referred to as *conditioning*.

From this simple experiment there developed a much more involved framework for stimulus-response analysis, added to and refined by Watson into a system termed *behaviourism*, which held that most patterns of thinking and action were the result of conditioning of some kind, and that all other behaviour was the result of instinct or emotions, which were basically a kind of inherited conditioning. Watson remained active within the field of psychology only till the late 1920s, after which time he turned his efforts towards the world of commercial advertising. (Perhaps it's not entirely surprising that he should have chosen that particular profession.) However, interest in his methods grew over time because, as had been his aim, it became possible to scientifically study these ideas by subjecting a person or animal to the process of conditioning in controlled circumstances and studying the results. This contrasted with the basic impossibility of finding a way for an observer to watch someone going through the psychodynamic stages of infant development within the private recesses of the mind.

From the standpoint of the twenty-first century, Watson's ideas may seem rather crude, making human beings into helpless puppets that are slaves to outside events. The basic message of this kind of thinking is that behaviour can be altered without any conscious effort on the part of the individual, and will change whenever a new situation (or therapist) dictates it. It now seems rather sinister to us that experiments were carried out by Watson and his followers to prove this by creating conditioned behaviours in children.

Nevertheless, these ideas remained popular until the 1950s, and were the prime motivation behind many now outdated therapeutic methods such as *aversion therapy* (being made to think negatively about something by, for instance, being given an electric shock when looking at a picture of that thing). Books were written which enthusiastically claimed that the actions of all future generations could be shaped by careful use of these techniques; these now seem frightening rather than enlightened. 'Pure' behaviourism of this type has long since been discredited because experience and common sense tell us that a person is much more resistant to change than these ideas seemed to acknowledge. The behaviourists did not consider probably the most important element in the stimulus–response event, namely the thoughts that occurred within the individual who was being stimulated and who then reacted. This middle step went almost ignored, despite the fact that human beings generally prize their status as reasoning beings and believe that they are different from animals because of their higher intellectual capacity.

Greater focus on this part of the process led to the school of *cognitive psychology*, which explicitly acknowledged the way that thoughts or 'cognitions' mediated feelings and behaviours. This later gave birth to the therapeutic model of *cognitive behavioural therapy* (CBT) as developed by **Aaron T. Beck** (1921–). Beck emphasised the free will of the individual to change conditioned responses that resulted from past or present stimuli, and the power of cognitions to overcome a tendency to behave in a certain way. This much more empowering stance holds that the conscious mind can target behaviours that a person wants to change by looking at the emotional and intellectual perceptions that surround them. This crucial relationship between thoughts, feelings and behaviours is sometimes called the *cognitive triad*. CBT is extremely popular in the UK today, and is discussed in detail later in this chapter.

3 Humanistic

Just as behaviourism was initially a response to psychodynamic thinking, in some ways the next major developments in psychology were a reaction to the limited ideas of pure behaviourism. The philosophy behind the new type of therapy was referred to as *third force* thinking, or *humanism*. It became a significant model for talking treatments in the late 1940s, significantly before the development of cognitive behavioural approaches.

Humanistic psychology was based on a belief in the uniqueness of the individual, and disagreed with the psychodynamic belief that we are all obliged to pass through the same potentially risky processes of development identified by Freud and Jung and the practitioners who elaborated on their work. Equally, it did not accept that we are slaves to external conditioning influences, and held that the response of a person to a particular stimulus is unpredictable, certainly not likely to be the same for every member of the human race. Humanism was as heavily influenced by schools of philosophy as by schools of psychology. It was based upon *phenomenology*, the belief that human observations are not objective or consistent, because every observer is different; and *existentialism*, from which came the belief that people determine their own destiny and lifestyle.

The most important early thinkers within the third force were **Abraham Maslow** (1908–70) and **Carl Rogers** (1902–87). Maslow and Rogers believed that personal problems were the result of distress rather than illness, and developed talking treatments based on gentle questioning and positive feedback. This was in contrast to the seemingly speculative interpretations of psychodynamic therapy and the practical reconditioning process of behaviourism. Many of their ideas still acknowledged the presence of some of the mental processes described in psychodynamic thinking, but these were now thought to occur in different ways for different people rather than in some pre-determined order. This meant that an undesired behaviour or emotion was just a response to a stress or trauma, rather than demonstrating a failure to mature.

It was extremely important to this kind of thinking to accept the individual as basically good, working towards positive aims, even if he or she was frustrated in achieving them. This was very different from the psychodynamic idea of the troubled individual as disturbed or perhaps somehow perverted as a result of childhood experiences. It must be pointed out that by the 1950s this was a very outdated view of analytical practice, but in any case it was very important to the humanists to promote an uncritical view of human experience. They believed that the ability to 'grow' and make huge changes existed within all people, and that often they just needed to be encouraged in this. Special techniques were not always needed to bring about this kind of growth.

However, this led to many questions being asked about this new way of working. Humanistic psychology was, and is still, criticised for being almost too positive a framework for counselling and psychotherapy, and it is sometimes dismissed as a naively optimistic set of ideas that sound nice but which do not necessarily help anyone. Humanistic therapists claim that this is a totally inaccurate picture of the way they work, and argue that a positive starting point does not mean that they ignore the uncomfortable realities of daily experience. At the same time, people using this approach explicitly do not see themselves as more developed human beings simply because of their status as practitioners.

The more equal relationship between the person seeking support and the person providing it that first developed within humanistic therapy has since been widely adopted across a broad range of talking treatments. The practitioners involved in therapy are often now seen as fellow travellers who are working towards an agreed aim, rather than as experts sharing their knowledge with their willing pupils. A significant contribution of humanism was to reinforce the idea that everyone – practitioners as well as clients – was on a journey towards greater self-awareness.

4 Eclectic and integrative

Over time, the major schools of psychology began to borrow ideas from each other and became less dogmatic in their standpoints. There are probably relatively few practitioners these days who work in a totally 'purist' fashion; most follow a model that has made at least passing use of ideas from the previous main movements within the world of counselling and therapy. This is probably inevitable, since the schools grew out of each other.

Even more significant than this exchange of ideas, however, has been the recent increase in methods of working that deliberately make use of techniques drawn from several distinct types of counselling and therapy within psychodynamic, behavioural and humanistic practice. This is often referred to as *eclectic* therapy, because it draws much more deeply upon a range of ideas, and may involve training in more than one type of therapy. However, it could be argued that ideas can be 'eclectic' without being consistent

The four main waves of historical development: summary

School of practice	Historical development	Rationale	Common terminology
Psychodynamic	Late 19th century to the present. First distinct 'talking treatment'. Most popular period: 1900–1920s. Still widely practised.	People must go through stages of psychological development; problems occur if this doesn't happen smoothly.	*Developmental stages* *Unconscious* *Id, ego, superego* *Archetypes* *Transference, countertransference*
Behavioural	Early 20th century to 1950s. Most popular period: 1930s.	Stimulus (event) leads to response (related result).	*Conditioning* *Association*
Cognitive behavioural	Largely replaced pure behaviourism from 1960s onwards. Most popular period: now.	Stimulus is interpreted by thoughts and feelings, and only then produces result.	*Cognitive triad* *CBT*
Humanistic	Late 1940s to the present. Most popular period: 1960s. Still widely practised.	Experience is totally unique, generalisations are unhelpful. Problems are not an illness or a sign of failure.	*Phenomenology* *Positivism* *Equality*
Eclectic and integrative	Of major importance since 1960s; ongoing process of development. Most popular period: now.	Ideas from all three schools can be used in conjunction if responsibly and safely combined.	All of the above

or easily workable when in combination; consequently, the term *integrative* therapy is becoming increasingly common, because integration indicates that the different ideas have been made to fit with each other rather than being just a 'pick and mix' approach. This does not mean that an eclectic therapist has not also achieved this integration, just that the label 'eclectic' is unfortunately open to a more negative interpretation.

Eclectic and integrative work form a large part of what is on offer in the UK today, and the boundaries between different models of therapy and counselling are still changing. This allows for a very positive exchange of ideas. However, it still does not mean that specific ways of working are all one and the same, or that it is likely that one 'super-model' of talking treatments will be created. It is arguable that the process of looking for ever more ways of mixing ideas together leads to an increase, rather than a decrease, in the number of counselling and therapy approaches on offer.

Specific theories and techniques

How have these ideas translated into modern talking treatments? The approaches outlined below are some of the most common ones used in the UK today. However, they are not all available from the same agencies, and few are available free of charge. They are described here because they are still popular and are being continuously discussed and refined, even if they were originally developed some time ago. Chapter 3 gives details on how to obtain these kinds of therapy and counselling.

Psychodynamic practice

There have been many developments within the psychodynamic approach since the early work of Freud, and the experience of practitioners has led over the decades to different ways of understanding the mind. Basically, however, the various psychodynamic schools all keep in common the core idea of an active unconscious, that can and does influence how we experience the world emotionally. All these schools also emphasise the fundamental importance of transference and countertransference as described above.

The technique of 'free association' (the arrival into conscious thought of a train of ideas, daydreams, images, feelings or memories) remains a key tool in modern psychoanalysis. Most **psychoanalysts** still use a couch, to encourage the client to associate freely in an atmosphere of quiet reflective privacy; they see clients intensively, usually three to five times a week over several years. Other psychotherapists use the same techniques, but slightly less intensively, and are called **psychoanalytic psychotherapists**. A great many other **psychodynamic therapists** base their work on the psychoanalytic model and its theories, but may see clients once a week or less frequently, and work face to face with their clients seated comfortably in a chair.

All these therapies have as their aim a fuller understanding of the unconscious 'inner' world, as a means of achieving change. In an intensive therapy, the transference relationship is likely to rekindle very early ways of relating to people and the very early 'defences' that the individual may have developed to ward off psychological pain and distress. The aim of the therapy is to make this process of achieving understanding happen in a way that carries emotional credibility, rather than just making intellectual sense. (The client may be only too well aware, at a conscious level, that his or her thoughts and behaviour are 'irrational' or problematic.)

By their nature, psychodynamic therapies are long and painstaking approaches to helping distressed people. The length of treatment, the cost, and the fact that these approaches do not easily lend themselves to being studied by modern research tools such as the randomised controlled trial (see Chapter 6) have, by and large, made them an unattractive option for healthcare managers in a cash-strapped National Health Service (NHS). This is unfortunate, but should not obscure the fact that psychodynamic thinking informs the work of many practitioners working in a variety of ways and in many different settings. Furthermore, mainstream intensive psychoanalysis, Jungian analysis and psychoanalytic psychotherapy continue to be practised widely throughout the UK on a private basis.

Freud and the post-Freudians

For classical Freudian and post-Freudian (people who later elaborated upon and developed Freud's ideas) analysts it was seen as essential to understand the client's unconscious drives and instincts, and his or her psychological defences against them or against conflict. This provided a starting point for understanding that person's world and difficulties. It was held that the way that the individual had been able (or unable) to negotiate his or her development through the oral, anal and genital phases, and through the Oedipus complex, and had learned to manage early sexual and aggressive impulses, was pivotal in shaping his or her personality and behaviour.

Curiously, however, while so much of Freud's writing focused on the earliest developments in the child's life, Freud himself never directly conducted an analysis of a child. It fell to his successors, notably his own daughter, Anna Freud, and Melanie Klein (see below), to make detailed studies of the psychological world of the developing child. In their observations of the child at play, they described the equivalent of the 'free associations' of adults, and in their writings they greatly added to the way that modern-day psychodynamic therapists work and think about the mind.

Notable post-Freudians are Karl Abrahams, Sandor Ferenczi, Anna Freud, Erich Fromm and Karen Horney.

Melanie Klein and object relations theory

The majority of psychoanalysts and psychodynamic therapists in the UK now work with an 'object relations' model. This was the name given to a new school of thinking that emerged in the 1940s and whose main figure is **Melanie Klein** (1882–1960). At the time deep divisions began to open up in the psychoanalytic movement in the UK, especially between followers of Freud and Anna Freud on the one hand and those sympathetic to the new theories of Melanie Klein on the other. Klein suggested that most major psychological development occurred in the first few months (or even weeks) of infancy. She maintained that a baby's normal 'bad' experiences (frustration, hunger, painful bodily sensations) were felt by the infant as 'attacks' on its survival by bad aspects of the mother, the father and the parents as a couple. The nourishing breast became the 'good' and idealised breast, while hunger and absence of the nourishing breast were literally experienced as attacks from a persecuting 'bad' breast. In healthy development, this splitting into good and bad eventually gave way to the baby's realisation that the breast that nurtures is the same as the breast that at times frustrates, and is simply a part of a whole other being (the mother). This brought the first experiences of guilt (for the infant's fantasies about attacks on the breast), mourning for the damaged or 'destroyed' good breast, and the wish to love and be loved.

While Freud had emphasised the overriding importance of instincts as the driving forces in the primitive mind, for the object relations schools what was important in human development was that, from the beginning, life's quest was for relationships with 'objects': the feeding breast, the mother, other people. The whole of life was directed towards *relating*, and the emotional experiences encountered in early relationships shaped forever the individual's internal life, and capacity to love and to cope with pain and periods of insecurity. The concept of 'object relations' has had a lasting influence on psychodynamic schools of therapy.

Other leading figures in the object relations school of thought are Ronald Fairbairn, Michael Balint, Donald Winnicott and Wilfred Bion.

Jungian analytical psychology

Probably the most significant division in psychodynamic thought occurred very early in the history of psychoanalysis, between Freud and **Carl Jung** (1875–1961), a Swiss doctor. Jung worked closely with Freud at first, and his development of word-association tests (where the client was asked to respond spontaneously to a series of words, with his or her responses revealing something of his or her unconscious thoughts) gave some scientific credibility to the concept of the unconscious mind. But Jung's ideas were later to diverge from Freud's, especially in respect of Freud's emphasis on infant sexuality. Jung eventually split from Freud in 1913 and founded a separate school of analytical thought, which came to be called *analytical psychology*.

For Jung, the personal unconscious was only a small part of an individual's unconscious world. Beneath this lay what he called the collective unconscious, which contained universally recurring myths and themes which he called the *archetypes* of the collective unconscious.

This would mean that we have an archetypal idea of what it means to be a man or a woman, just as we have an archetypal idea of what light and darkness, or life and death are. Trying to make sense of what life is, or to live up to accepted images of being a man or a woman, can lead to unhappiness or confusion in a world that is sometimes not so neat and tidy. Classically, Jungian analysis seeks not only to understand the prohibited and repressed thoughts of the personal unconscious, but by free association and dream analysis, to bring the client into contact with the healing qualities of the collective unconscious. Jung believed that the religious and spiritual dimension was very important to the individual's growth and development.

Jung also invented the terms *extrovert* (a very outgoing and socially confident person) and *introvert* (someone who is more shy and reserved) and saw all people as being somewhere on the continuum between these two extremes. This positioning greatly affected the desire for or ability to relate to other people.

Although Jungian work is normally intensive and long term, it is also possible to do briefer work, concentrating on dreams or receiving basic rather than detailed interpretation.

A major figure in this field is Michael Fordham.

Behaviourist practice

Although the earliest behavioural techniques are rarely practised in the UK today, cognitive psychology and cognitive behavioural techniques are probably at the height of their popularity. This is because research over the last few years has indicated that this is a very successful way of working with a lot of different problems. However, it is arguable that behavioural therapies are much easier to research than either psychodynamic or humanistic approaches. This is because they are often focused on very practical tasks such as filling in questionnaires, keeping diaries, and 'self-reporting' (where the client assesses how anxious he or she feels and gives these feelings a mark out of ten, for instance). It is inevitably easier to assess progress (or lack of it) if interventions are scored using ratings scales.

Chapter 6 provides more information on research methods for counselling and therapy, along with some thoughts on why any attempt to 'prove' the effectiveness of a talking treatment is such a difficult process. But the popularity of these approaches is unquestionable, and a great deal of NHS provision is geared towards this school of thought at present.

Cognitive behavioural therapy (CBT)

Cognitive behavioural therapy is centred around the idea that our emotions, thoughts and behaviours are closely linked. In other words, all three are shaped and strongly affected by the other two, and what we feel, what we believe, and what we do are dependent on each other. For example, you might see depression purely as a low mood that lasts for a long time – an entirely emotional problem. But a CBT practitioner would say that the depression is maintained by negative *thoughts* that reinforce the sadness, such as a belief that the situation will not change. In addition, *behaviours* may contribute to these feelings: for instance, you may cut yourself off from other people and in doing so become even more bored, isolated and unhappy. If emotions are dependent on thoughts and behaviours, there are obvious things that can be done to find a way forward. It may seem that feelings are often out of control, but this cannot be true if changing a pattern of thinking or behaving has direct results on what we feel.

A better understanding of these links can be gained by structured questions and answers from a trained practitioner, and out of this process can come a sense of greater self-control and the ability to manage a situation rather feeling helpless within it. CBT is a very practical approach that concentrates on the client's current situation and is less interested in the effects of his or her past experiences than are many other approaches.

The therapy often takes place over eight to ten sessions, but duration is determined by individual need. The client will often be asked to keep diaries and maintain records of his or her progress between sessions.

The major figures in this field are Aaron Beck, David Clark and Adrian Wells.

Rational emotive behavioural therapy (REBT)

REBT (previously called just rational emotive therapy or RET) is also based on the cognitive triad of thoughts, feelings and actions, and holds that the individual is responsible for his or her emotions and behaviours because these are the product of patterns of thinking, and thinking can be changed. For example: 'I think life should be stress-free, but I feel frustrated because it most definitely is not, and behave aggressively towards anyone who represents these stresses; my problem is that I am aggressive, but the reason is my faulty thinking, because it is based on an unrealistic expectation of the world'. REBT holds that most difficulties can be broken down to these kinds of unhelpful thoughts, and emphasises the client's ability to change if he or she reflects on what is wrong about his or her way of thinking.

This form of therapy often involves making lists of thoughts and feelings in relation to behaviours or events, and looking for things that can be altered or dealt with in a different way, sometimes referred to as *coping strategies*. It is usually offered as a time-limited talking treatment, generally in eight to twelve sessions over a period of a few months.

Major names in this field are Albert Ellis and Windy Dryden.

Cognitive analytical therapy (CAT)

Cognitive analytical therapy takes the ideas of REBT and combines them with looking at early-life experiences. The idea is to identify where negative or problematic thoughts originally came from. This improves the client's understanding of his or her faulty thinking by giving it a context, and so relates the process of changing destructive patterns in the person's life to the time and the place where these patterns first emerged.

It is possible to see cognitive analytical therapy as being similar to the psychodynamic approach because of this focus on early life. However, practitioners of CAT do not usually relate the client's experiences to the idea of stages of normal psychological development that form part of the theories of Freud, Jung and their successors. The main focus is on the events that happened in the person's environment rather than upon the unconscious conflicts affecting the client's mental processes.

The treatment usually continues for two to six months, most often with up to 25 sessions.

A major figure in this field is Anthony Ryle.

Interpersonal therapy (IPT)

Interpersonal therapy is based on the belief that psychological problems such as depression and anxiety develop because an individual has problems of a social nature. This means that the trigger for emotional pain will be something like the end of a love affair, the loss of a job, the death of a loved one, or any other event that changes our relationship with some or all of the people who are important in our lives. A client is asked to look at all his or her relationships, identify which are in trouble, and consider the emotional consequences of these bad relationships on a daily basis.

The aim of interpersonal therapy is to look for any reasonable way to change the situation, with the emphasis always placed on the social life of the client. This can often involve active decision-making about the future, and improved ways of communicating with people who are important to the client. Like REBT, IPT is seen as a very practical type of talking treatment, and the very active participation of the client is intended to improve confidence. It takes as a starting point the idea that the low mood or stress is an illness, and that the individual has the power to effect a cure by altering his or her lifestyle.

Treatment is usually limited to 12 sessions, with some flexibility in extending this.

Major names in this area are Myrna Weissman and Gerald Klerman.

Others

There are many other cognitive techniques, such as dialectical behaviour therapy, schema-focused therapy, biofeedback, autogenic training, stress inoculation and eye movement desensitisation and reprocessing. These represent a growth area within the therapy world, both in the UK and abroad. CBT and related approaches have been incorporated into many models of working, and are a very important part of eclectic and integrative counselling and therapy.

Humanistic practice

Asking practitioners to explain which psychological theories they make use of most often and why has been compared to asking them which football team they support. Perhaps this isn't a bad analogy, because you might admire players who currently play for clubs other than the one you support, and the transfer system allows for movement between teams just as ideas move between therapists. The analogy could be said to be particularly true for humanistic practitioners, who have used many different philosophical and spiritual ideas as a basis for developing new models. Not all these ideas will be of interest to everyone, but they have in common the aim that the client finds out about his or her personal strengths and uses them to change a situation for the better. This can be a little bewildering to a new client who has more experience of a traditional medical approach to psychological problem-solving.

The caricature of the unskilled humanistic practitioner is that of someone who paraphrases everything that his or her client says and offers him or her lots of clichés, comforting words and perhaps the occasional hug. Of course, bad therapists of all schools may limit themselves to this kind of ineffectual repetition of one or two simple techniques, and never vary what they are doing. But recognised approaches within the humanistic tradition have a clear theoretical basis and definite aims within therapy as practised, and are not merely 'feel-good' exercises. Common to most of these approaches is the creation of a comfortable physical environment for the client, a non-judgemental attitude from the practitioner, and an atmosphere in which emotions can be safely expressed and respectfully acknowledged but never demanded or 'dragged' out of the individual. As with the psychodynamic school, these basic conditions are broad enough to make research or external analysis very difficult; this kind of experience is not easily reduced to numbers and statistics.

Person-centred therapy

Person-centred therapy (also referred to as client-centred therapy) was the creation of **Carl Rogers**, who believed that every human being had a huge capacity for personal growth. He saw this ability to bring about positive change as being present even if you found yourself in a situation where it was difficult to believe that this could be true. Rogers felt that a practitioner could encourage a client to look for this inner strength by keeping to what he called the three core conditions of his model. These were *congruence* (being real and honest and open as a practitioner, instead of hiding behind a professional role); *unconditional positive regard* (being positive and accepting of the client whatever he or she may be saying, and looking for the good within the person instead of the damage or disturbance); and *empathy* (listening to the client and trying to see the world through his or her eyes instead of allowing your own ideas and beliefs to come to the surface).

Rogers believed that attitudes, rather than techniques alone, were what was important in a talking treatment. If the right environment was provided, the client would let go of his or her anxieties and fears, and begin to see his or her situation in a more realistic way. He used this model in a wide range of settings, including hospitals, schools and prisons, and saw it as a way to empower people to do their own therapy with a little outside help. This was thought to be much more satisfying for the client than learning to rely on someone else for answers. Rogers presented his ideas not as startling new discoveries, but as basic facts of human nature that people had forgotten and of which they needed to be reminded. His belief in a more equal relationship between client and practitioner was a very big shift in the world of counselling and therapy, and led to a new way of working for practitioners from many different approaches.

Person-centred therapy is often a long-term option, but Rogers strongly believed that even brief exposure to his model – perhaps only a single session – could help someone to gain a better under-standing of his or her potential for change. In the humanistic tradition, this kind of sudden transformation is sometimes referred to as a *peak experience*. Of course, practitioners of other approaches might simply call this 'progress' or the achievement of greater self-awareness and insight.

Existential therapy

Existential therapy developed from existential philosophy. This was originally a European school of thought dating from the mid-twentieth century, although its roots go back further than that. Existentialism believes that as individuals we are free and in control of our own destiny; although this sounds good in principle, it can also sound a little disheartening if taken to extremes. According to this way of thinking, we are responsible for all that happens in our lives, including all of our problems, and for the vision of reality that we construct around us.

As used in talking treatments, the existential idea is meant to be a much more positive starting point. Existential therapy holds that there are four major concerns on which we all have to negotiate some kind of understanding: free will; the inevitability of our own death; solitude – the fact that we are basically alone even when surrounded by other people; and the search for meaning or answers to the big questions that life raises for us. Unhappiness is the result of not finding a balance or peace in relation to one or more of these ideas, and any everyday problem can be traced to one of the four concerns. For instance, relationship difficulties may result from a fear of isolation that leads us to be over-protective of a partner; or anxiety about our health could stem from a fear of dying. The therapy involves looking at each of the major concerns and making choices about our lives that satisfy us and allow us to reach whatever goals are desired.

As with person-centred therapy, the individual is seen as having great inner strength and a powerful capacity for change. The existential approach is a 'phenomenological' model of therapy, meaning that – unlike therapies that contain the idea of universal stages of psychological development – it sees each individual's experience and worldview as inevitably and completely different from those of other people.

Existential therapy tends to be a medium- to long-term option, involving self-exploration over a substantial number of sessions.

Major figures in this field are Irvin Yalom and Rollo May.

Gestalt therapy

Gestalt therapy (*gestalt* is German for 'form') is based on the idea that what we see or believe *right now* is more important than interpretations or explanations that relate to our past or future. The fact that the approach places emphasis on the present (like several other humanistic approaches) makes it very different to psychodynamic thinking, which is mainly (but by no means entirely) concerned with the past. At the same time, it emphasises the belief that the whole person consists of mind, body and spirit, which together make up the self. Also very important are relationships between the individual and other people. The above ideas are therefore sometimes summed up as the 'Here & Now' and 'I & Thou' approaches to therapy.

Gestalt practitioners use techniques that focus the client on the present moment and what is being experienced in all these parts of the self. This is done in the belief that it will inevitably increase understanding of our patterns and the way we express ourselves, and give the individual the knowledge and the tools to make any desired changes. Often, but not always, this kind of therapy is carried out in groups rather than one-to-one. Role play (where people act out scenes or conversations to see what feelings and thoughts they lead to) is very common, because it helps the client to experience the Here & Now more intensely than just talking about it.

Because of this focus on the present moment, Gestalt work is not necessarily seen as a long-term therapy. Even so, people often feel that regular contact with a Gestalt practitioner helps them to stay in touch with what is happening in their lives. Many people experience the approach by attending several groups or sessions over a long weekend or in some similar short 'burst' of activity.

Major figures in this area are Fritz Perls and Laura Perls.

Transactional analysis (TA)

Transactional analysis is perhaps only marginally a humanistic therapy, although it was developed by psychologists who definitely shared humanism's belief in people as basically strong and able to find answers with minimal help rather than needing years of expert advice. TA sees the human mind as having three distinct elements called *ego states*: the parent (responsible and caring), the adult (reasoning and decisive) and the child (creative, demanding). These different aspects of the person take particular roles in daily situations and interactions with other people.

An exchange between the ego states of two separate people is called a transaction, hence the name of the approach. In a romantic relationship, for example, we may sometimes want to look after our partner (our parent has a transaction with our partner's child); sometimes we may want him or her to look after us (our child has a transaction with our partner's parent); and sometimes we may want to discuss things as equals (our adult transacts with our partner's adult). Problems result if there is a miscommunication.

The techniques of transactional analysis work by helping individuals to recognise when they are in one ego state rather than another, and what they routinely look for from other people and why. Part of the therapy process involves searching for what are called *scripts*, patterns of communication into which we may have become stuck. Perhaps a particular person at work makes you feel like a child every time he or she talks to you because he or she is very parental and does not give you credit where it is due or speak to you as one adult to another. Or maybe, although a particular person treats you as an adult, you prefer to respond 'childishly' because you feel overworked and have become tired of all that person's demands. Looking for 'scripts' is about increasing awareness. The approach helps the client to acknowledge that his or her emotional needs are not always the same, and may vary in relation to the situation and the needs of another person.

Generally this is a short- to medium-term approach, often with 'homework' to be carried out between sessions; homework involves trying to practise what you learn in real situations. Brief or one-off therapy is not uncommon.

A major figure in this area is Eric Berne.

Eclectic/integrative practice

Several of the approaches discussed so far can themselves be said to be examples of taking ideas from different types of talking treatments and mixing them together into a new and integrated way of working. The following are not so much distinct approaches as examples of models that may use ideas from a range of schools to achieve a specific end. New ways of combining ideas are always emerging, and this provides an exciting opportunity for clients to benefit from more flexible ways of working in the future. Increasingly, there is an understanding that practitioners of all schools are stronger when working together than when arguing about who's right and who's wrong.

Brief solution-focused therapy

Brief therapy takes a slightly different starting point from many other talking treatments by concentrating on the solution to a difficult situation and working backwards, rather than identifying a problem and looking for causes. An example would be to take as a starting point the wish to feel calm and get a good night's sleep, and to look for ways to make this happen, as opposed to analysing the underlying reasons for the anxiety that have led to the agitation and poor sleep. This is a very practical technique, searching for useful and manageable steps that can be put into action immediately. It also helps by encouraging people to overcome the negative thoughts that may have led to them losing sight of what it is they want from life. A gloomy view of the future can be replaced with positive ideas about how to achieve desired goals.

The solution-focused approach is more of a framework than anything else, and its principles have been used by psychodynamic, cognitive behavioural and humanistic practitioners. The basic idea of looking for answers rather than questions is an attractive one, and a wide range of talking treatments can be adapted to work in this way.

As the name suggests, 'brief' solution-focused therapy is practised over only a handful of sessions, with four to five often viewed as sufficient. This is flexible, however, and the approach is sometimes referred to just as 'solution-focused' because the word 'brief' can be seen as an unnecessary pressure on the client to make rapid progress.

Major figures in this field are Steve De Shazer and Insoo Kim Berg.

Multimodal therapy (MMT)

Multimodal therapy looks at different aspects of the individual that take in ideas from a range of theories and so encourage change from a variety of angles. It is based on an assessment of seven aspects of personality (referred to as *modalities*, hence the name of the approach). These are **B**ehaviour, **A**ffect (mood), **S**enses (sight, hearing and so on), **I**mages (pictures of the future or other important mental images), **C**ognitions (thoughts), **I**nterpersonal relationships, and **D**rugs/Biology (the effect of physical things on state of mind). The first letters of these modalities spell **BASIC ID**, and this assessment aims to give just that: a starting point for further work.

The process of looking at each of these aspects in turn helps to identify where a particular problem lies. It also gives both the client and the practitioner some idea of what kind of approach will be helpful in dealing with the identified difficulties, because it points to those areas (or modalities) of the client's life that need to be worked upon. So an alcohol problem might need to be addressed with help for the physical, mood and behavioural modalities; alternatively a bereavement might need work in the image, cognition and interpersonal modalities. This information can then be used to choose techniques from a particular school or schools of therapy that are suitable for the problem or problems, and which match the client's ideas about what would help him or her.

MMT gives a broad choice to people about how they can work with a practitioner, and is popular because it accepts that many different ways of working can have good results. As mentioned earlier in the chapter, the integration of different approaches can work better than just the use of ideas eclectically without making sure that they are consistent with each other. However, MMT takes a slightly different view, and holds that a practitioner should be skilled in several approaches in order to be able to give clients what they need and want. If appropriate, a practitioner might carry out a multimodal assessment and then refer a client to someone more experienced in the approach that is needed.

This therapy tends to be time-limited but is flexible because the techniques that may be used come from such a broad range of approaches. MMT holds that the nature of the problem will probably indicate the length of the therapy needed.

A major figure in this field is Arnold Lazarus.

Feminist therapy

Feminist therapy is a good example of how the introduction of a political or philosophical idea to the therapy world leads to the development of new approaches to working with personal problems. A big change in the way people see gender roles has taken place since the 1960s. This has led to many of the major theories underlying talking treatments being revisited and questioned by women who believe that these ideas are dated and often based on negative views of femininity. Practitioners have then found ways to address these flaws and create new theories that present both a more positive view of being a woman, and also a framework for looking at the way that gender stereotypes might lead to personal problems in the first place. Perhaps low self-esteem is caused by the low value previously placed on women in society, or maybe lack of opportunity and equal rights leads to anger and frustration. Under the feminist approach, these feelings are not seen as problems but accepted as necessary and reasonable responses to sexism.

Feminist therapy is sometimes thought of as a humanistic approach, and many practitioners who identify themselves as feminists do work from a humanistic perspective. But feminism as an idea has been introduced to all kinds of talking treatments – psychodynamic, behavioural and eclectic as well. A practitioner from any school may claim to be a feminist therapist, and in this sense the concept has been fully integrated with other ways of working. This is a good illustration of how counselling and therapy do not exist in isolation, but are reflections of the world around us, and of the social changes that have taken place in the last century. It also shows that the development of psychological theory can be as much about political ideas as it is about science.

Because feminist therapy is not limited to a particular technique, but can be seen as an attitude and belief that can be combined with any technique, the number of sessions will depend on the particular approach into which feminist ideas have been introduced.

Major figures in this field are Jean Baker Miller, Laura S. Brown and Susie Orbach.

Making sense of what's out there

Remember that the overview given in this chapter does not cover all the kinds of talking treatment that you may find available, and gives only the briefest introduction to the schools of thought included here. At this stage, the best advice that can be offered is:

- be aware that not all talking treatments are the same
- consider what seems to make sense to you and what does not
- be open to the idea that an approach that sounds helpful or unhelpful when you are reading about it can prove very different when you are working with a practitioner who is skilled and experienced in the field.

In the end, only practical experience can tell you what way of working is best for you.

Your choice of treatment will involve other decisions such as whether you prefer to see someone on your own, with your partner, or in a group, and whether to look for help in the public, voluntary or private sector. These options are explained in Chapter 3.

Chapter 3

Formats for talking treatments and where to find help

Choosing what kind of therapy to go in for is clearly very important. Chapter 2 explores the different schools of thought and Chapter 6 addresses the issue of what therapy is best suited for specific conditions. Another important choice for anyone considering a talking treatment is the format of the treatment. Would you prefer to see someone on your own, or would it be better for you and your partner to seek counselling together? Should the whole family be present? Would you prefer to have group sessions with other people seeking help for the same kind of problem as yours? This chapter outlines the choices available.

The second half of the chapter gives an overview of the organisations and individuals that provide talking treatments in the UK, and how you can gain access to them. Depending on your preferred format, you may have a greater choice of providers if you follow one route rather than another. Equally, you may be able to get help sooner from one sector than from another, and your choice may be constrained by your ability to pay for treatment. This chapter should arm you with enough knowledge to begin your search for support.

Common formats for talking treatments

The basic formats used by practitioners are often the same. Often we think of individual sessions as being the only kind of counselling and therapy available, but there are several other ways that talking treatments can be delivered. One or more of the following may seem attractive or appropriate to you.

Individual face-to-face therapy

The general perception of counselling and therapy is that it is a dialogue between one therapist and one client, taking place in a location convenient for both parties, at regular intervals, and in sessions of between 45 and 60 minutes. This is the format preferred by most practitioners because it allows for sufficient space and time for a client to enter into the process of self-examination in safety and without other distractions. These conditions are usually what individuals look for when they are seeking support; individual therapy also allows clients to disclose personal information, in confidence, to just one other person.

The focus of individual sessions can vary greatly, as can the overall intention of a talking treatment, and these will depend on the contract or agreement made between the client and the practitioner. There will be differences in the duration of therapy, the specific problems to be discussed and managed, and the school of thought in which the practitioner has trained. Individual therapy may be time-limited or open-ended, centred on one specific issue or looking at a much broader set of concerns. But the basic idea is familiar: two people get together to allow one of them to discuss personal difficulties in a supportive and constructive environment that will, it is hoped, allow for positive change.

Group therapy

Many schools of psychotherapy and counselling also practise in groups, with an agreed number of clients and two or more practitioners specifically trained or experienced in working with larger numbers of people. Here the aim is for group members to share experiences and difficulties, and gain support and understanding in a more dynamic and varied environment than could ever be possible with only one other person. Simultaneously, there is also the opportunity to offer help and compassion to others, meaning that participants can be empowered to become 'auxiliary' therapists. Finding that you possess the ability to support other people can be a very satisfying experience when previously you have been feeling out of control or thought yourself incapable of achieving anything useful.

Groups can be extremely large: 50 or even more people in some cases. More commonly they consist of perhaps eight to ten members. Sessions are often longer than is usual in individual therapy: anything from one to two hours is fairly common. Groups often have tremendous energy and may cover a wide range of issues in a short time. In the hands of skilful therapists, these can be very powerful opportunities for gaining insight.

Most groups function by emphasising feedback of reactions to what is said and done within the session, so that behaviours and any thoughts expressed aloud can receive a kind of 'reality check' from a sympathetic audience. The group should not become a competition as to who can talk the loudest or most often, or who expresses the greatest levels of emotion. It is intended to be a contained space, with clear limits on what the participants may do and say ('boundaries'), and in which there is time and opportunity for all members to gain something from the experience.

Groups may focus on one particular issue or problem, or may function with a very wide brief. Attendance is usually (but not always) time-limited; however, frequently a group may have a long life with a constantly changing membership – a so-called 'open' group. On other occasions a group will be created for a specific membership and will be disbanded after an agreed period of time. This is referred to as a 'closed' group.

Couples therapy

This is another common format for therapy and counselling. The two clients, who are experiencing some sort of difficulty in their relationship, are usually a married couple or partners, but they may instead be blood relations, or two people who work for the same organisation. The practitioner (or occasionally practitioners) acts as 'honest broker', not taking sides but making sure that both parties are able to speak and be listened to in turn. Problems between people are almost always partially, if not completely, about poor communication. The presence of an unattached participant is a safety net for both individuals to use when anger or confusion overwhelm the desire for change. The particular nature of the problems being encountered will determine the duration of this kind of therapy, but work with couples is rarely a long-term option.

Systemic and family therapy

This approach is based on the belief that the difficulties encountered by a family unit are best tackled by working with everyone involved, even where the difficulties appear to relate most obviously to one person within the unit. It is sometimes called a 'systemic' approach because all the people concerned are seen as parts of a complex 'system' of interrelationships. A systemic approach can be used for families or other kinds of 'family unit', such as people who work together in an office, or a sports team. This kind of therapy is arguably a distinct type of talking treatment. It is different from group therapy because the people involved already have relationships with each other.

Family therapy is often needed when either the people who are requesting support, or the practitioners who are offering them help, believe that the interaction within the family is worsening the overall situation and adding to whatever difficulties exist. For example, one person may be tired and stressed, and take out these feelings on the rest of the family. They in turn become anxious and unhappy and respond with anger. The stress levels of the original sufferer get higher, and that person dumps even more bad feelings on the rest of the family. The problem now feeds off itself, and a bad situation spirals downwards.

Family therapy, like couples work, does not aim at finding out who is to blame and punishing the guilty party. Neither does it assume that a family must be 'dysfunctional' if it needs help. Instead, it acknowledges that everyone is hurting, and that everyone needs support. Usually there are at least two therapists involved. As with all other formats for talking treatments, the nature of the sessions will depend on the specific training and beliefs of the therapists. Systemic and family work is generally time-limited, although this may mean regular attendance for quite a long period of time. Sometimes the outcome may be that individual therapy or counselling is recommended for one or more people in the family, or that couples therapy has a role.

Telephone counselling

Some people prefer anonymous support, and consequently there are practitioners who choose to offer telephone contact only (occasionally this is as a prelude to face-to-face work, although this tends to be a matter of choice rather than something forced upon the person seeking help). Talking over the phone may be the most practical way for someone to obtain support in the middle of a busy and chaotic lifestyle, and many of the benefits of other therapeutic methods are just as apparent when offered by a skilled practitioner.

Of course, telephone contact is by its very nature more impersonal than a meeting. This may be part of the attraction for many people, but it can result in a kind of emotional distance between the people involved. This could mean that some aspects of the client's situation remain invisible to the therapist and so do not get explored. Given that a major part of entering into a talking treatment is establishing mutual trust and respect, it is possible (although by no means inevitable) that the telephone can create and maintain a barrier between the people involved and so allow difficult issues – which may be the most relevant ones – to be avoided. This may further limit the effectiveness of the work being done. On the other hand, the lack of physical contact may even make it easier for some people to open up.

Telephone counselling is often very suitable for brief and crisis therapy, where help or support is needed immediately and can be offered right away. Some longer-term work is carried out by phone, but this is relatively unusual. Other practitioners would hold, rightly or wrongly, that significant therapy cannot properly be offered in this way, and that the phone is best limited to advice work and general support.

Self-help networks

Many agencies in the UK offer the self-help model. Often it is felt that while no real 'professional' help is needed to manage a particular problem, nevertheless some support might be welcome in the form of talking with other people who have had similar difficulties. This is basically the thinking behind group therapy, but not everyone wants to deal with the challenge of attending group sessions. Self-help can be easily accessed if one knows where to look. The growth of the Internet means that a worldwide community is now available to the ordinary person, although some cautions about this will be discussed later in this chapter.

The level of support that people obtain from self-help networks may be very great, and is not usually limited to one or two hours a week, unlike most talking treatments. Despite the potential benefits, it is often questioned (as is the case with telephone work) whether this kind of help is properly a type of therapy or counselling. Some people offering their time to self-help agencies may be

What to expect from different formats of treatment

Format	Number of people involved	Duration	Pros	Cons
Individual face-to-face	Two: one therapist, one client	Varies according to training of therapist and problems of client; may last several years	May be less intimidating than group activities. Focus stays always on needs of the individual	Feedback and ideas are limited by absence of others. Most expensive type of help if obtained privately
Group work	Variable: at least two therapists, any number of clients up to several dozen	Usually attendance is time-limited, although group may continue with new members	Possibility of hearing lots of new ideas and multiple feedback. May be very intense with rapid results	Can seem confusing, especially at first. It may be difficult to open up to a lot of people
Couples therapy	Two clients, one or two therapists	Usually of limited duration, as negotiated by parties involved	Ensures both parties have a voice, aids constructive dialogue	May have limited aims, focused on problems in relationship, not problems of individuals
Family or systemic therapy	All affected members of family or unit, at least two therapists	Usually of limited duration, as negotiated by parties involved	Offers support to everyone in need, aims to give equal time to all	Some of the family may not want to get involved. Fear of being blamed
Telephone counselling	Two: one caller, one counsellor	Generally brief contact, with some exceptions	Discreet. No travelling. Greater anonymity	Limits counsellor's knowledge of client. Can reinforce isolation
Self-help and support networks	Varies: may involve group or one-to-one contact	Usually open-ended, often long term when desired	Informal. Allows client to meet people with similar problems	Often no professional training. May be judged not to be 'proper' therapy

very experienced and highly trained in talking treatments; others may have limited or no training, and this may become a problem if the individual who is looking for help has complex needs.

The time spent on self-help or with a supportive network is usually entirely up to the individual seeking help.

Comparing formats

All these formats can be said to have advantages and disadvantages, and whether the pros outweigh the cons is down to individual judgement and choice. The table on page 70 gives a summary of the formats covered here.

There is room for overlap between some of these categories, and, for the most part, several of these different formats may be used by practitioners from any of the four major schools of psychological thought described in Chapter 2. This means that if you are looking for help you may have to decide not only what school of therapy sounds most useful for addressing your problems, but also what format you think would suit you personally. When you begin a course of counselling or therapy your practitioner will help you to assess whether you have chosen the most suitable form of treatment, and will advise you about alternative, more suitable forms of help if appropriate.

Who provides the treatment?

There are basically three major sources of support in the UK at present:

- the public sector (statutory services)
- the voluntary sector
- the private sector.

The table below gives a summary of which of the major formats of talking treatments are usually available from each of these sectors.

Availability of therapy in different formats

Format	Public sector	Voluntary sector	Private sector
Individual	Yes	Yes	Yes
Group	Yes	Yes	Yes
Couples	Less common	Yes	Yes
Family	Yes	Less common	Less common
Child/adolescent	Yes	Less common	Less common
Telephone	Less common	Yes	Less common
Self-help networks	Increasingly common	Yes	Less common

Of course, your choice of sector may be very limited by your location and how near you are to suitable voluntary projects. Other factors may include financial considerations, and the fact that the specific kind of help you want is more likely to be provided by one of these sectors than another. In fact, the choices that you have will often be narrowed down considerably; at worst, you may have almost no choice. Despite this, it is worth trying to find what you think will suit you. General sources of information are examined later in the chapter.

Public sector

You can try to find what you need from within the National Health Service (NHS), the social services, or (in the case of children) the local education authority. The government is legally obliged to provide this kind of help to people in need. The statutory services are guaranteed funding from taxation of the general population, and have their working policies dictated to them by the Department of Health and the Department of Social Services. At the same time, the process of decision-making about what should be provided for local communities is now being passed downwards. Smaller bodies made up of employees of these government departments and local 'stake-holders' – people within a geographical area with interests as to what services are provided – now have an increasingly large say in how money should be spent.

Until very recently, the public sector made a clear distinction between healthcare and social care, in terms of how services were funded, and these responsibilities were managed by the NHS and social services respectively. This situation is now changing. In the last few years the usefulness of the distinction has been questioned, and with good cause. In the area of disability, for instance, it was usually social services that assessed a person's practical functioning and requirements for support or practical aids, even where the cause of the disability was strictly medical. Conversely, care of the elderly was seen as predominantly the responsibility of the health service, even though the problems most difficult to address were often those of housing or companionship, which are clearly social rather than medical needs. In many areas, healthcare and social care staff found themselves working side by side, often carrying out almost identical tasks.

To address this situation, more recent legislation and policies have been often based around what is termed 'integrated care', where services on offer are provided by institutions and teams that represent both the social care and healthcare professions. This has helped to promote the idea of the holistic approach, where the whole problem is addressed without separating the different causes of illness and distress. It is now generally accepted that such multi-disciplinary teams provide the best care for patients or clients. However, different parts of the UK are at very different stages of developing this model of working. Because the relationship between psychological distress, physical health and social situation is a complicated one, this overall change in philosophy may have many consequences for talking treatments and the political deci-sions influencing public spending.

Government policy regarding mental health has to look at the subject in a very wide-ranging way. This means that proposals usually have to promise help for everything, from minor personal issues that pretty much everyone will experience at some time, through to major and lifelong mental illness. Chapter 4 says more about this bigger picture, which goes beyond counselling and psychotherapy.

Help from your GP

In the UK the 'gatekeeper' of most healthcare and related services is the family doctor, and it is often your GP who will be the most obvious person to go to and ask for support. However, although your GP will have encountered many individuals with psychological and personal difficulties, and may have spent part of his or her medical training working within a psychiatric team, he or she will not usually be a specialist in either talking treatments or the broader issues regarding mental health. Relatively few GPs have received any formal teaching in therapy or counselling other than a basic understanding of listening and communication skills. This being so, the GP's role is often to assess the individual patient's difficulties and decide what assistance is needed, and then provide this support either within the local practice, or by referral elsewhere.

Many GPs' surgeries now offer a wide range of interventions for promoting psychological health. The doctors themselves will prescribe suitable medication if desired, but in addition many practices now have a practice counsellor to provide talking treatments, and some also have complementary therapists (such as aromatherapists) who visit for occasional sessions.

Practice counsellors are often employed by GPs on a part-time basis, to offer talking treatments in a number of one-to-one sessions over the course of the week. The label 'counsellor' is the one used by the NHS to refer to these practitioners because it is the term most familiar to the general population. However, they may be trained in any of the schools of therapy mentioned in Chapter 2, and may prefer to describe the treatment they offer as therapy rather than counselling. It is entirely reasonable to ask your GP what kind of therapy the practice counsellor can offer you, but do not to be too surprised if the GP doesn't know.

Frequently, the GP will request a more detailed assessment of an individual patient's needs to ensure that the right kind of support is given. This assessment could involve seeing a mental health nurse or psychiatric social worker, and is discussed in Chapter 4. The assessment may show that you would benefit more from a talking treatment different from what the practice counsellor provides, in which case you will be referred to the appropriate service.

Specialist help from the NHS

The NHS usually has a number of local specialist departments that give counselling and therapy free of charge. These are organised so that each offers help with particular kinds of problems, or provides access to particular kinds of talking treatments. More details are given in Chapter 4. What is available varies in different parts of the UK, but should include some or all of the following.

Psychotherapy

In most regions of the UK, the NHS employs a department dedicated to offering group and individual psychotherapy to patients referred by other health professionals, including GPs. Sometimes self-referral is also possible, but this is less usual. The treatment on offer is usually (but not always) based on the psychodynamic approach (see Chapter 2), and in some cases, psychoanalysis is also available. Occasionally, long-term work (of up to several years' duration) is possible. All employees should have received full training in psychotherapy or analysis, or be in the process of completing training and working under supervision. Decisions as to what is suitable for your particular needs will be made in an initial assessment interview.

Psychology

All local health authorities have clinical psychology services working in partnership with both psychiatric teams and primary care doctors such as GPs. A clinical psychologist will have studied psychology at undergraduate degree level and then taken a higher degree in the practical application of his or her knowledge to clinical problems. Most clinical psychologists work using the cognitive behavioural approach (see Chapter 2), but often with other ideas that they use in an integrated fashion. The psychologist assesses a new client and then offers a fixed number of sessions to meet his or her individual needs. This time limit is generally agreed at the start of treatment and can be shortened or extended by agreement between the psychologist and client. Clinical psychologists often have the title 'doctor' because of their higher degree (doctorate); this does not mean they are medical doctors – they cannot prescribe medication, and are not trained in physical health matters.

Family therapy services

As described above, this particular format of talking treatment is provided by a team with specific training in working with families and groups. Practitioners may be nurses, social workers, psychologists, or counsellors and psychotherapists, but all will have chosen to specialise in this field. They will be knowledgeable about different approaches for family work, probably including the systems model described earlier in the chapter. Therapy tends to be more open-ended, depending on the nature of the difficulties being experienced. Taking up family therapy does not bar you from also seeking individual help for yourself, although it is best to discuss this with the therapists involved.

Child and adolescent services

Teams also exist for working with young people with psychological and emotional difficulties. The age range that is served varies, but is usually up to 16 or in some cases 18. Again, staff can come from a variety of health and social work backgrounds, or they may have trained in counselling and therapy. All practitioners will have either undergone specialist learning in this area or have gained a lot of experience of working with young people. Children's services are often linked to family therapy teams so as to provide support for parents and siblings. Again, the length of therapy tends to be dependent on the severity of the problems being encountered. Treatment for children is discussed in Chapter 10.

Substance-misuse services

Health authorities also provide specialist treatment services for people with alcohol and drug-related problems, and often for other addiction-related conditions such as gambling, compulsive sex, and eating disorders. The links between the physical, social and psychological needs of someone with a pattern of substance misuse are often very complex. This means it can be hard to prioritise and decide where to start in offering help. Consequently, these services tend to offer a mixture of social work, medical and counselling interventions, but generally employ clinical psychologists and nurses, doctors and social workers with different levels of skill and training in providing talking treatments. Chaotic use of drink or drugs is likely to cloud or even completely confuse a person's emotional and intellectual perceptions, and intensive therapy is often delayed until the individual has achieved a degree of stability. See Chapter 10.

Limitations of the public sector

Chapter 10 gives more information about the way in which specialised therapy can be targeted at particular sections of the population (such as adolescents), or can deal with highly specific types of problem (such as addiction). But generally the public sector is given the task of working with all kinds of psychological and personal difficulties, and in theory is supposed to be able to offer support of some description to anyone in distress. In practice, there are clear reasons why service provision is not always so wide-ranging. For one thing, all these services have to be paid for with public money. The overall budgets for healthcare and social care, although massive, are not big enough to deal with the almost infinite needs of the population. It is commonly believed that the NHS and social services are under-resourced and overworked. If this is true, then however unpopular the idea may be, choices have to be made as to which of society's problems will be given the greatest priority and which will be seen as less worthy of attention.

Typically, the broad area of mental health (including talking treatments and a great deal more) has often been considered to be a 'Cinderella service' in the UK. In other words, it is a poor relation of more headline-grabbing fields such as, say, cancer treatment or transplant surgery. This does not mean that those problems are necessarily well funded either, only that they may be more likely to arouse public interest and support. In recent years, there have been some high-profile cases indicating the struggles of the public sector to meet the mental health needs of the population. But even with this publicity, there is still a lack of funding in this area.

Policy and planning are often geared more to dealing with severe and enduring mental disorders such as schizophrenia than to the daily experience of personal suffering encountered by many millions of citizens. The upshot of this is that while structures exist to 'fast-track' individuals presenting with major psychiatric conditions (which is, of course, entirely appropriate), there is little else for other people. The services listed above, which are intended for everything except the most severe of disorders, often have small professional teams, inadequate premises, and lengthy waiting lists. The only good news is that efforts are being made to address this, and that waiting lists vary a great deal from area to area. When you are referred, or refer yourself, ask how long you may realistically have to wait to be seen.

Voluntary sector

Some people like to keep psychological problems separate from their more obvious physical health needs, or are worried about a treatment within the public sector becoming part of their permanent medical records. Others may want to meet people with problems similar to their own, or at least address their difficulties in a more informal environment, and choose to stay away from clinics or hospitals. If this is how you feel, you can look for support from charitable organisations, perhaps run by professionals or by interested and experienced lay people. These are commonly referred to as the voluntary sector not because these agencies are staffed by volunteers (although this may be the case), but because the organisations developed independently of the statutory services. They came into being not as a legal and political requirement, but because of the interest and enthusiasm of a group of people. Well-known examples of such organisations are RELATE★ (the former Marriage Guidance Council), Childline★ and CRUSE Bereavement Care.★

Voluntary-sector organisations do frequently receive at least some funding from central or local government. However, this money has to be applied for and is either granted (or not) on the basis of how useful a project is thought to be. Unlike the public sector services, funded voluntary organisations can create their own management structures and ways of working, provided they continue to deliver a service that justifies their funding. Many voluntary projects receive no government financial support at all, and can therefore do whatever they like (provided their actions remain within the law). The voluntary sector is by definition non-profit making.

While the statutory sector is staffed by personnel with professional and vocational qualifications and is directed by political decisions and economic policy, the voluntary sector is filled with a much broader mix of people who have chosen to collaborate towards aims determined by their own perception of need and of what is useful. This has some advantages, because although voluntary projects do not have a completely free hand in determining their working practices, they are often more able to respond rapidly to local need, and are more inclined to do this. Instead of having to wait for a change in public opinion, or political priorities, concerned individuals who want to set up a new agency within the voluntary sector will usually follow one of these basic patterns.

- A person (or persons) with particular skills or experience identifies a deficit in local or national provision and sets up premises and recruits staff to meet this need.

- An individual (or individuals) with no specific background in relevant professions or fields of endeavour nevertheless identifies an interest or deficit in provision and co-ordinates the efforts of others. Appropriate staff can then be employed, greater knowledge of the issue can be acquired, and useful interventions aimed at dealing with it can be planned.
- A person (or persons) establishes an information network dedicated to a particular need, with help and advice being spread by any easily available means. Contact between interested or affected parties can also be encouraged.
- An existing non-statutory agency decides to expand its current services and uses its knowledge and experience to achieve this, either widening the choice of services on offer, or offering more of the same to a greater variety of clients.

Each of these models of development (which may overlap, of course) has led to the creation of many new projects offering support to people with personal problems. In fact, so successful has the voluntary sector been in promoting the use of local knowledge in the planning of services, that the NHS and social services now work more and more in tandem with voluntary organisations. This ensures that there is no unnecessary duplication of what is on offer, and allows the public sector to learn from voluntary organisations' experiences and management decisions. The two sectors have never worked so closely together as they do now.

This is why central and local government are frequently a major source of funding for voluntary projects. They provide capital funds with which to set up agencies, and support them over time with large contributions towards costs and overheads. The people setting up a project often 'top up' this money by registering as a charity and inviting donations; tax concessions are available on this kind of income. The government gets a service without having to foot the entire bill, and the future of the project is assured. However, the agency has to continue to prove the success of, and need for, its services at regular intervals.

Voluntary-sector projects vary hugely in size, from those that employ thousands of full-time workers to others that consist of two people working out of their own home. Some projects may even exist without any government or local council funding, relying either on charity status alone or by meeting costs out of the pockets of the staff themselves. Maintaining an information service for sufferers from a particular problem may require no more than one person, a computer, a website and a few hours of effort per week, but this can still provide a vital service. The voluntary sector continues to grow within the UK, both as the result of rising demands that are not being met elsewhere, and, more positively, because the benefits of this approach are becoming clearer.

Types of voluntary-sector organisations

This section outlines the three main types of voluntary-sector projects dealing with personal and psychological problems.

Agencies providing organised therapy and counselling

Given the increasing popularity of talking treatments, and the length of waiting lists within the statutory sector, it is not surprising that many organisations have been set up to provide alternative means of accessing therapy and counselling. These organisations usually obtain convenient premises and aim to offer a range of services to prospective clients. Some employ staff who all work from the same specific school of therapy and others employ people trained in different schools so as to broaden choice. Practitioners may be on a salary or may give their services free of charge. Similarly, sessions may be entirely free, or the agency may request donations (fees that are not fixed or compulsory, but paid according to what the client can afford). Work may be very time-limited, or open-ended; they may be entirely one-to-one, or a mixture of individual and group sessions. Often therapists are senior students, in the process of completing a professional training in talking treatments.

These organisations can be created to deal with a very broad range of issues and clientele; alternatively, they may aim to work with a particular kind of problem, or may be limited by age group, gender, or sexuality. Most agencies will work within codes of practice appropriate for their staff and clients so as to provide safe-guards and also a structure to examine and assess their ongoing work. However, it is advisable to ask about the training, experience and supervision of a therapist. Chapter 9 gives you information on safeguards and training, and a list of questions to ask. As mentioned in Chapter 1, the overuse of the term 'counsellor' has become so great that it is possible to meet someone offering 'counselling' whose sum total of training is a weekend course in listening skills. (This is true among doctors, nurses and social workers, as well as among voluntary-sector staff.) People may in all good conscience carry out what they think of as 'counselling' despite having undergone no significant training, and despite receiving no useful feedback from a supervisor about their actual level of technical skill.

Regrettably, the more successful and better organised a voluntary project is, the more likely it will be that it too has acquired a waiting list.

Agencies providing useful information

Many organisations within the voluntary sector offer more general information to help deal with personal difficulties. This may be with a view to preparing people for the experience of a therapy appropriate for them, or could instead be aimed at helping empower them to make active choices as to how best to tackle their difficulties. There is a significant difference between offering advice and practising counselling or psychotherapy. But contact with people knowledgeable about the experience of talking treatments can be a very reassuring step in the larger process of obtaining help.

Some agencies may offer very short-term contact with a therapist that can help someone to decide whether longer or more intensive work is needed. Informal groups may also be available that provide a similar 'taster' of what is to come if you commit to a more involved therapy in the future. Again, these projects may be very specific about the issues they cover or clientele to whom they offer their services, or they may have a very broad remit that includes a range of personal problems. Because these organisations often give only brief contact, waiting lists do not exist for all of their services. Charitable contributions are usually welcome.

Agencies providing opportunities for self-help and social contact

The model of different people affected by a common problem getting together and offering support to each other was pioneered in the voluntary sector. The social services and the NHS have increasingly adopted this approach in recent years, using professional staff as a channel of communication through which this kind of contact can occur. There are now countless self-help groups available at national and local level, via telephone, the Internet and in person, and which offer support both in groups and on an individual basis. Many of these organisations, for example Alcoholics Anonymous,★ are sufficiently large that they provide a programme of help available almost 24 hours a day. Because they usually rely on the goodwill of huge memberships, they can give support and advice unmatched in quantity by even the best developed of public-sector services. Others have much more modest aims, and hold occasional meetings or maintain limited contact to allow for an exchange of useful information.

Although this is probably not organised counselling or therapy as defined in this guide, it is certainly an experience found to be highly therapeutic by many people. This kind of support may be an ideal alternative to, or provide additional help alongside, in-depth talking treatments. The downside, especially where no public funding is received, is that frequently no agreed codes of conduct are required to be in place. This is not to suggest that guidelines do not exist, or that self-help groups are likely to be run by irresponsible or dangerous people. But someone who organises a supportive network cannot really be reported to a professional body or disciplined. This may mean that different expectations and a different sense of professional limits will apply than would be the case in dealing with a doctor or nurse or social worker. Chapter 9 explores the issue of accountability in the counselling and therapy world.

Waiting lists as such do not really apply here, and contributions towards costs or offers of practical assistance are very welcome.

Private sector

Despite the existence of public-sector services and the growth of the voluntary sector, there is still room for a flourishing private sector (also known as the independent sector) for those who can afford it. You can obtain the therapy you need by paying a trained and qualified self-employed practitioner, or a suitable organisation, to provide it. Many private practitioners are members of professional associations such as the British Association for Counselling and Psychotherapy,★ the British Association of Psychotherapists★ or the United Kingdom Council for Psychotherapy.★ As well as setting standards for membership and professional conduct, and providing a body for the client to contact over any complaint, these professional associations can help arrange assessment of your needs and can refer you to a suitably qualified practitioner in your local area. Chapter 9 gives more details on the professional standing of practitioners, and your safeguards.

You can expect to receive a much wider range of healthcare options, and be treated much more quickly, if you pay to 'go private'. This means that ability to pay, rather than need, can all too often determine the level of service you receive. However, many counsellors and therapists work privately out of necessity rather than choice, because there are still far more people who want therapy than there are practitioners employed to provide it free to the client. This is despite the fact that there is an increasing recognition of the usefulness of talking treatments.

On the other hand, the changes that have taken place in healthcare since the 1980s mean that the demarcations between public, voluntary and private sectors are not as clear as they used to be. The public sector may often pay for a person to receive counselling or therapy from the private sector. Usually this happens because it is seen as a cheaper option, and gets the best out of limited resources. It can be a cost-effective way of dealing with waiting lists, or may happen when highly sought-after skills or experience are most easily found outside the public sector. This does not, of course, mean that you can select a therapist and expect the NHS to pay for your treatment. Sometimes this kind of arrangement is possible if you have private health insurance, so it is worth checking the small print of any policy for which you are paying. The growing popularity of private health insurance will probably extend this blurring of the lines between the sectors.

Voluntary professional associations and charities, too, may keep lists of suitably qualified practitioners working within an agreed ethical code of professional conduct, and may help people to arrange private treatment if it is not available in the public sector.

At the same time, no private venture will be developed if those who offer it cannot see a reasonable financial return. As with most other areas of healthcare and social care, a broad range of therapy and counselling can be obtained if you can afford to pay for it. It is usually not an option for anyone on state benefits. However, people with some ability to pay will find that costs can vary enormously. Not all private services are very expensive, and it is well worth investigating what is available.

Individual therapy

For individual face-to-face work, costs in the private sector can range from £5 to £10 per hour for a few subsidised sessions, through to the more typical rate of £30 to £60 per hour, and upwards to well in excess of £100 per hour. A few practitioners see their clients several times each week, but fees that could total in excess of £1,000 monthly are probably affordable only by the super-rich. More usually, a fortnightly visit to your therapist for an hour's session at £30 would work out at a more manageable £15 per week. Costs can sometimes be negotiated with therapists, and you may find that they offer a sliding scale of fees according to clients' means. Fees are usually paid after a session, rather than in advance. There may also be charges for cancelled or missed sessions – this should be discussed with a practitioner before the first session.

These amounts are not a guarantee of how much therapy will cost, nor are they a recognised standard that can be used to beat down prices; they are simply a rough guide to what is being charged by many people at the time of writing. It is best to make no assumptions about cost until you hear what the therapist has to say. Although £40 per hour may seem a high fee, you must bear in mind that most responsible practitioners would not see more than four or five people per day, and some not even that many, in order that they can offer high-quality work and concentrate on what they are doing. In addition, self-employed therapists must pay for premises, supervision, and ongoing training (the last two of which can cut considerably into the hours available for offering sessions), and – like all self-employed people – they earn nothing when sick or on holiday. It is true that some practitioners make a very good living from their work, but most private therapists and counsellors earn less than skilled tradespeople, and a few struggle to make a living at all.

If payment is the most obvious disadvantage of private therapy, the most obvious advantage is that you can choose what school of therapy to engage in and approach people with relevant training. There may also be greater freedom in terms of the duration of the therapy and the time of day you are seen, and you may avoid a waiting list. These are not absolutes: a well-liked and effective practitioner may be very popular, and may have to turn prospective new clients away; or he or she may be able to see you only at the less popular times of day.

Private practitioners may see their clients in the practitioner's home or in a consulting room at a centre or clinic.

Couples, family and child therapy

Most of the above information on individual therapy holds true for work with couples, families and children or adolescents. All these formats for counselling and therapy are available privately, and with a widely varying scale of costs. However, these therapies are much less commonly offered in the private sector than is individual work. Many practitioners who work in these specialities in the NHS or other statutory services also do private work.

Groups

Private group work is also available, and tends to be cheaper than individual sessions, for the obvious reason that more people are paying. In return for getting a cheaper therapy, however, you have to share the focus of attention with other group members. (You may, of course, choose group therapy specifically for its benefits.) It is hard to place a specific figure on costs for attending a private group, but it is likely to be more reasonable than one-to-one sessions.

Residential programmes

There are private clinics and hospitals that offer therapy in a residential setting, but they are generally beyond the financial means of the average person. It may cost you hundreds or even thousands of pounds a week to receive therapy while enjoying hotel-standard board and lodging. Therapeutic programmes often include a mixture of group and individual work, perhaps lasting for many hours each day. Occasionally a programme is designed around daily rather than residential attendance, and you can go home at night. These kinds of clinics, whether they involve overnight stays or not, are sometimes referred to as 'therapeutic communities'.

Readers may be familiar with these kinds of programmes from media stories about celebrities who book in for extended treatment, but they are not a realistic option for most of us. An exception would be where residential treatment is indicated for long-standing drug or alcohol problems. Sometimes the NHS or social services will pay for a limited stay in a clinic if it is believed that this is the only realistic method of successful treatment. This is decided upon the basis of an extended assessment, but must be requested via a GP or an addictions team. The assessor's decision is final, and a programme will not be available on demand.

Paying for treatment from health insurance

At present there is a lot of talk in health and social planning circles about creating more and better partnerships between the public and private sectors, just as closer links have been achieved between the public and voluntary sectors. This will probably happen only if there is an increased uptake in private health insurance, a subject on which the public is very divided. Many insurance packages will now provide for talking treatments of limited duration, and also for non-talking approaches to personal problems as discussed in Chapter 12.

Company-sponsored counselling

This method of obtaining talking treatments from the private sector started in the USA, but is increasingly available in the UK. Larger businesses provide medical insurance cover for their employees that includes a comprehensive package of counselling, therapy and psychological assessment services. Employers consider this worthwhile because so many working days are lost through employees' personal difficulties and mental health problems. Originally schemes were created only for problem drinkers, but now help for a broader range of issues is available.

Workers whose companies have Employee Assistance Programmes (EAPs) can often bypass long waiting lists for talking treatments by contacting a private practitioner. At the most basic level, telephone counselling is provided and an employee can receive support anonymously. Other employers have an account with a practitioner or professional practice and can provide a limited number of sessions from a therapist. Confidentiality is maintained, with no feedback to the employer.

The quality of the support available and the level of training and qualification of practitioners in company-sponsored counselling schemes may vary considerably. At the top end of the scale there may be access to a practice with clinical psychologists and other highly trained practitioners and medical personnel. Other EAP schemes may only be able to provide basic and very brief interventions from less experienced counsellors and therapists. While these schemes may be very helpful to employees in dealing with surface issues and by offering support at times of crisis, they may not be able to provide the in-depth help that some individuals require. Long-term psychotherapy and psychoanalysis are not usually available, although assistance can sometimes be offered with finding a suitable practitioner for longer-term work.

Companies that do not operate an EAP as described above may still offer private health insurance that covers all kinds of physical and psychological problems.

Services provided by each sector

Sector	Provided by	Managed by	Costs to users	Breadth of services
Public	Central and local government. Provision guaranteed by legal statute	Government-appointed staff. Recently, greater involvement from local population	Usually free at point of delivery; some minor fees payable by user, e.g. prescriptions	Aims to provide for all needs and wants; in practice, funding issues mean some needs have priority
Voluntary	Concerned and interested individuals; charitable organisations. No guarantee of existence unless service is useful	Interested individuals and local population; occasional input from government, Charity Commission	Often free at point of delivery; some fees charged or donations requested	Based entirely on interests and concerns of management; often target a specific need
Private	Self-employed practitioners, commercial businesses, professional associations. No guarantee of existence	The providers. Legal statutes and codes of practice may oversee standards of care	Generally all costs met by user or private insurance. Many low-fee schemes or sliding scales of fees. Costs occasionally met by public sector	Determined by costs and the skills available among practitioners

Finding appropriate help

It is not always easy to start the process of looking for help, and it may require considerable effort and time to locate the kind of support you need, at a cost you can afford, and at a place accessible to you. Yet often the very reason you are looking for help is that you are finding it hard to manage your daily life, and probably don't have the energy or concentration to take on this extra, unfamiliar task. The Resources section at the end of the guide will help you locate some first points of contact, and includes a list of publications and websites that will give you more information. The paragraphs below give a brief overview of good initial sources of guidance, and some words of caution.

Your GP and other primary care services
Your family doctor and his or her nursing and social work colleagues are usually responsible for co-ordinating onward referrals to other public-sector services, and will often have a good knowledge of voluntary projects as well. Their awareness may not be ency-clopaedic, but they should at least be able to offer you a starting point and, if necessary, refer you to an appropriate agency that will meet your needs. GPs' surgeries are also a useful source of leaflets and posters advertising places to go to when you need help. Some doctors and nurses are happy to recommend private services from particular therapists, while others avoid doing so because of the possibility that they may not be the best choice for you.

Professional bodies
Most schools of psychotherapy and counselling, and the major divisions within those schools, have professional bodies that provide information on training and guidelines for practitioners, and usually maintain a register of qualified members. Often this is available to the public and will include brief details of the geographical area served by a therapist, and special skills or interests.

Chapter 9 explains what kind of safeguards you can expect from your therapist's membership of these professional bodies. Contact numbers and addresses are in the Resources section at the back of this book.

Telephone directories
The phone book can be a surprisingly rich source of information in seeking help for psychological problems. Many major organisations

are listed in the opening sections of phone books, along with their helpline numbers; you will also find information on support and self-help projects.

In *Yellow Pages*, you will find local practitioners listed under 'Psychotherapy & analysis' and/or 'Counselling & advice'. However, it is impossible for most people to discern from an advertisement whether or not the advertiser is properly qualified. If you wish to make direct contact with a practitioner, it is best to contact one of the professional bodies, including those listed in the Resources section of this book, to find a qualified practitioner in your area.

Local library

The library is another good place to find leaflets and posters with useful information. It is possible to research schools of therapy and guides to dealing with common problems from the bookshelves themselves. This can include audio-visual aids such as videotapes and CDs. A selection of relevant publications is listed at the end of this guide. Libraries also offer access to the Internet, although you may need to book time on the computer.

Self-help networks

Several self-help networks are listed in the Resources section of this guide. Once you have contacted a network for people with the same difficulty as you, it will often be an excellent source of further information about other available agencies and services, including appropriate counsellors and therapists. Many people prefer to obtain advice from other service users rather than from professionals because they believe that they may get a less biased viewpoint. Self-help networks are often nationally organised, but with local branches. Your first exposure to them may be calling someone in another part of the country to ask about assistance available nearer to home.

Publications

The 'Self-improvement' or 'Counselling' sections of larger bookshops can also be a good place to look for information about what's out there. Although most books on these shelves are about the theory of counselling and therapy rather than places to obtain it, they can still be a good starting point for useful addresses and telephone numbers.

The Internet

The World Wide Web must be the largest single source of information ever known, and there are certainly many useful sites giving details of professional organisations, opportunities for self-help and support, and in-depth explanations of the kinds of therapies available. Some good websites are listed at the end of this guide. The Department of Health's website – www.doh.gov.uk – has contact points and guidance on obtaining support, and local government sites often have similar information. Alternatively, if you enter a key phrase relating to a particular problem or talking treatment into an Internet search engine, you are likely to get a list of dozens or even hundreds of relevant websites. In order to get information specific to the UK, include 'UK' (or a more local geographical location) in your key phrase.

Remember, however, that while the Internet can provide a great deal of information and contains responsible and professionally sanctioned sites, it also contains pages written by cranks and people with odd, sometimes sinister, agendas. You may find a well-presented website with an official-sounding name, only to discover that its authors are supporting offensive (even illegal) viewpoints. Or a site that seems genuine may in fact present inaccurate, or at least questionable, information. The Internet's strength, that it gives a voice to almost everyone and allows for free access to all kinds of information, is also its central weakness, for precisely the same reasons.

Word of mouth

Possibly the most encouraging of all sources of information about an agency or practitioner comes in the form of a personal recommendation. A good experience of therapy or counselling, or of the person or organisation that provided it, is a very concrete assurance of standards and practical usefulness. Of course, personal taste can vary a great deal, and what suits one person may not suit another. Moreover, a treatment that was effective for one kind of problem will not necessarily be effective for other problems. Obviously it is wise to get as much detail as possible from the person making the recommendation before investigating further.

Testing the water

If you are still not sure what type of therapy to choose, you could complete the two questionnaires supplied in Appendix II. These are headed *Opinions about Psychological Problems* and *Help for Psychological Problems* and they have been developed by psychologists to help people make decisions about therapy. If you complete the two questionnaires and score them with the template provided in Appendix III you will get an indication of the match between the main types of therapy available and your own thinking about psychological problems and the help required for them. This may offer some guidance about where your preferences lie.

You could try out different types of therapy, but this option can be very expensive and time-consuming. Although you should certainly change therapists if you feel you are not achieving anything useful, this has to be balanced against the risk of adding to your confusion. Testing out types of therapy is not the same as test-driving cars, even though great care has to be taken to find the right therapy for you.

Chapter 4

Mental health services in the NHS

The overlap between talking treatments and the broader range of services for mental health is not always very clear. Practitioners from different schools do not always agree on whether the kind of personal problems that are addressed in therapy and counselling are anything to do with 'illness'. Some think that when diagnoses are used to describe these life issues – a process referred to as 'medicalisation' – it does not help, because it stops us from looking at our situation from a number of different angles. Instead we see ourselves as 'unwell' and are encouraged to want a tablet or other physical treatment to 'cure' us.

But talking treatments in the UK are widely available from the NHS, and are paid for and organised by people who are responsible for overseeing mental health services. This means that inevitably there is a link between talking approaches and the medical world.

What is mental health?

In the UK, the NHS is the main provider of services for people with psychological and personal problems. This is because it has the statutory responsibility to provide help and support to the entire population, and must provide a range of options that are available to everyone. This is different from the voluntary and private sectors, which are more able to specialise in areas of their own choosing. Chapter 3 gives more details on the structure of the statutory (public), voluntary and private sectors.

The NHS offers both talking treatments and also many of (although definitely not all) the non-talking approaches described in Chapter 12. Altogether, this means that a wide-ranging attitude to working with individual problems is currently to be found in the statutory sector. However, the health service generally does not talk about offering services to 'people with psychological problems'. Instead it uses the umbrella term 'mental health'.

For the first several decades of the NHS's history, services developed not from within the talking-based approaches of psychology, but from within the medical field known as psychiatry – that is, the branch of medicine concerned with mental disorders. More recently, the term 'psychiatry' has come to be thought of as not very user-friendly. In the past, a person seeing a psychiatrist was assumed to be 'mentally ill' and this was a source of stigma, something to be ashamed of. This was behind the change to the more popular term 'mental health', with the emphasis on promoting overall well-being and a positive lifestyle rather than on sickness and disease.

What would be a reasonable definition of 'mental health'? The word **mental** means something to do with 'the mind', most commonly understood as those aspects of our psychological functioning that are taken for granted – memory, intellect, personality, and so on. As Chapter 2 explains, there always has been, and still is, a lot of debate and disagreement about psychological theory. 'Mental' is a convenient term because it does not distinguish between these theories, or tell you which is thought to be best. However, it does make a distinction between the psychological elements of a person's make-up and those that relate to the body, or the purely physical. But many conditions considered to be 'mental health' problems within the NHS, and under British law, are actually disorders with a clear physical cause. These include Alzheimer's disease, pre-menstrual syndrome, and various types of learning disabilities. So 'mental' does not *only* mean 'mind' or 'psychological' when used in this particular way.

The term **health** is equally loose. The World Health Organisation (WHO), which co-ordinates and advises on medical issues internationally, defines health as '*a state of complete physical, mental, and social well-being and not merely the absence of disease or infirmity*'. This may be a helpful definition when looking at personal problems, because it acknowledges that illness is not only concerned with the body. But by opening up the range of things that 'health' can mean so that they include social well-being, the WHO statement becomes rather impractical. All human beings have at least some difficulties with their body, their mind or their relationship to the world as a whole. This is true whether the difficulties are serious (cancer, suicidal depression, total isolation and abandonment by others) or minor (eyesight that needs glasses, a stressful day at work, temporary problems in a relationship). It is unlikely that, at any one time, anyone is completely free from any condition or concern that by this definition could be seen as threatening 'health'. This means that by the WHO standard, it is arguable that no one could ever be said to be healthy. Instead, 'health' is a kind of imaginary state, something for which people may hope but which exists only as a concept rather than as a day-to-day reality.

Definitions of illness

When we start looking at ideas like health and illness, it can be surprising how easy it is to get stuck in circular definitions:

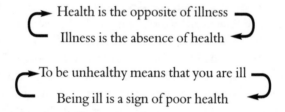

Health is the opposite of illness

Illness is the absence of health

To be unhealthy means that you are ill

Being ill is a sign of poor health

None of this gets us very far, other than to demonstrate both how much we take these kind of words for granted, and also how little they actually tell us. Perhaps another approach to understanding the concept is to look at how one moves from a state of 'health' to a state of 'illness'. If we can understand this in the more general sense, perhaps we can also understand how it works in terms of 'psychological' or 'mental health' problems.

We can use the WHO definition of health, for all its limitations, as a starting point. The WHO states that types of health involve physical, mental and social well-being. Thus types of *illness* will include:

● **physical illness** – part or all of the body does not respond or 'work' in the accepted way. This leads either to reduced ability, or unwanted limitations being placed on daily activities, and, at worst, ongoing deterioration and death

- **mental illness** – the processes of the mind do not appear to function in the way that is commonly considered 'normal' from a psychological standpoint. This may cause problems with emotions, self-expression, memory and reasoning skills, or behaviour. Again, this can vary in seriousness or duration
- **social 'illness'** – the individual struggles to deal successfully with other people and social structures or organisations. The person may have difficulties in managing areas of his or her life such as family relationships, romantic attachments, employment, or finding a meaningful existence within society and the world as a whole. Once more, this is not limited to serious issues or long-lasting problems, and could include minor or short-lived struggles.

This tells us how a person may experience illness. But if it is accepted that the 'ill' or 'unhealthy' person is someone who has problems in one or more of the above areas, it is also necessary to state what the causes of those problems are.

What causes illness?

Chapter 1 looked at common explanations for the kind of problems that can be helped by talking treatments. That overview can be widened out to look at the causes of all kinds of distress, not just psychological or personal difficulties. The table on page 96 shows some ways in which the causes of illness can be explained and categorised.

It is worth adding that for the most part these explanations are not mutually exclusive and do not have to be seen as contradictory. Many of them clearly overlap, and it is generally a matter of emphasis that is important, the belief that one factor is the *major* rather than the *only* cause at work. At the same time, the more enthusiastic champions of any one of these ideas may be convinced that it is an authentic explanation for all illness and personal suffering. The current trend of looking for genetic causes for many behaviours is a possible example of this.

The interrelationship between problems

Whether or not people believe that personal problems are a kind of illness, it is often a real struggle to identify what kind of help might

Explanations of illness

	Origin	Immediate cause of illness	Examples
Medical	Illness has a clear biological and scientific basis	Infections, physical trauma, hereditary factors	Common cold, broken arm, cystic fibrosis
Interpersonal	Illness results from work, relationships and resulting stresses	Significant people in our daily life	Anxiety, bereavement, stomach ulcer
Intra-psychic	Illness is the result of uncontrolled urges or feelings or unresolved internal conflicts	Dysfunctional or conflicting mental processes	Drug and alcohol problems, eating disorders, smoking-related illness, obsessive compulsive disorder
Socio-political	Illness occurs because society is disorganised or uncaring	Governments, big business, dysfunctional families	Famine, CJD, asthma caused by pollution
Spiritual	Illness is caused by divine intervention, fate or retribution	Religious codes, cosmic justice	Almost anything

be needed in a specific situation. This means that it is not always clear who is best suited to give support: the medical services, or counsellors and therapists, or social workers. Consider the following cases.

- A 38-year-old man is diagnosed as having very serious liver disease following 20 years of heavy drinking. He is informed that if his alcoholism is not treated, he has a limited time to live, and that no surgery or medication will otherwise be of help. He tells his doctor that because he is homeless and without friends or family, he does not have a stable enough situation from which to start to make this huge change. Is this a mental, physical or social problem?
- A 13-year-old girl is pregnant and has been rejected by the 15-year-old father of the child. She has tried to kill herself by

taking an overdose. Her mother, a lone parent, suffers from multiple sclerosis and feels unable to cope with the situation. Are mental health services alone going to be enough in this case?

- A 49-year-old woman has been diagnosed with breast cancer and is undergoing radiotherapy. She is told that maintaining a positive attitude and a relaxed lifestyle is at least as important a factor in her recovery as the radiation treatment. Why, if this is clearly a physical illness, should that be so?

These cases show how the distinctions between 'mental' and other kinds of health problems often (perhaps almost always) seem to become blurred. All these people require psychological help, and may be treated within the mental health services of the NHS, but their difficulties also relate to physical and social needs. It would not only be hard but also probably irresponsible to pretend that we could state categorically what the main issue was for each person, and whether each person's problems were mainly psychological or otherwise.

If the causes of a problem can be explained in different ways, or if the problem has more than one cause, it goes without saying that the service providers might need to offer several different things to help deal with it. Not all of the NHS, and not all users of the NHS, see talking treatments as the best way to manage personal difficulties. This is why Chapter 12 lists many alternative, complementary and additional ways of dealing with life's challenges. Perhaps it also goes some way to explaining why 'mental health services' exist: sometimes people need a more complex approach for their situations, and talking alone may not be in any way sufficient for their needs. This is why a doctor, nurse or practitioner of counselling and therapy may recommend you for a mental health assessment (see the section later in this chapter).

Structure of NHS mental health services

Overall management of mental health services in the UK is provided by the Department of Health (DOH) in England and Wales; the Scottish Executive Health Department in Scotland; and the Department of Health, Social Services and Public Safety in

Northern Ireland. Services on offer do vary within the home nations and sometimes even within regions of each country, although they are largely similar throughout the UK.

An overview of NHS care

Chapter 3 lists the kind of practitioners to whom GPs can refer patients for talking treatments. These include counsellors, psychotherapists and psychoanalysts, psychologists, and family and children's services. All these services are paid for out of the overall budget for mental health services. The intention is to provide help and support for people as locally as possible: professionals will usually be based in small **clinics** within the community, and sometimes work in more than one place. They may visit several different clinics in the course of a week and carry out sessions near to where people live, rather than making their clients travel a long way. Often this includes visits to GPs' surgeries.

Some **specialist services** have to operate on a less flexible basis, because they are offered to quite small numbers of people and may be run by very few staff. As a result, teams work out of one building and clients may need to journey greater distances to see them; the alternative would be for specialist practitioners to spend more than half their time travelling, seeing only one or two people each day.

A large proportion of the money allocated to mental health is spent on **hospital-based services**, especially in-patient wards. This is not because great numbers of people are admitted to hospital for treatment of mental illness or distress, but because, compared to community services, hospital wards are extremely expensive to run. This is one of the major reasons that, where possible, 'community care' is preferred over hospital admission. The other reason is that attitudes have changed, and it is no longer considered necessary in most instances to admit people to hospitals for assessment. Previously it was not uncommon even for people with quite mild depression to be admitted for a few days so that a full assessment could be made. Today this is rare. The period of assessment is believed to be better accomplished at home, with the individual in a familiar setting where a clearer picture of his or her difficulties can emerge. In-patient treatment is only thought necessary when a person has become incapable of caring for himself or herself (or his or her children) even with maximum support being offered at home, and now only a tiny percentage of people is admitted to a ward because of mental health problems.

The NHS also funds **day hospitals**, which are community-based clinics that people can attend on an occasional – or sometimes a frequent – basis. These centres can provide group and individual talking treatments, reviews by doctors and nurses, and some of the creative and social therapies mentioned in Chapter 12. NHS mental health services may refer people to voluntary-sector projects or self-help organisations. These are separate from the NHS itself, but they often receive some government funding.

In most parts of the UK, the public services are co-ordinated by **community mental health teams** (CMHTs). Often people are referred to a CMHT by their GP for an assessment of their needs, especially when their problems are complicated and are seriously affecting their daily lives. Continuing contact will be provided where this is desired and necessary. Crisis intervention teams may also be in place to support people who are struggling to care for themselves but who want to avoid a hospital admission. Forensic psychiatry teams are a specialist service, providing help in situations when mental health problems have led to criminal behaviour. All of these groups are multi-disciplinary in nature, and are made up of people from a number of different professions.

Staffing

Mental health services may employ any or all of the following:

- psychiatrists
- psychiatric nurses
- approved social workers
- clinical psychologists
- counselling psychologists
- occupational therapists
- psychotherapists and child psychotherapists.

Psychiatrists

A psychiatrist is a qualified doctor who, after seven years of medical training, has decided to specialise in treating mental health problems. An NHS consultant psychiatrist will have overall responsibility for the care of patients referred to the mental health services (whether in hospital or in the community), and will be assisted by junior doctors (house officers) and more senior doctors (registrars) in his or her team. Psychiatrists can prescribe medication, arrange hospital admissions or day care, and may refer patients to other specialists. The consultant psychiatrist is often seen as the head of the mental health team because this person has primary legal responsibilities regarding diagnosis, prescribing and treatment (see 'Mental health legislation', later in this chapter). Some consultant psychiatrists will have undertaken specialist training in psychotherapy.

Psychiatric nurses

Registered mental nurses (RMNs) are nurses who have decided to specialise in mental health. Most of their training will have been spent working with different kinds of mental illness and psychological problems. Some will have completed a general nursing training, and many will have had some experience of caring for people with physical illness. RMNs are trained to carry out procedures such as administering medication when necessary. Some nurses can also prescribe medication, but this is not yet very common. An RMN will often have regular contact with clients in the community to assess their continuing need for support.

Approved social workers

Approved social workers (ASWs) have a wide training that includes child protection, care of the elderly and residential work. They have also taken a second qualification in mental health, and, like nurses, they are frequently assigned as case workers and have ongoing contact with clients. Social workers are not medically trained, but they will probably have knowledge of housing issues, welfare rights and social security benefits.

Clinical psychologists

Clinical psychologists take an undergraduate degree in psychology and then a second degree in using psychological principles in order to provide treatment and support. As pointed out in Chapter 3, they are often referred to as 'doctor' because they have completed a doctorate in their field of study, but they should not be confused with a psychiatrist or any other kind of medical doctor. Clinical psychologists can offer testing of mental functioning such as memory or IQ. They are also trained in talking treatments, usually cognitive behavioural therapy.

Counselling psychologists

Counselling psychologists have a similar career path to clinical psychologists, but their second degree is in eclectic and integrative therapy, meaning that they train in more than one school of counselling. They may offer a range of talking treatments but are not qualified in the testing of mental functioning.

Occupational therapists

Occupational therapists (OTs) have a specialist qualification in the assessment of individual ability in physical, mental and social functioning. Many work in the field of physical health, but those working in mental health assist clients in planning lifestyle changes. This can include looking at a balance of work and leisure time, seeking out educational opportunities, and providing skills training (for instance, social skills or budgeting) in group and individual settings.

Psychotherapists

The mental health team will also include psychotherapists, and there may be a Department of Psychotherapy (or psychological treatment services) attached to, or working alongside, the Department of Psychiatry. NHS consultant psychotherapists are consultant psychiatrists who have specialised in psychotherapy. They may head a department that includes many trained psychotherapists, some of whom may also be medically qualified or trained in clinical psychology. The psychotherapists may include practitioners who specialise in long-term (psychodynamic) therapy or those who use brief therapies such as cognitive behavioural therapy, cognitive analytical therapy, or interpersonal psychotherapy.

Other mental health professionals

You may also be referred to see a professional working in a specialist area such as addictions or child and adolescent therapy (see Chapter

10 for more information about these services). Mental health psychotherapy teams may also employ practitioners of creative therapies (see Chapter 12 for an outline of some non-talking therapies available).

A mental health assessment

The large majority of patients who go to their GP for support with an emotional problem will not require a mental health assessment, and will never meet a psychiatrist, nurse or social worker while they are getting help for their difficulties. However, a mental health assessment is useful when people have complex problems that are difficult to manage with a single or low-key approach. It may be felt that you need several different kinds of treatment or support, and this is often best co-ordinated within the mental health services rather than by a GP or counsellor alone.

If your GP or another professional suggests an assessment, try to keep an open mind. An assessment could be a way to receive more immediate and more comprehensive support in the NHS. If your difficulties are getting out of hand, it could be exactly what you need. Many of those who are referred to the community mental health team are likely to have short-term problems, and will not require ongoing contact with a psychiatrist or case worker. Seeing any of these professionals does not mean that you must have a serious mental illness, or that you will automatically be labelled with a mental health diagnosis. In asking for an assessment, it may simply be that your GP is being cautious, or wants a second specialist opinion, or does not feel especially skilled in dealing with personal problems and wants someone else to decide what kind of help is best.

What happens

The assessment process will probably begin with a single interview with a nurse or social worker, or sometimes with a psychiatrist or psychotherapist. This may take place in your own home but more commonly will be at a local clinic, day hospital, or occasionally at your GP's surgery. The assessment aims to find out more about your mood and emotional state, family matters, past history and significant life events, and any current issues that are giving rise to concern. Following the assessment the assessor will generally discuss the findings with colleagues in the mental health team and with the practitioner who made the referral. Plans will then be made as to what kind of further help and treatment are most suitable.

Often this interview is the only contact that you will have with the mental health team, and the only support given will be advice and information. If your initial assessment was not with a psychiatrist, but if medication is thought to be helpful, an interview with a psychiatrist, who is the only professional in the team who can prescribe, will be arranged. This will frequently be followed by more regular contact, because it is necessary to review medication. On other occasions, the staff member you see may recommend a talking treatment, and refer you to a psychologist, counsellor or therapist. A benefit of this assessment is that sometimes the mental health team can help to bypass the waiting lists for counselling or therapy. You could also be referred to the occupational therapist, to a practitioner for therapy with your partner or family, or for regular attendance at a day centre or day hospital. All treatment should be discussed with you in detail.

Although hospital admissions are rare these days, this may sometimes be necessary to give you a complete break or if your physical health has deteriorated seriously as a consequence of your mental distress. People are frequently very scared that they may be forced into hospital or have to accept treatment against their will. This is uncommon, but the situations in which it can happen are described in the section on 'Mental health legislation' later in this chapter.

Types of mental illness

Having a breakdown

Sometimes people talk about having had a 'breakdown' because of stress or other mental health difficulties. Although this is a very commonly used term, it is hard to define, and seems to mean any kind of situation in which someone feels unable to carry on. Mental health professionals do not generally use the term because it is imprecise.

Psychiatrists and their colleagues are trained to work with a range of different conditions, many of which are similar to the kind of personal problems discussed throughout this guide, and some of which are not. The role of a mental health professional is to assess the individual's situation and see if a clear diagnosis is possible. A diagnosis will help determine what kind of overall treatment is needed, and – if a talking treatment is appropriate – what kind of counselling or therapy is likely to be best for you.

Psychiatric diagnosis is complicated, but most diagnoses fall into three main categories:

- neuroses
- psychoses
- personality disorders.

More information on diagnosis can be found in Appendix I.

Neuroses

Neurotic disorders are very common. They are disorders of mood and emotion, which often severely interfere with the way the individual functions in life and in relationships. People with a neurosis are aware of their difficulties, and usually have some insight into themselves and their problems. This may be buried under their emotional strain, but it means that talking treatments can be at least part of the solution. There are many types of neurosis, but these are the most common examples:

- **depression** – a constant low mood and slowing down of mental functioning. A traumatic event or loss is often the cause; the individual cannot learn how to deal with what has happened, and sinks deeper into their sad feelings. This is commonly accompanied by feelings of hopelessness and worthlessness, and sometimes by suicidal ideas
- **anxiety** – a state of panic and agitation leading to negative thoughts and expectations. High levels of stress are usually the cause, especially when there are few opportunities to relax or change the situation
- **phobia** – an unreasoning fear of something or some situation. The fear is deeply felt even if, on an intellectual level, the

person may be aware that it makes no rational sense. Phobias can relate to places, animals, situations or even certain types of thoughts

- **obsessive compulsive disorder** – repetitive thoughts and feelings that often lead to strange habits and behaviours aimed at making the thoughts go away. For example, worries about household dirt could lead to daily rituals of excessive cleaning, or washing hands until they are red and raw. Usually this develops when a reasonable fear or concern gets gradually more out of control; small steps in this process eventually add up to very severe changes in personal routines and well-being
- **eating disorders** – these include *anorexia nervosa* (excessive dieting), *bulimia nervosa* (binge eating and forcing yourself to vomit) and being chronically and significantly overweight. Often there appears to be an underlying emotional problem such as relationship difficulties or sexual worries, or a history of trauma.

Neuroses often seem like extreme versions of common personal problems. We all get depressed, we all feel stressed, we have fears, we may eat for comfort, we may worry excessively – obsessively, sometimes – about particular things. Although these diagnostic labels are strictly defined medical terms, they are used loosely in everyday conversation. But it is when these difficulties have become very exaggerated and long-lasting that they are sometimes said to have become an 'illness'. At that stage support is needed – and quickly.

There are other types of neurosis, but these are the most common examples.

Psychoses

Psychoses are major mental illnesses, and are experienced by many people in the UK.

What causes psychotic illness is poorly understood, but there is evidence for important chemical changes in the central nervous system. A psychosis can be caused by external factors such as taking drugs or drinking too much alcohol. Stress, unhappiness and other personal difficulties also seem to be significant factors in causing psychotic illnesses. There is also some evidence that people can be genetically disposed towards these kinds of conditions, and that high stress or other traumas can lead to these symptoms emerging. Psychoses are most likely to be seen for the first time during the teens or early twenties. Many psychotic episodes are short-lived, although without treatment (and, sadly, even with treatment) they can become a lifelong problem.

These are the two most common types of psychosis.

- **Manic depression** With this condition the individual experiences alternating and unpredictable mood swings: periods of extreme depression alternating with equally extreme 'highs' when he or she is elated and very energetic ('manic'). A depressive or manic phase usually lasts for months at a time. Occasionally people experience only the severely depressed phase, and do not have manic episodes. This is called 'endogenous' depression, to distinguish it from 'reactive' depression, where the sadness is more obviously traceable to some life event. Endogenous depression appears to occur suddenly and for no obvious reason, rather than as a reaction to an unpleasant event. Such depression may be very severe, difficult to treat, and has features closer to psychosis than neurotic illness.
- **Schizophrenia** This is a condition where the sufferer not only experiences mood changes but also hallucinations and delusions. A *hallucination* is a false sensory impression caused by a malfunction of the central nervous system. People suffering from schizophrenia perceive something that is not actually there, but their senses convince them that it is. In schizophrenia, the hallucinations frequently take the form of 'hearing voices'. The person is not imagining it or making it up, but really does hear, see, taste, smell or feel the non-existent something. *Delusions* are rigidly held beliefs that are clearly untrue or irrational; again, they are completely real to the person. The person may be convinced that (for instance) he or she is someone else, or married to a celebrity, or is being persecuted by his or her neighbours, or watched or spied upon. Hallucinations and delusions are bewildering and sometimes terrifying, and can lead to chaotic situations very quickly. Schizophrenia, too, seems to be caused by chemical imbalances in the brain, although there is a great deal of disagreement

about why these imbalances happen. Medication can bring chemical levels back to normal, and sometimes this is achieved through an injection that is needed only once every few weeks. Previously the drugs used had many unpleasant side-effects, but improvements have been made in this respect in the last ten years. See Chapter 12 for more information.

Psychotic illness is a very frightening prospect because the symptoms often involve what might be described as 'being out of touch with reality'. The idea that we cannot trust our senses or memories, or that our mood can change from high to low without any clear cause, is very disturbing. Many of us, when faced with high levels of stress and sadness, can begin to feel that we are losing control or 'losing our minds', but this does not usually mean that we are experiencing a psychotic episode. However, it may mean that our problems have reached crisis proportions, and that we need to seek help.

A great deal of the work of mental health teams involves helping people who have a psychosis. Medication is usually needed to relieve symptoms, but talking treatments can be an effective way of providing emotional support and play an important part in the multidisciplinary care of people with schizophrenia.

Personality disorders

Certain patterns of behaviour seem not to relate to any underlying neurotic or psychotic disorder and tend to be attributed to some flaw or problem in the individual's personality. For instance, the individual may seem to habitually function in a disruptive or destructive ('antisocial') way, or to behave in an impulsive, self-centred, or even callous ('psychopathic') way, with no depth to any of the usually important relationships. However, many mental health professionals and practitioners of talking treatments disagree with the diagnostic concept of 'personality disorders'. The belief that there can be a 'disorder' of the personality is based on the idea that there is such a thing as a 'normal' personality, but nobody has defined what this is. The argument is circular: since there is no clear sense of what a normal, healthy personality is, it is difficult to be sure what a 'disordered' personality would be.

Although the terms 'psychopath' or 'sociopath' are often used to describe people with 'severely disordered personalities', these words are generally unhelpful because in people's minds they are linked with violent and other antisocial behaviour. The clinical meaning of these terms is different, and does not necessarily imply that someone is dangerous or criminal.

Whatever the appropriateness of the concept of 'personality disorder', individuals with features such as those described are most likely to require a long-term talking treatment. Mental health services sometimes have specialist teams to support people with personality problems.

Learning disabilities

Conditions in which people have limited or reduced mental functioning as a result of injury, hereditary factors, or damage following illness, are legally referred to as 'mental impairment' and are not a kind of mental illness or personality disorder. Disorders such as Down's Syndrome, Alzheimer's disease and autism are quite different from mental illness, and services for people with these problems are usually separate from services provided by mental health teams. It is sometimes forgotten that people with learning disabilities also suffer from the same personal problems as the rest of the population. Talking treatments and music, art or drama therapy have been shown to be effective in helping these clients deal with emotional and social difficulties, and some counsellors and therapists specialise in working with these individuals.

Mental health legislation

Mental health has been the subject of laws since the mid-1800s. Before that time there was no agreement in society as to how people with psychological and personal problems, whether severe or minor, should be treated. In practice, sufferers were often treated very inhumanely. In the mid-nineteenth century an Act of Parliament established that it was the responsibility of local authorities to provide for people with mental illness. Mental health matters can also become the concern of the courts when a family's welfare is involved and when a person's mental illness is considered a contributory factor in law-breaking.

The single major piece of legislation currently relating to the management of psychological problems in England and Wales is the Mental Health Act of 1983. This replaced the earlier 1959 Act, and has been updated every five years to take on board changes in society and NHS provision. It is probable that a new Act will be introduced in 2003, and this has already been drafted for a process of consultation, but the new legislation is likely to be a revision of the existing Act rather than a significant rewriting of any of the legal matters involved. In Scotland the relevant act is the Mental Health Act (Scotland) of 1984, and in Northern Ireland, the Mental Health (Northern Ireland) Order of 1986. Ongoing reviews of these documents, with a view to new and revised legislation, are also taking place at present. Further information on this subject is available at www.mentalhealth.org.uk/html/content/legislation.cfm

The legislation does not really have anything useful to say about the kind of personal difficulties discussed in this guide, nor does it make any complex statements about talking treatments. Much of the legislation covers hospital-based services, and defining the terms under which people can, in law, sometimes be compulsorily admitted to a psychiatric ward for care or treatment. When this happens a person is said to be 'sectioned', which refers to the sections of the Mental Health Act that describe how it happens. The only situation in which people with psychological problems can be forcibly detained is when they are assessed by competent professionals as being a danger to themselves or to others, *and* they will not accept help voluntarily. If someone is suicidal or aggressive to the degree that hospitalisation is required, but is willing to accept help, he or she does not need to be admitted against his or her will. Only a small number of people in psychiatric hospitals are held under the sectioning arrangements.

The Mental Health Act also goes into great detail in defining treatments available for mental illness, and whether these can be administered against the will of a patient. The situation can be summarised as follows: most treatments can be given only with the consent of the individual; the very few exceptions are nearly always in hospital settings; these exceptions apply almost exclusively to sectioned patients in emergency or urgent need; and finally, not even an emergency treatment can be given if it has effects that last beyond the immediate situation – for instance, a violent person might be given calming medication, but could not be forced to have surgery. Decisions about sectioning and giving treatments against a person's will can only be made by doctors, sometimes with the co-operation of psychiatric nurses and approved social workers.

Legally a diagnosis is only acceptable when made by a medical doctor (not necessarily a psychiatrist, given that a GP may also diagnose) and in some circumstances by a clinical psychologist. A psychiatric nurse or approved social worker can assess – and make suggestions about – what may be happening, but only a doctor or psychologist's diagnosis carries any legal weight for housing letters, insurance reports and long-term sick notes. It is important to bear this in mind if you need to prove to an official body, or your employer, that personal problems or mental illness have had serious consequences for you.

Common perceptions of mental illness

It is interesting to think about why many people are extremely reluctant to consider that mental illness might affect them and not just other people. In West European cultures, and certainly in main-stream society in the UK, major disorders such as manic depression and schizophrenia – indeed, psychological problems of all kinds – are not always dealt with sympathetically. People diagnosed by a doctor as suffering from a 'mental illness' are often patronised, excluded from society, and looked down upon. Many commonly used insults demonstrate the underlying attitudes and fears: 'He's barking', 'It's a madhouse', 'The guy's crazy', 'She's a total nutter', 'They're a bunch of morons'. In other words, we describe a person or group that we do not like as somehow not mentally 'right'. This suggests that someone who is not mentally 'right' is someone we would not like.

If asked, many people would say that they are sympathetic towards people with mental health problems, that it isn't someone's fault if they are mentally ill, and that society should provide sufferers with as much support as possible. But at the same time, because we are concerned about what other people would think, most of us would deny that we ourselves have ever had serious mental or emotional problems. It is as though we are ashamed to admit that we have been in pain, are less strong than we would like to believe, or have been unable to cope. However, the truth is that we have all lived through situations that we could not cope with, and it is an illusion (if a comforting one) that we can avoid problems through our personal determination and strength of character. Traumatic events and losses can happen to any one of us, and, when they do, there will be a point at which we need help and support.

Chapter 5

Common concerns and practical considerations

When we are feeling distressed, often our first reaction is to hope that the cause will go away of its own accord, and sometimes this does happen. But if the problem persists, we have to work a little harder at convincing ourselves that we are feeling fine, or at least managing to get by. Usually the energy and effort involved in maintaining this pretence (which is often considerable) would be much better spent in looking for solutions. The first section of this chapter considers some of the reasons that can lead us to avoid asking for help.

If you have identified that you may have a problem that could benefit from a talking treatment, and if you have decided what kind of therapy you think will be suitable for you, it is still a good idea to consider a number of important practical issues before starting a talking treatment. The second section of the chapter aims to help you make sure that this is the right step to be taking at this particular time. Finally, the last two sections cover common anxieties about the process itself and about how useful it is likely to be.

It may sound as if counselling and psychotherapy are 'risky' ventures that should be avoided where possible. While talking treatments carry none of the risks of surgery or taking medication, it should be understood that there are implications to beginning a course of therapy, and the longer and more intensive the therapy is, the greater those implications become. Thinking about this can raise a lot of anxieties, but the issues do nevertheless need to be thought about. Ideally this can be part of a process of empowerment, helping you to avoid pitfalls and later difficulties. The explanations also provide an opportunity to destroy a few myths about what therapy is, and about the kinds of people for whom it is, and is not, suitable.

Will therapy be right for me?

Many people who have decided that they could probably benefit from a talking treatment still have very mixed feelings about whether they should go ahead with the process. This is understandable, and is a very common experience. Almost everyone, when starting therapy for the first time, will be wary about the usefulness of the treatment. Below is a list of just a few reasons people find for not starting the process. Most people considering seeking help for personal problems have been convinced that these are valid objections, at some time or other. But while some of them are reasonable concerns, others may be attempts to avoid facing the situation.

1 *I'd rather cope by myself. I'm a strong person, and I've always coped before.*
2 *I'm too old and set in my ways.*
3 *I can't take the time to indulge my problems. I have to be there for other people.*
4 *Therapy would be useless for me. I find talking to other people very difficult, and I'm not good with words anyway.*
5 *I don't have any really serious problems, I'm just a little unhappy about some things that have happened to me in the past.*
6 *I do have some difficulties right now, but the idea of a talking treatment leaves me cold – all that lying on a couch and touchy-feely stuff isn't for me.*
7 *Why should I go and see a therapist? The problem isn't with me, it's with the people in my life.*
8 *Someone I know went to see a counsellor and told me afterwards that it was a dreadful experience, and didn't help them in any way at all.*

Despite these reservations, however, many people do find that a talking treatment helps. There are always reasons for not doing things, and making the decision to look for help with a psychological problem is often the most difficult step. Some clients reach this stage simply by asking themselves: 'What do I have to lose?'. If you are in need of some kind of change in your life, or at least some opportunity to reflect on your experience of life and your feelings, a talking treatment may help.

I'd rather cope by myself. I'm a strong person, and I've always coped before.

Wanting to talk about our problems, or feeling psychological pain, are not signs of weakness. They are signs that something feels wrong, and that things may need to change. In Western cultures, many people believe that it is admirable to be silent and uncomplaining, and this even extends sometimes to physical illness. However, people are often much more understanding of the difficulties caused by a broken leg than they are of the difficulties caused by stress. 'Coping' is often seen as an important skill, and we all find ourselves in situations where we have to get by as best we can. But 'coping' can sometimes mean that we are ignoring a problem and suppressing the distress and pain that it causes. Because these things continue to accumulate over time rather than conveniently go away when we choose not to think of them, we may reach a point when a situation we could have handled a year ago has now become overwhelming and unmanageable. It is worth taking action before we reach this kind of a crisis.

I'm too old and set in my ways.

People are never so old that there is no chance they will not benefit from talking about their problems and feelings. Sometimes it can seem as if it is too late to look at changing our life situation and the choices we have made, and it is true that the past cannot be undone and made to go away. But our perceptions of the past and the effect it has on us most definitely can be changed. Past disappointments, regrets and experiences can be come to terms with, leaving an individual free to enjoy the present and the future. Age and experience are not in any sense a handicap in being able to make use of whatever help is available; they will probably be a big help when the process gets under way.

I can't take the time to indulge my problems. I have to be there for other people.

Therapists and counsellors tend to accept without too much thought the idea that the 'healthy' individual should learn to put his or her own needs first, and not base decisions on what is best for other people. Of course, in many respects this is entirely correct, and learning to prioritise your own needs can be an important lesson when receiving counselling or therapy. However, individual clients are entitled to decide how to balance their own needs against those of their family, partner, children and friends. The important point is that other people's needs are rarely a good reason for you not to engage in therapy. If you have reached a stage at which you are finding it difficult to function as you go about your normal daily routines, and find it impossible to meet your responsibilities, it is better to do something about this. If you do not take good care of yourself and attend to your own problems, you are unlikely to have the strength to take care of other people.

Therapy would be useless for me. I find talking to other people very difficult, and I'm not good with words anyway.

The good news is you don't have to be good with words to engage in a talking treatment, and you don't even need to be good at talking at all. It is the job of the therapist to help you to describe what you are feeling and thinking, and he or she does not expect you to use long or interesting words. It is very difficult for all of us to describe accurately what we think and feel. But even if you think you may struggle more in this respect than other people, it will not be a big problem. All that is needed is that you stay committed to trying as hard as you can to involve yourself in the process.

I don't have any really serious problems, I'm just a little unhappy about some things that have happened to me in the past.

This may very well be true. Although books about counselling and therapy (including this one) have a tendency to talk about 'problems' as though they are the main or only focus of a talking treatment, this is an over-simplification. Being unhappy or stressed are extremely 'normal' experiences and do not indicate that anything is necessarily seriously wrong: it is a matter of degree. Therapy sessions may focus on looking at positive changes, rather than managing a crisis; or they could be a way to let off steam, talking about things that sometimes preoccupy you or exist as painful memories. Talking treatments are certainly very effective in managing the more extreme kinds of anxiety and depression, but they can also be useful in working with many less obviously serious kinds of experiences, or reflecting on any challenging or unsettling situations you are facing at home, work, or in life in general.

I do have some difficulties right now, but the idea of a talking treatment leaves me cold – all that lying on a couch and touchy-feely stuff isn't for me.

You certainly wouldn't be alone in feeling this. Most people have media-influenced ideas about what counselling and therapy are. Hollywood and our own domestic film and TV industry seem to have an endless fascination with the more lurid aspects of the therapy world, and this leads to some strange and thoroughly inaccurate representations of practitioners and their clients on both the small and large screens. But even if we acknowledge this, it is true that some therapists use a couch, and some do believe that an occasional hug is a good way to express concern for a client. (More is said about this in Chapters 8 and 9.) If you have a really major objection to these or any other aspect of a practitioner's way of working, then that particular type of therapy is probably not for you. There are lots of others available, and it is rarely a good idea to accept a particular method of working simply because it is the only one offered to you.

On the other hand, it can be useful to ask yourself why you object so strongly to the type of work in question. If you are satisfied that your reasons are good ones, fair enough. But consider whether it might be because the method of working relates to a problem that you wanted to address by arranging therapy. Although you should not engage in something that worries you, just as a means of challenging yourself, it might be worthwhile discussing your concern with your therapist.

Why should I go and see a therapist? The problem isn't with me, it's with the people in my life.

Making the decision to see a therapist or counsellor does not mean that you are accepting the blame for something. It may be entirely correct to say that the real difficulties lie elsewhere – perhaps your partner or a parent is violent towards you, or has a drug problem, for instance. But if this behaviour is causing you distress (as would be expected), then at the very least there is some value in talking about it and trying to determine what you can do to take care of yourself or manage the situation. Unfortunately, just because something is not our fault does not automatically mean that we can avoid having to deal with it.

Someone I know went to see a counsellor and told me afterwards that it was a dreadful experience, and didn't help them in any way at all.

There are several reasons why someone could give a bad report of his or her experience. Perhaps your acquaintance wasn't ready to engage in therapy, or at least in the kind of therapy that was on offer. Perhaps his or her particular issues would have been better dealt with in a different way. Or perhaps he or she was unfortunate enough to see a very bad counsellor – there are bad practitioners in all professional fields, and this certainly includes the therapy world. (See Chapter 9 for more information on how to deal with this situation if it should happen to you.)

It is easy to assume that because someone else has had a bad experience of therapy you will too, but this is really not sensible. Finding and working with a counsellor is like finding any suitable professional help. Establishing a good professional relationship is dependent on a number of factors, not least of which is the uniqueness of the two people involved, and you cannot expect your experience to be inevitably similar to someone else's.

Is it the right time?

The simple answer, of course, would be that if you believe you need therapy, then now is a good time to start. But given that most people are in a less than ideal situation, there are other questions that need to be answered before therapy or counselling gets under way. Consider whether any of the following might apply to you as you begin to look for a practitioner.

1 *I haven't yet decided whether to approach the public, voluntary or private sectors to find the help that I need.*
2 *Whichever choice I make, is this going to cost me more money than I can reasonably afford?*
3 *Can I make the time to keep to regular appointments, and is the journey involved one that I can make easily without the risk of being late or missing sessions?*
4 *Can I manage childcare?*
5 *Can I take the time off work?*

6 *Can I foresee anything that might seriously interrupt my sessions in the near future (holidays, people coming to visit, family events)?*

7 *For what period of time can I commit myself to therapy? What if I'm expected to make a long-term commitment?*

Some of these matters may seem self-evident, or be irrelevant to your situation, or relate to choices that you do not have. Alternatively, they may make you suddenly feel that there are lots of reasons why you cannot see a counsellor or therapist, at least not now. There is no ideal time to begin a talking treatment, but there are factors to be weighed up once you have made the decision to seek help. In determining what seems the best arrangement, given all the factors involved, you may have to make some compromises. This can seem disheartening, but in fact it is a positive assessment of your situation, allowing these variables their due significance but not letting them become reasons to avoid getting the support you need. In reality, solutions can usually be found.

I haven't yet decided whether to approach the public, voluntary or private sectors to find the help that I need.

Leaving aside the cost, in most cases, this decision will be heavily influenced by what is easily available locally, and perhaps also by the nature of your particular problem. For example, if you are dealing with a particularly distressing bereavement, and an agency that offers bereavement counselling is just around the corner from you, it is likely that you will look no further. But many problems are not so easily labelled, nor are most people fortunate enough to find an appropriate specialist service on their doorstep. In any case, to be able to choose the right sector you should do some research and be aware of what is available. Chapter 3 outlines these possibilities. If you are not sure what kind of help you need and/or don't know what is available locally, you can always approach your GP and ask to be referred to a therapist.

However, when you are ready to discuss your problems, and a therapist has been identified, you may find that there is a significant waiting list, or that the private therapist you want to see is not currently taking on new clients. This can be deeply frustrating and leads many people to consider abandoning the whole idea of talking treatments. So an important criterion in choosing a therapist should be his or her availability. Try to find out not just who does this kind of work locally, but also whether they can always offer immediate assistance, how long they generally see people for, and how these variables compare between the statutory, voluntary and private sectors.

In other words, if you have mixed feelings about engaging in therapy right now, but think that it might be a good idea in a few months' time, it is well worth exploring the possibilities straight away. This does not in any sense commit you to anything, but it avoids your having to suffer an unexpected and frustrating delay when you feel ready to start.

Whichever choice I make, is this going to cost me more money than I can reasonably afford?

Private therapy of any school or model of working can turn into an extremely expensive proposition. When you engage with a practitioner and begin to unravel your problems in a way that you find helpful, it goes without saying that to end this process prematurely would be unwise and entirely counter-productive. So it is necessary to commit yourself to the treatment for as long as the job is going to take. Many practitioners offer only time-limited work, and this means that the client is in a good position to decide if the costs involved are manageable. A great deal of therapy is open-ended, however, and so it is worth discussing with the therapist any limits on your financial resources. Only then can you decide whether you can afford a sufficient period of time in which to achieve what you hope for. If you have enough funds to be able to continue indefinitely, you are in a strong position, although this is not to imply that therapy should continue indefinitely. Some people may feel that they need support for longer than others, and seeing a therapist for months or even years is by no means unusual. It is up to you and your therapist to decide.

Chapter 3 gives some idea of the fees charged in the private sector. Many private practitioners operate a 'sliding scale' and charge clients according to their means; or, in some cases, they subsidise a few clients, charging them a much reduced fee (or even nothing) by charging full rates to others. If your finances are very limited, it is a good idea to ask if this facility is available, although most practitioners will advise prospective clients of this as a matter of course. It is strongly advised that you are entirely honest about your money situation. Distorting the truth in any way to obtain support at a cheaper rate is a poor way to establish a trusting relationship with someone to whom you may be revealing your innermost fears and emotions.

Obviously the above applies mainly to people who have opted to see a practitioner from the private sector, but there can be financial considerations even where therapy is provided free of charge. Perhaps a long or expensive journey is involved, or maybe you need to reduce working hours to be able to attend your sessions. Consider both the obvious and the hidden costs, and factor these in to your decisions about who you see and when.

Can I make the time to keep to regular appointments, and is the journey involved one that I can make easily without the risk of being late or missing sessions?

Entering into therapy is a commitment that has to be taken seriously. If your problems are a serious matter, then so is the process of looking for solutions, and this means that it will be expected that you make your sessions a priority in your weekly (or fortnightly) routines. Of course there is always the unplanned difficulty – we fall ill, a family crisis develops, a strike halts public transport. But outside such unusual circumstances, regular attendance is important if benefits are to be gained. Very little positive work can be done if a client attends only every other booked session, or often arrives 15 minutes late.

Journey time is an important element in all of this. Occasionally it may seem a good idea to see a particular practitioner with specific skills or experience, and you may be willing to travel some considerable distance to achieve this. But this can have real consequences in terms of the time needed to manage a regular session with that therapist. Even an hour's journey can turn a 45-minute session into a half-day exercise, and this can be both inconvenient and tiring if undertaken on a frequent basis. Think about what you are taking on and all the ramifications involved, and make decisions in an informed way rather than assuming that everything is bound to work out for the best.

Some private therapists will charge for sessions that you have missed, on the grounds that a contract has been made: the practitioner has put aside professional time for you, and this time cannot simply be given to another client. (Others will even charge when a client is on holiday, although this is becoming less common.) Even where no fees are involved, the existence of a waiting list or pressure of numbers can mean that your therapist terminates the arrangement even if you have missed your appointment only a few times. It is also quite common to refuse to see people if they are late, because the length of a session is determined by the minimum sufficient time in which you can discuss your problems carefully and in detail: a reduction in this time can be seen as making the session pointless. The finishing time cannot be extended to make up for a client's lateness, however unavoidable.

These arrangements exist not because the practitioner is unsympathetic to the client's problems, but owing to the inevitable consequences of scarce resources and the importance of the work being done. Difficulties are best avoided by clear limits being established at the beginning of a therapeutic relationship. Ask about arrangements for cancellations, make sure you know who to contact and how, and give as much warning as possible if you are unable to attend a session. If you feel that regular attendance is going to be difficult at the moment, consider whether this is the right time to start. If you believe that your problems are significant enough that you simply cannot wait, be sure that you give your sessions a priority in your life that matches that belief.

Can I manage childcare?

Parents of young children obviously have to build most of their routines around the children, and it is no different in the case of therapy and counselling. Generally speaking, therapy sessions are conducted between the practitioner and the client with no one else present, and this includes children, on the grounds that a parent is unlikely to be able to focus on talking if he or she has to keep an eye on a bored child. Depending on the child's age, you will probably also be reluctant to discuss personal issues in front of him or her. If, despite these cautions, you would prefer to have a child or children accompany you (or you have no alternative), this needs to be negotiated with the practitioner, and will not always be easily manageable. Some clinics, health centres and voluntary-sector projects have crèche facilities, but this remains somewhat rare and certainly cannot be relied upon.

Finding adequate childcare is a constant struggle for many parents. Trustworthy friends, close family or a helpful partner are not always available, and many people cannot easily afford a babysitter or childminder. Unfortunately, there is no magic-wand solution here, but addressing this openly with a therapist may reduce or remove the potential complications involved.

Can I take the time off work?

Under current UK law you do not have an automatic right to attend a regular appointment for any kind of medical or pastoral care during working hours. If you want to see a counsellor during your normal working hours this can be done only by prior arrangement with your employer or by taking sick leave or annual leave. Your boss has the choice to refuse you this favour. Since for most of us it is difficult to arrange time off on a medium- or long-term basis, most people working regular hours choose to see a therapist at weekends (if the practitioner works at weekends) or in the evenings. Evening appointments, not surprisingly, are thus more difficult to obtain than daytime sessions.

Can I foresee anything that might seriously interrupt my sessions in the near future (holidays, people coming to visit, family events)?

This may sound entirely obvious, but it is surprising how eagerness to start therapy can blind us to potential complications. One of the prerequisites for engaging in a talking treatment is focus, and concentrating as rigorously as possible on the goals that you set for yourself. This may be very difficult if you are in the process of moving house, are planning a wedding, or are completing a series of examinations. If you are just about to take a three-month holiday in Bermuda, there will be a rather large break in focus. Of course, many such events are highly stressful occasions in themselves, and may be part of the reason that you are seeking support in the first place. On the other hand, it is likely to be at best frustrating, and at worst extremely upsetting, to start a process of self-examination and then put it on hold for a period of time, or to find that you have to cancel sessions frequently because of other commitments. It is far preferable to delay the whole business for a few weeks rather than start at the wrong time and have a negative experience of therapy, be forced to abandon sessions and have to start again at a later date.

This is not to suggest that everything else can or should stop when you begin to see a therapist, nor that you cannot take holidays or devote your attention to other matters. But there is also an issue of urgency here. Are the matters you want to discuss so central to your future that they cannot permit any delay; and are they so important that they deserve time, consideration and freedom (as much as is possible) from external pressures? Only you can judge this.

For what period of time can I commit myself to therapy? What if I'm expected to make a long-term commitment?

A successful episode of talking treatments takes as long as it takes, no more or less. However, often a timescale is built into the particular model of counselling or psychotherapy. Many approaches are based around working through a specific series of steps in relation to the client's problems, and use a limited number of sessions in which to achieve this. (This is particularly true of a number of approaches found within the NHS at present.) Others also specify particular steps, but are more flexible in determining how long it may take to work through them. The majority of models are open-ended, and may last for years, by mutual agreement between client and practitioner. Unsurprisingly, the deciding factor in all this lies in the complexity of the aims of the sessions. For example, learning to control panic attacks might be the subject of six sessions, one per week. Trying to resolve a state of chronic unhappiness caused by poor relationships and a negative self-image could take a great deal longer.

When starting the process of therapy, it is vital to plan how long you are likely to be involved with the therapist. This will allow you to ensure that the required resources – time, money, energy – are available, and, equally importantly, will help make the aims of the therapy as clear and explicit as possible. Many people choose to tackle their problems in stages instead of all at once. It is better to have realistic aims than to take on the burden of trying to resolve too much in too limited a timescale. Similarly, having no agreed aims means that the talking treatment could go on almost forever, and it would never be clear whether you have achieved what you set out to do.

Anxieties about starting therapy

The process of beginning to see a counsellor or therapist can be quite intimidating. We may be quite sure that we need support, and even be desperate for some kind of change, but it can still be a little scary to meet someone for the first time and begin to reveal very intimate matters to him or her. It may feel as if the whole of your life and efforts are suddenly under scrutiny, or even 'being judged' – though this is never the case. The following questions may resemble some of the internal dialogue people may have with themselves at this time.

1 *How can I share my most personal thoughts and feelings with a stranger?*
2 *Will my problems seem petty compared to other people's problems?*
3 *Will my therapist be upset by what I tell him or her?*
4 *Should I try group therapy? It sounds scary.*
5 *Am I going to be open about what I'm doing – tell my friends, family, partner, employer?*
6 *Are there any issues or things that have happened to me that I'm unwilling to talk about, and if so, what are they?*

These are valid questions, and should not be dismissed as mere 'nerves'. In fact, thinking them over can be viewed as a necessary and normal step in the overall process of seeking help, and can be an empowering experience. In many ways, entering into any kind of therapy goes against our natural inclinations. Few of us are keen on the idea of revealing too much of ourselves to another person until we are very familiar with and trust him or her, and yet this is exactly what we are required to do when we visit a therapist, right from the start.

How can I share my most personal thoughts and feelings with a stranger?

In some ways it can be easier to talk with a stranger than with someone you know very well. The unfamiliarity of the practitioner with you as an individual means that he or she comes into the professional relationship without any history, without any perceptions of your situation being shaped by any shared experiences that might blind him or her to what is going on for you. There is a significant difference between confiding in a family member or close friend, however sympathetic, and talking to a trained practitioner with clear standards of confidentiality and a method for tackling problems. But of course some things are just very difficult to talk about. Doing this in a strange environment (a clinic, community centre, or therapist's consulting room) can make it doubly difficult. After all, this may involve talking about things that you have never shared with anyone, and you may fear being judged or dismissed out of hand.

It is important to remember that listening to people's problems and offering useful feedback is the counsellor's chosen job, not just something he or she is doing because he or she accidentally met you at this particular time and place. Whether he or she does this full time or part-time, for an income or as a volunteer, he or she is interested in what makes people 'tick' or troubles them. He or she will be interested in you and hearing about you, and aims to offer you space to discuss your concerns, and to provide as safe an environment as possible. This time is yours, and it is about you and for you, a place to let go of the stresses and anxieties that you are holding. Any capable practitioner will work hard to make you feel sufficiently comfortable to be as open as possible with him or her, and to assure you that what you say is dealt with respectfully and seriously. This may require a considerable leap of faith on your part, and by all means work at a pace which you find manageable. But do try to accept the opportunity that a talking treatment offers you and believe that the therapist is there to offer assistance, not simply because he or she is nosey or has nothing better to do with his or her time.

Will my problems seem petty compared to other people's problems?

It is a constant fear of many people who see a counsellor or therapist that their problems will seem like nothing in comparison to what other people are going through, and that consequently they do not really deserve the help being given to them. This is a good example of taking a partial truth and distorting it into an untruth. It is very possible that someone else has even bigger and more complex problems than you. In fact one of the few things of which we can be certain is that there are always people worse off than we are. But this is entirely irrelevant, because you still need help anyway. If two people go into a busy casualty department, one with a broken leg and the other experiencing a heart attack, the person with the heart attack will no doubt be seen as being in more urgent need. However, this does not mean that the person with the broken leg will be ignored, or told to go away and stop feeling sorry for himself because there is someone else in greater pain than he is. It is the same with psychological and personal difficulties: the existence of other people's problems does not wipe away the existence of your own.

Sometimes we find it difficult to accept that we deserve the attention of others. Sometimes this may even be a cause of the build-up of stress in the first place, because insufficient attention has been paid to our needs, a situation leading to a point at which we can no longer get by without support. But ultimately the need, and therefore the justification, for receiving therapy or counselling are self-defining. If help is required, help should be looked for and received, because it is *your* life that you are trying to manage. And it is your own life for which you are responsible, not the lives of other people who may also need help.

Will my therapist be upset by what I tell him or her?

The level of emotional responses shown by the practitioner can vary a great deal from one practitioner to another. This level of response is often puzzling to someone experiencing a talking treatment for the first time. Some kinds of therapy hold that practitioners should be guarded about showing their emotions, because this can be a distraction for the client. Others think the exact opposite, and believe that honesty in this and all things (sometimes referred to as 'congruence') is necessary for a good therapeutic relationship. Still others think that a spontaneous response, rather than a carefully thought-through display of feelings, is even more honest and advisable. It is easy to see how these different viewpoints could have developed, especially when you consider that they all seem to place the needs of the client as central to the decision made by the practitioner.

Nevertheless, and whether your therapist is open or guarded with his or her thoughts and feelings about what you say, it is a certainty that he or she does in fact have emotional responses to your problems. Only a very bad practitioner (not to mention a highly dysfunctional human being) would never feel sympathy at hearing about the suffering of others. This can also be a worry for clients, who may feel concern at their counsellor's daily routine of having to listen to what they might imagine to be an endless series of tragic stories. In some cases, this may even discourage the client from being open about his or her situation in case it upsets or angers the therapist unnecessarily.

It should be understood that all practitioners working from an organised model of therapy or counselling receive regular professional supervision. This is a session held with another qualified practitioner (or practitioners) trained in the same way of working. Together they can discuss any matters arising from the work that the practitioner under supervision is doing, and relating to that practitioner's current clients. If this sounds like a kind of therapy-for-the-therapist, then that is pretty close to the truth. In fact most training schools insist that trainee practitioners receive a course of therapy as part of their learning experience. Some even insist on therapy being continued on a regular basis for as long as the practitioner continues to work within the field.

Whether or not the practitioner is in therapy, supervision is always recommended. It is a confidential setting in which clients will not usually be referred to by name, and certainly not as part of a written record, and it gives all therapists the opportunity to deal with their own needs in a safe and professional manner. Do not let your concern for a therapist lead you to censor what you say. Therapists are experienced in this kind of work, and should know what to do to take care of themselves. It is perfectly reasonable to question your practitioner as to whether he or she receives supervision, and what level of confidentiality is maintained with the supervisor. If no supervision is being undertaken, it is fair to ask what other safeguards or 'reality checks' the practitioner is using to judge his or her work. If the answer is 'none', you may well reconsider whether this is the right person for you.

Should I try group therapy? It sounds scary.

The option of group therapy (outlined in Chapter 3) is often a daunting prospect. Talking to one person about personal matters may be nerve-wracking enough. To do so with a whole bunch of people can seem terrifying to some people. But there are some real gains to be made from working with groups, if this is a possibility on offer for you or if it is the format suggested to you.

First, a therapeutic group is made up mainly of other people like yourself, people who are experiencing problems and need support. One or two therapists will also be present, but most of the group will be ordinary people, not trained professionals. This means that there is a much larger opportunity for the sharing and comparing of experiences, and perhaps also for receiving practical help from others in the group. Second, by their very nature groups are a more social experience, and lead to greater interaction both during and outside the session itself. This does not mean that a group should be seen as a likely place to make friends, and some groups would strongly discourage this, but it may be an opportunity to address any general difficulties you have in dealing with other people, or making your voice heard. Third, the energy of a group can be very intense and stimulating, and can be a great opportunity for making big steps in a very short space of time.

Obviously you may see all the above as good reasons *not* to engage in a group. But very often the experience of being in therapy is about challenging oneself, and even though this should never mean putting yourself through painful situations just for the sake of it, sometimes it does mean that you have to push yourself to do things in spite of your fears.

It is important to understand that working along with other people is usually as much about listening as talking. Hearing other people's experiences can help you to reflect on your own, and this in itself may make you feel less isolated and more able to talk about yourself. The 'rules' of the session, including levels of confidentiality, starting and finishing times, and what is and is not expected of participants, should be decided during the first meeting. Although everybody will probably feel nervous at first, skilled practitioners should be able to give reassurances, put people at their ease, and make the session into an opportunity for positive learning.

Am I going to be open about what I'm doing – tell my friends, family, partner, employer?

Given that one of the intentions of this book is to 'normalise' the whole experience of going to see a counsellor or therapist, it may seem a little hypocritical to suggest that this is a process that we might consider hiding from other people. In fact it is generally not a recommended or necessary course of action. At the same time, discussing the contents of sessions in detail may cause feelings to 'leak' and so cause distress in your relationships. Keep your feedback to friends and family brief. There is a difference between being deliberately dishonest, and taking steps to maintain privacy.

Regrettably, narrow-minded views about psychological problems still persist, and you may be aware of a stigma attached to those who are known to have problems. If you feel that seeing a counsellor is a very personal thing and no one else's business, this is entirely understandable.

However, consider the significant people in your life and the relative importance of keeping them informed about your state of health and well-being. It is hard to imagine that you could keep from a partner that you were seeing a counsellor, or would wish to, unless perhaps it was to discuss some major destructive aspect of his or her behaviour, such as violence or substance misuse. Even then, maintaining a secret like this would be difficult and perhaps even hazardous. The more intimate you are with someone and the more time you spend together, the more complex and problematic it becomes to hide things from him or her. The stress of avoiding the truth might become greater than the stress of dealing with what you fear might be a negative reaction from him or her.

This is likewise true of close family with whom you are in regular contact – anyone you see on an almost daily basis may begin to wonder about these unexplained absences that occur at fixed intervals. You may be able to make excuses, but unfortunately excuses frequently turn into lies, and a web of half-truths and untruths that can rapidly ensnare you and arouse suspicion. The same is true of employers – perhaps it starts with you asking for permission to take time off, telling your employer that you need regular sessions with, say, a physiotherapist. Then a couple of months later the employer wants to know what kind of progress you are making and asks for a report from the physiotherapist. An employer does not have the absolute right to obtain medical reports without your permission. But without concrete information your employer is likely to make assumptions about your health, and this might place you in a real quandary.

It is arguable whether discretion, rather than distortion, is the best policy. If you wish to maintain privacy, involve as few people as possible in the process, and so avoid even brief explanations. But also consider whether any such steps are really necessary. Anyone who will dismiss your problems and the ways that you have chosen to address them is not being supportive of you, so perhaps worrying about their opinion of you isn't so important after all.

Are there any issues or things that have happened to me that I'm unwilling to talk about, and if so, what are they?

Not all kinds of therapy and counselling demand that you describe everything that has ever happened to you, or require complete 'unburdening' and lots of self-disclosure. In fact, most do not, and the limits that you place on what you say are entirely a matter of your own choice. For example, unless directly relevant, it is not necessary during a brief course of bereavement counselling to talk about the major events of your childhood. Neither do you have to describe all your personal relationships in detail if you are seeing someone to discuss excessive levels of stress caused by overwork. Not all talking treatments are concerned with 'global' views of your life, past and present. Many are focused on a very specific issue or issues that you have decided to address, and in fact it can be somewhat reckless to attempt to sort out other long-standing problems within a short-term course of therapy. The aims of seeing a therapist should be agreed when you start the therapy, and re-negotiated if necessary, but not changed without discussion.

This may sound impractical. Are we all so self-aware that we know where one problem ends and another begins? Or is it possible that issues are interrelated in some complicated fashion that will become apparent only at a later date? The latter is a very common experience, and some re-negotiation of the goals of therapy is frequently necessary. This is not a failure, but a positive sign of your increasing understanding of yourself. This being so, and given the unpredictable course of many episodes of therapy and counselling, it is perhaps best to be *willing* to talk honestly about anything that may become relevant without necessarily *setting out* to do so. This may seem a fine distinction, but it is an important one.

Ultimately no one can, or should, try to force information from you. It is perfectly reasonable for a therapist to ask you if you are willing to discuss specific issues, but he or she must respect your answer whether it is yes or no. In some cases this might lead to a mutual decision that it is best not to proceed with the professional relationship. In others it will be seen as being merely a step in the ongoing development of that relationship. You are in control of what happens in your sessions, although it must be understood that a therapist may firmly believe that it is necessary that you look at a particular concern if progress is to be made. Ask yourself what aspects of your life would fall into this category for you, and why you are unwilling to look at these concerns. If your reasons seem sound to you and you are willing to accept the consequences, you are completely entitled to stand your ground.

How might therapy help me?

It is not always easy for the client to believe that therapy will be beneficial, and this is perhaps the most basic anxiety when thinking about starting a talking treatment. Therapists sometimes forget that not all prospective clients are convinced that coming to see them is a good idea, or even that they have a clear sense of why they are coming. The original idea may have come from a friend or family member, or another healthcare professional. Deciding to go along with the suggestion is not always because a clear agenda has been established, but merely because the individual knows that *something* has to be done to alleviate his or her distress, and hopes that this might be it. Addressing the following questions should help to disperse some of the confusion and lack of clarity.

1 *How big or small do I believe my problems to be?*
2 *What kind of control do I have over my life?*
3 *What resources and strengths do I have to help me in this situation?*
4 *Do I want just to learn how to manage my difficulties or do I want them to go away altogether?*
5 *What changes would I not be willing to make to solve my difficulties?*
6 *Do I believe that talking treatments can work?*

These questions are relevant because the extent of your present difficulties determines the extent of change that you hope to achieve: if you think you have a major problem you will hope it is possible to achieve a major change. In turn, how far you believe in the possibility of these changes will underpin the entire process of engaging in a talking treatment.

How big or small do I believe my problems to be?
It is perfectly possible to be extremely troubled and concerned over an issue that seems highly specific and limited to only one area of your life. Perhaps a relationship has ended unhappily, or

you are attempting to change what you perceive to be a bad habit or behaviour, or maybe you are overstressed by the demands of your work and becoming increasingly anxious. None of these problems, or anything similar, should be underestimated or ignored. They are potentially serious and emotionally draining experiences that can easily lead to despair. This is not to suggest that someone with one of these difficulties must be feeling despairing or that despair is the inevitable consequence of personal difficulty. But it does mean that any source of distress should be respected, deserves to be acknowledged, and that there is a case for addressing it via counselling or therapy. It can be short-sighted to ignore your problems on the grounds that they are less complex than those of other people.

It is essential to have a real sense of how deeply imbedded in your life the problems that you are facing may have become, because unless this is faced honestly you may settle for methods that are inadequate to the task. Big and enduring problems are unlikely to respond to a brief therapy. Be prepared to allow yourself enough time and space to address your situation properly and do not expect sudden or miracle cures. Talking treatments involve commitment and energy, and a skilled practitioner will help a client to work at an appropriate pace, and will not try to 'jump-start' this process. Low levels of motivation or insight are often present when someone has been struggling with his or her problems unaided for a long time.

Of course, the bigger your problems feel, the more hopeless it may seem to begin addressing them. But all journeys begin with a single step, and the best way to proceed can be to view the time spent with a therapist as the start of a longer voyage of discovery, or even as the first act in a play that may be running with significant breaks and intervals. Maybe you want to take a good, long run at a talking treatment and see someone frequently for a year or two. Maybe you realise that your problems are complex but think that taking smaller bites, seeing someone for a few sessions at a time with breaks in between, is the way to go. Or maybe you aren't at all sure, and need to make this decision with the help of your practitioner. Feeling at ease with the process of therapy can take time and needs patience – it will probably be a while before you find out how the process 'works' and how to get the most from the opportunity. If this is not rushed it often comes more naturally and no longer seems so strange and unfamiliar.

What kind of control do I have over my life?

A great deal of the psychological theory surrounding counselling and therapy is based upon the assumption that people believe they have the power to make decisions. In turn, this means that they can influence their own lives for good or bad, and take an active role in determining their future. This is in many ways a highly Eurocentric viewpoint, not shared by all of the world's population. It is, however, the default position in Western Europe and other parts of the world dominated by West European philosophy, such as North America. Chapter 11 provides more on the manner in which cultural expectations can shape the nature of therapy.

This notion of control can be very important in shaping your experience of a talking treatment. If you feel completely out of control (which is not uncommon when faced with stress and anxiety, or any life crisis that makes you question your abilities) then it may be very hard for you to convince yourself of the usefulness of seeing someone and talking through your problems. As with most things in the therapy and counselling world, these feelings are best talked about and managed rather than ignored. If you have made the decision to see someone but feel that you are largely incapable of influencing your current situation, tell your therapist this and take the opportunity to explore what it means. For many people, this sense of helplessness and the belief that positive change is impossible is almost a defining symptom of depression and unhappiness, a sign of how hopeless their worldview has become. Accepting that this is the case and trying to move beyond it may be the first thing that you need to focus on with a practitioner, and can be a stepping stone to further changes.

This is not to suggest that the mere fact of talking will make you capable of dealing with any problem. A physical disability cannot be talked away, for example, and neither can the death of a loved one, or the events that lead to many other crises. But how we deal with such a crisis, the way we think and feel about it and the significance that it has for us in the present, most certainly can change through talking. To experience even the first signs of this, however long it may take, can be a means towards establishing the kind of control that we may fear we do not possess.

What resources and strengths do I have to help me in this situation?

Although it may sound childishly simplistic, there can sometimes be a sense of achievement or comfort to be found in doing a simple inventory of your life, and reminding yourself what you bring to a therapeutic relationship. What are the positives in terms of your daily existence: relationships, work, material resources, health? What are your personal qualities: resilience, the ability to cope, a sense of humour, compassion for other people, insight and understanding? What experiences have you had that made you grow and learn in the past? What do you believe is important and worth fighting for?

This is not just a 'feel good' exercise, or a thinly veiled way of saying 'Look on the bright side!'. It is, in fact, an important part of entering into a working relationship with a counsellor or therapist. It is a means of focusing on what areas of your life are lacking, and which are at least satisfactory. It is easy to identify a vague sense of unhappiness or stress, but frequently much more difficult to determine what specifically is causing you psychological pain or disquiet. This brief kind of self-examination may offer some guidance as to the direction needed in therapy, or at least give you a starting point, even if it turns out that the actual causes of your difficulties are unclear. But more than this, it may help to emphasise your achievements above and beyond your problems. This will allow you to get a more balanced view of the significance of your difficulties within the context of your entire life, past as well as present, and indicate what you have been able to deal with previously. Even the most unhappy and despairing of us can perhaps find some hope in the way that we have risen above suffering in the past and kept going.

Because therapy is something that involves the active participation of at least two people, the belief that both people can bring skills and knowledge to the professional relationship is very important. Even when our lives seem endlessly complicated or confused, we can search for ways to find and use our strengths and abilities towards positive ends.

Do I want just to learn how to manage my difficulties or do I want them to go away altogether?

In many ways the answer to this question seems entirely self-evident. Of course we would like all our problems to go away and never return so that we could be at peace with ourselves for evermore. But our resources, both financial and personal, are limited, and we may often have to settle for learning how to live with our issues rather than resolving them altogether.

Indeed, it could be said that the whole idea of identifying major life issues and patterns and then finding a way to 'resolve' them is another rather Hollywood concept of what therapy is about. Some people do engage in three or four sessions of a talking treatment each week for a period of perhaps many years, and move towards huge personal growth. But this is not a realistic plan for most people given the costs in terms of fees, energy and time. In any event, this guide does not define therapy and counselling as necessarily meaning either a long process or something that inevitably involves working with deep and complex issues. Just as the term 'surgery' can encompass processes as far apart as a heart transplant and the removal of an ingrowing toenail, so too the terms 'counselling and therapy' represent a very broad and inclusive range of talking treatments.

Sometimes the only course available to us is learning to live with a sadness and giving up the hope that it will go away. A traumatic event can touch us so deeply that its consequences will never entirely leave us. But with time and help, those consequences can be made bearable, and managed in a way that does not allow them to dominate every waking moment and every dream. On other occasions, we may be faced with several choices, none of which offers an easy solution to a current problem, and therapy may be a way to examine those choices and move towards a decision. Part of that process may include having to accept that none of the choices is ideal, and that we are looking for a compromise rather than a total cure. Only a bad or hopelessly naïve therapist will tell you that the work you do together can solve all your problems. Knowing this, and deciding at what level you will set your sights, is very important indeed.

What changes would I not be willing to make to solve my difficulties?

Change is a fact of life, but is often resisted because it is simply too painful or too frightening to consider. Change, or the need for change, is an equally major part of therapy, and sometimes the alterations to your routine and daily life that may arise from a talking treatment will go beyond what you are willing to consider. An example: someone pursues a career that he has always dreamed of, encounters a great deal of stress when this goal has been achieved, and, with the help of a therapist, reluctantly comes to see that the stress is entirely caused by his choice of career. Does this mean the person should abandon his plans and do something else instead? The answer is that people in this position have to do what they think is right. But if making this decision brings them to the understanding that they have hit a wall, or reached a point at which an action that they are unwilling to take is indicated, the matter is best dealt with openly and honestly.

A similar crossroads is often reached when discussing relationships. A partner or family member can be a source both of great support and great frustration, and abandoning or disowning the partner may be out of the question. In any case, therapy should never be about telling someone what to do, or making clients feel bad if they do not take up a particular suggestion. It should involve moving towards solutions that are acceptable, and this may sometimes call for a change in objectives. The focus may become learning how to live with a stress rather than removing it, if the price of removal is seen as being too high to pay.

Knowing where these boundaries lie for you personally, or working towards discovering what they are, will help determine your needs and intentions. Once more, this is about accepting compromise rather than absolutes; frequently this is the most realistic and achievable of aims in therapy.

Do I believe that talking treatments can work?

It is fitting that this is the question to end the chapter, because it is, after all, the most basic of considerations for a person thinking of engaging in therapy. Many people are cynical of the effectiveness of what seems, from the outside, 'just talking about something in the hope that it will go away'. This is an entirely reasonable standpoint given the way in which far too many people in the counselling and therapy world over-enthusiastically sell their profession to the public (however well intentioned they may be in doing this). Talking treatments are not a universal cure for even the most basic of problems, and no one should try to persuade you otherwise. But it is equally indisputable that they can be, and are, effective for many people suffering from a wide variety of personal difficulties. Chapter 6 explores this question in some detail.

Taking a healthy dose of caution into a therapeutic relationship is no bad thing. But at the same time, and without implying that you are likely to deliberately sabotage an episode of therapy, it is also true to say that going to see someone when you have little or no faith in what he or she has to offer can very easily create a self-fulfilling prophecy. Challenge yourself in this respect. Ask yourself what you think the benefits of going to see someone will be. Decide whether you are willing to carry on as you are now, or are hopeful (perhaps desperate) for something to change. Do you find the ideas underlying the approach that your counsellor or therapist uses convincing or relevant? If the answers to most of the above are positive, it will at least have given greater weight to your decision to start a talking treatment. If the answers are negative, you can address this directly with the practitioner and try to gain some greater understanding of what it is that you want. If therapy really isn't for you, you are free to draw a line under the experience.

Closing thoughts

In a roundabout way, this chapter emphasises what many readers will already suspect – which is that talking treatments can be complicated to arrange, to maintain, and to make good use of. The information here is intended to cut through some of those complexities and assist you in making choices that can help your own therapy to be a positive and useful event within your life. The more aware you are of potential difficulties, and how to overcome them, the more chance you have of gaining from the experience ahead of you.

Chapter 6

Do counselling and therapy work?

Chapter 2 discusses the schools of thought behind various approaches to counselling and psychotherapy. This chapter outlines what is known about the effectiveness of different approaches; it also aims to cover what is known about determining the best therapy to use for a particular kind of problem.

What is meant by 'effective' treatment?

Research into the effectiveness of a treatment is carried out to promote what is called *evidence-based practice*. In other words, practitioners are expected to work in ways that have been proven to be effective, and this is now the normal expected standard within the public sector. When a talking treatment is said to be effective, it means that there is evidence of improvement in the way that a person functions as a result of having that kind of therapy. This could be seen in his or her relationships, work, or quality of life as a whole. It may also be demonstrated by a reduction in distress or pain, or a relief from symptoms. In some cases a reduction in harm caused to the self or other people may also be an outcome. Other changes could be an improvement in overall health or a return to work after an enforced absence from employment. In general, as a result of effective therapy, the individual would be expected to develop a greater sense of well-being, and cope with life's difficulties and tackle problems more successfully.

When questioning the effectiveness of talking approaches, researchers use the same language and criteria that they do for studying physical medical treatments: Is this approach more effective than another approach? What is the best treatment for this problem? Are there any side effects? Could it be damaging?

Sometimes the questions are the same as when researching surgery: Will it be painful, and if so, is there a less difficult but effective treatment? Of course, the issue of choice and client preference for a particular talking treatment can also be very relevant here, perhaps more so than in the case of physical medicine.

In 1952, at a time when talking treatments were developing and growing rapidly in popularity, a controversial article by Hans Eysenck prompted a wave of research into the effectiveness of these approaches. Eysenck was an eminent psychologist working at the Institute of Psychiatry in London, and he argued that patients receiving psychotherapy made no further steps forward than people receiving no treatment. Thousands of research projects have been carried out since then, and they demonstrate clearly that talking treatments are, in fact, effective for a wide range of psychological and personal problems. The general consensus is that people who receive therapy are better off than 75 per cent of untreated individuals. This means that according to research, only 25 per cent of untreated people get better without help, and that the other 75 per cent who were untreated make no apparent improvements.

While it is clear that talking treatments do work, research is much less clear when it comes to showing the difference in effectiveness between different approaches. No single study has answered the question of what treatment (and when given and by whom) is most effective for specific problems, but reviews of research done in this area have gone some way towards answering this question. However, it would be going too far to say that there is complete agreement as to which approach is best for which problem. Some of the problems encountered in this kind of research, and some of the precautions necessary when considering it, are mentioned at the end of the chapter.

Gathering research evidence

Just as the questions posed in researching the value of talking treatments are the same as in the realm of physical medicine, the evaluation of that evidence is today commonly carried out in the same way as it would be done for drug treatment or other medical interventions. The usefulness of these methods has been questioned, particularly as applied to something as complicated as counselling and therapy, but the current academic and political climate continues to endorse this kind of research.

In the UK, the Department of Health (DOH) assembled a panel of experts (the Guideline Development Group) to review the evidence for effectiveness of talking approaches and to make recommendations for healthcare policy in the public and voluntary sectors. The report produced by this group in 2001, *Treatment Choice In Psychological Therapies and Counselling: Evidence-based Clinical Practice Guidelines*, gives a detailed account of how the experts analysed the evidence to arrive at their conclusions. This section gives a summary of the methods used to obtain research evidence and the level of importance given to these different methods by the panel when they were making their recommendations.

When it is said that you are receiving *evidence-based* treatment, it usually means that the evidence of the treatment's effectiveness has been demonstrated by a randomised controlled trial (RCT). The results of this kind of trial are sometimes referred to as having established a 'gold standard', or clear proof that the treatment works.

In an RCT, individuals with the same problem are randomly allocated to two or more groups. One of these groups receives the treatment under investigation. The other group or groups receives either no treatment or a fake treatment (known as a placebo). The results for these groups are then measured and analysed. It is then possible to compare the improvements (if any) made by the individuals who received the treatment being investigated with any improvements in those people who received the placebo or no treatment at all.

If there is no difference between the group which was treated and the group which was not, the treatment would appear to have been ineffective. If there is a positive difference, this is evidence that the treatment seems to have some benefits. This comparison is made by studying measurable changes, referred to as 'outcomes'. These measurements are made using tried-and-tested scoring systems that can be applied rigorously and as objectively as possible.

The 'gold standard' approach is believed to provide the best evidence for the effectiveness or otherwise of a treatment. The next best evidence accepted by the scientific establishment is obtained from what are referred to as *controlled trials*. In such a trial, the treatment is evaluated by comparing it not with placebos or with no treatment whatsoever, but with another treatment or treatments. The outcomes mentioned above are measured in the same way for each of the treatments being studied.

Often researchers establish findings by looking at what research has previously been carried out regarding the treatment in question. This is referred to as a research *review*. When carried out on a large scale, this process is referred to as a *meta-analysis*. These kinds of reviews consider not only research findings but also the quality of the research carried out and the level of faith that should be placed in its conclusions.

The work of the DOH mentioned above was a review of most of the existing research evidence. The panel considered the research findings of a very large number of studies, and sorted through the available evidence carefully. It was thus able to draw positive conclusions about the effects of talking treatments and gave a 'seal of approval' to particular interventions based on exactly how much evidence supported that way of working. Each of these conclusions was graded at one of four levels of approval depending on how much research supported the conclusion. This means that an 'A' grade recommendation had more evidence to support it than a 'B' recommendation; a 'B' recommendation had more evidence than a 'C' recommendation, and so on. Treatments for which there was little or no positive evidence were not graded at all.

The following table gives some idea of what levels of research evidence these grades were based upon.

Criteria for Department Of Health recommendations

Grading	Research findings supporting grade
A	A consistent finding in a majority of studies in high-quality reviews or evidence from high-quality studies (such as RCTs)
B	A finding of at least one individual high-quality trial, with at least some support in high-quality reviews or strong support in reviews not meeting the standards of high quality
C	A finding from individual studies that do not meet all of the criteria of high quality
D	Based on evidence from structured expert consensus

The DOH review is available online both in full and in a much more user-friendly shortened version at www.doh.gov.uk/mentalhealth/ treatmentguideline The conclusions fall into two main categories – specific recommendations about the use of particular talking treatments, and general guidelines about the use of talking treatments. These are considered in detail throughout the rest of the chapter.

What type of therapy works for what problems?

If research is to be carried out into the comparative effects of particular talking treatments, it is necessary to make that comparison by studying the effectiveness of those treatments on a specific problem. For example, if a researcher analysed the outcomes of a psychodynamic counsellor working with a depressed patient, and a cognitive behavioural therapist working with someone with an obsessive compulsive disorder, the comparison would be a 'peas and apples' one. The kinds of problems looked at in the DOH review were of a limited number, and the recommendations made applied only to the following:

- depression, including suicidal behaviour
- anxiety, panic disorder, social anxiety, and phobias
- post-traumatic disorders
- eating disorders
- obsessive compulsive disorders
- personality disorders
- some physical complaints such as chronic pain and chronic fatigue.

These are diagnostic labels, and represent only one rather than all of the different ways of categorising personal problems as described in Chapter 1. (For more information on diagnosis and the symptoms that are involved in each case, see Appendix I and the information it contains about DSM-IV, which is the most commonly used international classification of mental health conditions.)

It is immediately apparent when looking at the table below that cognitive behavioural therapy (CBT) and related approaches score very highly, often receiving 'A' and 'B' ratings from the DOH review panel. The general absence of recommendations for psychodynamic and humanistic therapy is not because these have been proven to be ineffective, but because much less research has been carried out into these approaches.

This is because, as was stated earlier, it has been possible through research to establish the general benefits of talking treatments but difficult to establish what type of therapy was most effective. This was sometimes referred to by researchers as 'the equivalence paradox', meaning that despite huge differences in training and techniques, outcomes were often found to be very similar for a wide variety of approaches. The nature of CBT – the ease of training, the structured and time-limited qualities of the treatment – means that many more studies have been carried out on this approach than on the other schools of practice. As a result of this, there has been a lot more evidence accumulated for its effectiveness.

Problem	Effective therapies	Type of evidence	Comments
Agoraphobia	• Cognitive behavioural therapy	A	
Panic disorder	• Cognitive behavioural therapy	A	
Social phobia	• Cognitive behavioural therapy	A	
Generalised anxiety disorder	• Cognitive behavioural therapy	A	
Post-traumatic stress disorder	• Eye movement desensitisation and reprocessing (EMDR) • Cognitive behavioural therapy • Psychodynamic therapy	A A B	Differential effectiveness of different types of therapy has not been established There is also 'B' grade evidence that hypnotherapy is effective for this kind of problem
Obsessive compulsive disorder	• Cognitive behavioural therapy	A	
Depression	• Cognitive behavioural therapy • Interpersonal therapy • Couples therapy • Psychodynamic therapy • Humanistic ('non-directive') counselling • Family therapy	A A A B B/C B	Very good evidence for psychological therapies in treating depression Psychological therapies in combination with antidepressant medication has also been shown to be effective

continued overleaf

Problem	Effective therapies	Type of evidence	Comments
Eating disorders	● Cognitive behavioural therapy ● Interpersonal therapy ● Family therapy	A B B	
Personality disorders	● Dialectical behaviour therapy ● Psychoanalytic therapy ● Schema focused therapy ● Cognitive analytical therapy	A B C C	Personality disorders often co-exist with other problems. Whether these problems are addressed may influence outcome
Somatic complaints (chronic fatigue, chronic pain)	● Cognitive behavioural therapy ● Rational emotive therapy ● Psychodynamic therapy ● Family & marital therapy	A B C C	

Conditions not considered in the DOH review

Although not included in the DOH review, other recent research reviews have suggested that cognitive behavioural approaches and family therapy are also effective for treating addictions, schizophrenia and manic depression. The research evidence for this would be comparable to 'A' and 'B' standards as defined above. However, those suffering from these conditions should have these talking treatments in conjunction with medication and other physical treatments.

Other recommendations supported by research evidence

The more general guidelines about talking treatments that the DOH panel was able to make were also based on the review of existing research, and were likewise graded using the A-D system described above, depending on the quality of research evidence available.

Factors affecting good outcomes

1 Therapeutic relationship

'B' grade evidence was found that the relationship between client and practitioner (also referred to as the therapeutic alliance) is a powerful element in determining the effectiveness of a treatment episode. This was seen to be the case across the entire range of talking approaches and the single best predictor of good outcome.

2 Length of therapy

How long an episode of therapy lasts is another important factor in predicting outcome. Some approaches such as analytical psychotherapy are seen as long term and may also involve seeing a therapist more than once a week. Longer-term therapies are generally offered by practitioners in private practice although there is limited provision in the NHS, which along with voluntary-sector service organisations, favours short-term or time-limited therapies. The DOH review concluded that there is 'C' level research evidence that very short-term therapy (fewer than eight sessions) is ineffective except in the case of uncomplicated phobias and panic disorder. The review also concluded that often 16 sessions or more are required for the relief of symptoms, and that longer therapies may be required to achieve lasting change in social functioning and personality-related issues.

3 Therapist's level of skill

It is generally assumed that more complex problems require more skilful and experienced therapists. The DOH review found only 'D' level evidence to support this, meaning that while experts strongly support this position, there is no strong body of research to back this up. The lack of evidence is blamed on difficulties in carrying out this kind of research, because it is hard to find ways of rating practitioners based on their experience.

4 Client characteristics

The DOH review found 'C' level evidence indicating that clients with an interest in self exploration and a capacity to tolerate frustration have better outcomes with psychoanalytic and psychodynamic therapies. There is no evidence that age, sex, social class and ethnic group are factors in better outcomes in therapy.

5 Client preference for type of therapy

As with any other product or service, it is difficult to establish a preference for a particular style of talking treatment unless you have had an opportunity to sample or experience different approaches. But the DOH panel found only 'D' level evidence that client preferences were significant in determining positive outcomes. There remains a professional assumption, but no clear research evidence, that giving a client his or her preferred type of treatment should favour a better outcome.

Therapies that have been shown to be not effective

The DOH review found very little evidence that indicated a clear *contraindication* for a talking approach, meaning that it was harmful in a particular situation. An exception was that critical incident debriefing following traumatic incidents has been shown to be not effective and possibly even harmful. This is a single-session intervention following a trauma, mostly used in a group situation when the event has been experienced by a number of people. 'A' grade evidence was found suggesting that this kind of intervention was unlikely to reduce symptoms of traumatic distress.

Difficulties in researching talking treatments

Research is not an exact science. There are many factors that can confound a research study, and make its findings open to question. It can be argued that trying to research something as complicated as talking treatments is even more prone to difficulties. Problems that might be encountered in this process could be as follows:

- comparisons between different schools are hard to make because some approaches offer only short treatments and some offer only long treatments
- comparing the problems of one person and another person and the effects of therapy upon them is questionable because no two people are alike
- making comparisons between the work of two practitioners (even if they are both trained in the same approach) can also be open to question because no two people work alike
- comparing positive changes from one person to another is hard because things like 'success in relationships' or 'satisfaction with life' cannot easily be expressed as numbers or percentages
- the co-operation of both clients and practitioners is critical, and it may be very difficult for them to remain objective when talking about the effectiveness of the approach used
- what goes on in the minds of clients and practitioners is not visible to others and cannot be scientifically reviewed with total confidence or certainty

- detailed research of what happens in therapy and counselling could be considered unethical because it involves analysis of too much sensitive and intimate information
- assigning people to random groups (as explained above in the case of RCTs) can also be seen as unethical because it may require people to be offered a placebo or no treatment when in fact a perfectly good treatment is available
- the basic assumptions of research (sometimes called the research *paradigm*) may not be a good starting point for looking at matters of a personal, spiritual and philosophical nature.

Of course researchers are aware of these limitations, and try to compensate for them in the work that they do. In fact, most of the above considerations would be heavily disputed by people researching talking treatments. But there is still a great deal of debate as to whether these problems have been overcome, and this is likely to continue to be a hotly contested argument. In any event, the findings discussed in this chapter can only represent a kind of consensus of opinion at the time of writing. New research and new reviews regarding the effectiveness of treatments will be carried out, and the body of evidence will inevitably change. The current trend in evidence-based practice will undoubtedly stimulate more research into all forms of talking treatments.

Chapter 7

Preparing for your first session

Once you have made the decision to engage in a talking treatment and found a suitable counsellor or therapist, the next step is to make sure you get the best outcome from the treatment. This chapter explains some of the homework you can usefully do before you begin the therapy. Organising your thoughts about your current situation can be helpful when you are feeling confused or unhappy. More importantly, thinking beforehand about some of the issues in this chapter will help you to explain your situation more easily when you first see your practitioner and ensure you make a good start.

For some forms of therapy it is a good idea to keep some kind of file, workbook or diary of your therapy work. This is not something you would want anyone to see, so you should make every attempt to keep it in a secure, private place. Start it off with the notes you make in preparation for your first session.

Throughout this guide, the word 'problem' is used as a shorthand for the reason you are seeking some form of talking treatment, and the treatment is generally viewed in terms of its use in helping you to overcome problems. It is worth repeating that this is not the only, or even the best, way of looking at counselling or therapy. The final section of this chapter may be a useful reminder that your reasons for seeking help, and your expectations of the treatment, may have little to do with so-called 'problems'.

The assessment session

The more you put into your relationship with your practitioner, the more you will get out of it – as with any relationship. The first step is to be clear about the problems you are trying to get help for. This may not be as easy as it sounds. You may be seeking help because of non-specific feelings – such as just feeling 'low' or lacking energy or feeling fearful – and may not be able to pinpoint the problem. This is not something to worry about. Your first session with a practitioner is generally treated as an assessment, when you and your therapist will be aiming to clarify the problem and identify your particular needs. Sometimes this assessment continues during the first few sessions.

Many well-established professional bodies (such as those listed in the Resources section at the end of this guide) can send you an assessment questionnaire for you to fill out. These are designed to gather as much relevant information as possible before you have a face-to-face assessment with a practitioner, so that maximum use can be made of your first meeting. Your responses on the questionnaire may also help the organisation to decide whether its particular type of therapy is suitable for you. Ideally, the questionnaire will help you to structure your thinking and prepare you for the assessment. If you decide to see a practitioner without going through one of these organisations, or see someone who does not use a pre-assessment questionnaire, the information in this chapter is intended to help you prepare for the start of your therapy.

Some therapists, whether or not they use a questionnaire, carry out the assessment by asking questions in a structured way, and deal with each of the areas outlined below. Other therapists, particularly if they work within an analytical framework, are likely to be less active and will not put many questions to the client; instead, clients are invited to give their own account of what they see as important about themselves and why they are seeking help.

Describing your problems

The reason why you are seeking counselling or therapy may not always be easy to pinpoint or put into simple words. The problems listed in previous chapters and Appendix I may help you to identify your own situation and help you describe it, as you see it. However, a bald label such as 'anxiety' or 'depression' may not be that helpful in an assessment. What is necessary is to find a form of words to describe why you have decided to seek help at that moment. For some types of therapy, it may be useful to take prepared notes to your first session, with some description of your problems;

however, therapists working in an analytical framework will normally prefer you to come without notes.

Most people seeking therapy have more than one problem they want to work on. You may find it useful to fill in the template on page 151. List your main problems in order of importance and rate how severe you think each of them is. The box below shows how you might fill in one section of the template. It is a good idea to keep blank copies of the template, and fill them out at different points in your therapy. This could be one of the best ways of measuring the outcome of your treatment. By filling this out periodically, or at the end of the therapy, you can judge for yourself what changes have taken place.

Example

> **Problem 1** (description)
> *Feeling very low in mood, very unhappy, finding it very difficult to cope at times.*
>
> My rating of severity
>
> 1   2   3   4   5   6   7   (8)   9   10
>
> Not severe   Moderately severe   Very severe

Information useful for your therapist

Before you meet your therapist for the first session, spend some time thinking about the following issues and writing about them if you can. In order to make a good assessment of what kind of help you need, the practitioner needs as much information as possible about the nature of your difficulties. It may be hard to answer some of these questions, or at least to answer them clearly, but this can be a very useful starting point for further dialogue.

- How long do you think you have experienced the problem?
- When did you first realise that there was a problem?
- Have other people pointed things out to you, or did you realise yourself there is a problem?
- Have you had periods in between when things have been better?
- Are there any particular things that trigger the problem?

Your own problems

Description of my problems

Problem 1 (description)

My rating of severity

1   2   3   4   5   6   7   8   9   10

Not severe   Moderately severe   Very severe

Problem 2 (description)

My rating of severity

1   2   3   4   5   6   7   8   9   10

Not severe   Moderately severe   Very severe

Problem 3 (description)

My rating of severity

1   2   3   4   5   6   7   8   9   10

Not severe   Moderately severe   Very severe

Things you have already tried

Your therapist may also ask the following:

- Have you done anything in the past to cope with this problem?
- What did you do?
- How successful were the outcomes?

For example, if you have tried any of the self-help options discussed in Chapter 1, these would be relevant. If you have had counselling or therapy before, your new practitioner will want to know what kind of counselling it was, how long ago you had it, the duration of the counselling, and how often you saw the counsellor.

Try to assess the outcomes of all this previous work so that you can give a summary to the therapist.

Family background

You may be asked to tell the therapist about your family background. It will be helpful to collect your thoughts about your family so that you can give a brief description of your father, mother, your relationship with them, and your perception of their relationship with each other. If you have any brothers or sisters, your thoughts about them, and about your relationships with them, will also be important. Clearly, information on your partner and children (if any) will be crucial. You should mention any significant family events that stand out in your life, such as periods of separation, deaths and illnesses. Has anybody else in your family suffered from the type of problem that you are experiencing? Has another member of your family had specific problems with their physical or mental health, including depression or a psychotic episode, or problems with alcohol or drug addiction? This would also be relevant information, even if you have none of these problems yourself. You may be asked about your memories of childhood (schooling and education), and sometimes specifically for memories of your early childhood.

These questions are not intended to pry, or attach blame to other members of your family – far from it. They will, however, give the therapist an impression of what it was like to be you, growing up, and of what stands out for you as being significant, not significant, or a 'blank'.

Your resources

Make a mental note of the resources you have (see the diagram on page 15). Your feelings about your support network are particularly important here. What would you say about your lifestyle and leisure activities? What things do you enjoy in life?

Medication

If you are currently taking medication – antidepressants, for example – or if you have taken medication in the past, it will be helpful if you can remember the name of the drug and what dosage was prescribed. In NHS and other medical settings, it is possible that the subject of medication will be discussed as a routine part of the interview, and it may be worthwhile thinking about this before your assessment. More information on commonly prescribed drugs can be found in Chapter 12.

Your assessment of the practitioner

The assessment should always be considered a two-way process. While the therapist is attempting to assess your problems and to clarify things for you, you should also be making an assessment of the therapist – especially, whether he or she is someone you could work with. Does the person seem understanding? Can you sense empathy and respect? The psychologist Carl Rogers (see Chapter 2) said that therapists should have 'congruence, empathy and unconditional positive regard for the client' and these are now considered the basic qualities of a practitioner from any school of thought. Chapter 11 examines the question of any cultural differences you may need to be aware of: these are not simply matters of having a different ethnic background, for example, but of age and experience, social situation, educational background and so on.

On a more practical level, and particularly if you have approached the therapist without a referral, now is a good time to ask whether the practitioner is affiliated to, or a member of, any wider professional association. It is reasonable to ask if he or she can give you some literature about that association. Membership of a professional association means that the practitioner is properly trained and will be bound by the association's code of ethics and professional conduct, and it gives the client a responsible body to turn to in the event of a complaint or grievance. This is a very important safeguard for individuals who are entrusting their care to a stranger. You may also wish to clarify the situation on confidentiality. These matters are dealt with more fully in Chapter 9. If you are having therapy in the private sector you will need to discuss charges, cancellation policy and holidays (see Chapters 3 and 4).

Expectations and goals

When you see a counsellor or therapist for the first time it is worth thinking about what you are expecting from the meeting and what you would like to come out of it. It is natural to feel quite anxious about the first meeting. Some of this anxiety might give rise to rather negative expectations, which in turn can make you feel even more anxious. For instance, you may find yourself thinking: 'The therapist will say my problems are not important enough to warrant therapy', or 'I'm going to be embarrassed by questions about very personal things', or 'The therapist is going to put me on the spot'. Chapter 5 explores the typical reservations people have about seeing a therapist. If you are still worrying, remember that these are all common fears reported by people when they first embark on therapy. If you focus on the reasons that you decided to seek help it may help you to overcome these thoughts and feelings. In fact, as trust in your therapist develops, you may well be able to share some of the negative and anxious thoughts you had. Exploring them may later prove very helpful.

The other kind of expectation you will have is about what you want to get out of the process – the 'goals' of your therapy. Chapter 5 describes some commonly expected outcomes, such as reduction in distress and relief from symptoms. Apart from these general expectations, each client will have his or her personal goals. For some, these may be improvements in how they feel, a reduction in the severity of their problems. For others, the hope may be simply to find someone who will listen and understand. Some may be looking for some feedback from an objective person. Sometimes the goal may be to make sense of a situation or sort out one's feelings and reactions.

People starting short-term counselling or therapy may expect to find solutions for very specific problems, while those embarking on long-term treatment may have goals such as a change in enduring patterns of behaviour or finding a sense of meaning to their life. It may be that short-term therapy will focus more on problem-solving while long-term therapy will concern itself with broader or more global issues.

Unrealistic expectations or goals – for instance that the therapist has a 'magic wand' and can make all your problems disappear – are, needless to say, bound to be met with disappointment. A fundamental assumption in the therapy world is that people seeking help from counsellors and therapists are capable of solving and managing their problems, and that the aim of therapy is to help people help themselves. So it is strongly recommended that you spend some time reflecting on your expectations before you first meet your practitioner. If your expectations match what the therapist believes he or she could help you with, then you are on the right track.

Chapter 8

Troubleshooting

This chapter continues the theme of Chapter 5, and is intended to give you some strategies for dealing with difficulties that may surface once your therapy is under way. Surprising things can happen in counselling and therapy sessions and although this means that you may find the process a little unpredictable, usually the surprises are pleasant ones and will be helpful to you in achieving greater self-awareness. However, some unexpected situations can be confusing or worrying, and may need careful attention to help stop any problems developing. Although many of the questions here may seem more appropriate to individual one-to-one sessions, most could apply in almost any format of therapy. The issues raised at the end of the chapter are specific to groups, couples and family work.

Fortunately, the experience of therapy and counselling is not usually one of constant crises and problems developing between client and practitioner. Difficulties can often be headed off by thinking them through before they happen, and so long as you maintain open and honest communication with your practitioner, any serious difficulties should be avoided.

Failures in communication

Very often difficulties between client and practitioner occur because what has been said during sessions was unclear, or does not follow the client's expectations of what therapy should be about. It is easy to take offence when none is meant, and also to ignore things when they should be challenged. What kinds of things could practitioners say or not say that might confuse or worry their clients?

Should I expect to receive advice from my practitioner?

The code of the British Association for Counselling and Psychotherapy* states quite clearly that practitioners do not usually give advice. This may seem a little odd, because, after all, we generally start a talking treatment to learn about things that are troubling us, or to find different ways of managing our problems. Why would it be wrong for a counsellor or therapist to tell us what changes we need to make?

The answer lies in both philosophical reasons and practical reasons. Most practitioners believe that simply telling someone what to do is wrong because it would give them a sense of authority over their client that would not be justified or needed. Most adults resent being told what to do, anyway, although this may be different if they are despairing or very anxious. Giving advice would also imply that the therapist is an expert on how people should live their lives, which is a rather bold claim. Your practitioner is more likely to be an expert on how to reflect on the problems of living, and that is a very different skill.

On a more practical level, the danger in advising people what to do is that if the advice works, the client may feel that he or she should consult the counsellor about everything. If it does not work, the client may blame the counsellor for any consequences. Most practitioners have had to face these situations at least once, when they have unwisely or accidentally strayed into advice-giving.

You may feel that if you are not going to receive any advice there is no point in seeing a counsellor. But there are ways of learning other than being told what to do. The therapy process is generally about thinking things through, and it is much more satisfying to find your own answers through the skilled questions of another person than through following the advice or instructions of that other person. The practitioner will often make suggestions, or mention ways of achieving things, or discuss strategies that he or she knows have worked for other people. But he or she should not actually advise you to do any of those things, even if you are desperate for advice. The practitioner may feel tempted to give you his or her opinion, but it probably would not help. It is your own assessment of your situation that matters most. If your feelings seem completely uncontrollable, and you are finding that a talking treatment is of little help in managing your situation, you are advised to see your family doctor and ask whether a mental health assessment is needed.

Why am I being told that I'm resisting change?

Sometimes almost the reverse of the above situation can happen. You are not looking for advice or criticism, yet your practitioner appears to be telling you off, and warning you that you are resisting progress. This can feel very hurtful, and may not seem to make sense – if you weren't interested in moving forward, why would you be seeing someone in the first place?

There are two possible reasons why this kind of conflict can develop. First, the practitioner may have overstepped his or her role and started giving you his or her opinions rather than listening to you and reflecting back what you say. Asking your practitioner why he or she believes you are 'sabotaging' your therapy may help him or her to reflect on what he or she is saying and lead to better communication. The second possibility is that there is something in what the practitioner is saying but it is not easy for you to hear. Often, when we are stuck in patterns of behaviour or ways of thinking, it is hard to see how changes could be made. Sometimes it is more frightening to think about moving on than it is to think about staying where we are, however bad the 'stuck' place may be. The devil you know may seem less frightening than the devil you don't know, especially if you have been living with a problem for many years.

Many therapists also believe in something called 'secondary gain'. This is a situation in which an otherwise difficult and dissatisfying aspect of your way of living your life may somehow be felt to be giving rise to some conscious (or more often unconscious or unacknowledged) benefit or satisfaction. In this situation there may be mixed motivations about dealing with the difficulties. One part of you may consciously be striving to make progress, while another may be 'putting the brakes on' any change. An example would be having an illness that limits your energy levels, but which also means that other people step in and do things for you, and give you a lot of attention. Getting well again might open up new possibilities, but it could also lead to your losing all the help and attention you are getting.

Most examples of secondary gain are not as obvious as this. Nor is the situation a sign of weakness or failure. The opposition to change may be something you are wholly unaware of. There may be real anxiety about change 'upsetting the apple cart', or even that changing your way of dealing with things might cause a breakdown. Many situations in life are a balance sheet rather than all good or all bad. Part of therapy might be to bring such concerns to light in a way that they can be thought about. The practitioner should never raise the subject in an accusing or aggressive way, however, and if you feel that you are being attacked, you will need to discuss this as openly as possible.

What if my therapist tells me that we have to talk about issues that I find uncomfortable?

No practitioner should make you talk about anything that you do not want to talk about. It is unprofessional to make these demands of a client. In fact, the practitioner would find it impossible to force you to discuss things with which you are not comfortable. In this respect, the power to make the necessary decisions lies with you.

However, sometimes a talking treatment will be effective only if you are willing to look at areas of your life that are complicated, painful or which you would rather leave well alone. This does not mean that you have to go ahead against your will, but it does mean that you will have to accept the consequences of not discussing whatever the subjects are that you want to avoid. Occasionally this is a major block to progress. Someone with a drink problem, for instance, will not make many positive changes if he or she is unwilling to discuss alcohol. The possibility that you are missing an opportunity has to be acknowledged whenever you decide to impose these kinds of 'no-go areas' on sessions.

Sometimes we avoid subjects out of loyalty. Perhaps we do not want to talk about our family because we think that it is wrong to criticise the people we love. On other occasions a trauma may be too distressing to discuss in detail, or even to mention. There are many reasons why it can be easier to stay silent. You may nevertheless find it helpful to discuss the reasons why something is difficult, and you can do this without necessarily discussing the issue itself. A discussion may reassure you that the practitioner is sympathetic and will not judge you. It may be useful just for both of you to know that there are areas that have to be left untouched, because this could be an important 'boundary' to agree upon. This may also leave the door open to returning to these subjects later in the therapy, when talking about them may feel less threatening or less uncomfortable.

The practitioner should never try to drag words out of you, and there is no pressure on you to walk into your first session and immediately tell him or her the story of your life. It may take time to get round to all the things that you want to talk about. Try to keep an open mind on what you may eventually want to discuss, but remember that you are the one in charge.

Why is my therapist trying to convince me of something that I don't believe is true?

A practitioner should never try to convince a client of anything. He or she may raise an issue or suggest an interpretation (possibly on several occasions), but if you are sure that it does not apply, he or she should accept that it is probably best left alone. Take the example of someone who drinks alcohol because he or she believes it helps him or her to relax, and does not want to discuss this. This may be one situation in which the refusal to discuss an issue could bring into question the usefulness of continuing with a talking treatment, but even then this can be put to the client in a friendly rather than confrontational way. Bear in mind that discussing something is not the same as agreeing with it. You are entitled to stand your ground, and to tell your practitioner that you do not find something a useful subject to talk about.

It is not unknown for bad therapists to have interests or agendas that they want to discuss with all their clients, regardless of whether these issues are relevant or welcome. In one television sitcom a few years ago a group therapist always asked new group members 'Were there any sexual problems?'. Although this kind of amateurish obsession is fortunately rare, it may sometimes be necessary to point out to a practitioner that his or her model of working, and/or the questions he or she asks, do not match your expectations of what would be helpful. The sessions are for your benefit, not for an over-enthusiastic practitioner to talk about the kinds of problems or issues that he or she finds most interesting. This may even lead to a situation in which you feel that a complaint to a professional body is necessary. See Chapter 9 for more about complaints.

Chapter 11 explains the cultural differences which could lead an inexperienced practitioner to assume you have values and expectations that in fact you do not hold. If you think this could be the reason for your unease, discuss these matters with your practitioner.

Why does my therapist say so little? It really disturbs me.

Just as it is common to be concerned about something a practitioner says to you, it can also be the case that you feel a little unnerved by what he or she does not say. Often we interpret silence as a sign of discomfort, or think that the person who is looking at us but saying nothing must be thinking unpleasant thoughts about us. But it is frequently the responsibility of the practitioner to be quiet, to try to give you space and let you think through your problems. Sometimes you may not have anything to say either, and this double silence can feel very strange indeed.

We are not really used to silence in Western society. Most of the time we are surrounded by noise, and we may not realise just how much of a distraction this is until we find ourselves in a quiet room with the conversation having stopped. Sometimes this can be a very peaceful experience, and help us to relax. At other times it is intimidating, and we may feel the need to fill the space with the sound of our own voice. This is not always a bad thing, especially for a client who finds it difficult to speak or be heard in other situations such as at home or at work.

A silent practitioner may be reflecting on what you have said, but more often will be offering what is called 'active listening', a deep and welcoming kind of space for you. Not everyone is comfortable with being the centre of attention, but it should be remembered that this time is for you, and it would be wasted if the therapist's talking gave you no opportunity to express yourself. Long silences do not always happen, but when they do it does not mean that you are failing as a client or that your therapist is being lazy. Perhaps a few minutes' peace is just what you need.

If I lose my temper, will my therapist start to dislike me?

People often worry about the feelings of their practitioner and whether they might be upset or offended by what happens during sessions. As explained in Chapter 5, therapists and counsellors should attend professional supervision to discuss their clients (in confidence) and to deal with anything that has come up during the course of their work. This means that they are responsible for their own state of mind, and should be able to take care of themselves.

This does not mean that practitioners do not have feelings or never have strong reactions to what is said to them. Some may even be keen to tell you how they feel, whereas others will be more reserved. This usually depends on the kind of talking treatment in which they are trained. If you get very deeply in touch with your own emotions during a session, it is possible that you will feel a lot of anger or sadness. It may seem to you that showing these feelings would be 'offloading' them on to your therapist. But there is a clear difference between displaying sadness or anger about an event or a situation in which you find yourself, and *acting* aggressively or threateningly towards your practitioner. Getting annoyed, raising your voice, or even shouting may be perfectly acceptable if these actions are not meant to scare, shock or threaten someone.

To some extent this is a cultural issue, because some sections of society are more comfortable with emotional display, and some are less so. Chapter 11 explores cultural differences in more detail. Practitioners may have different ideas about how feelings are best expressed, but they should be skilled enough to accept your feelings without judging you. This does not mean you have a licence to attack your practitioner verbally (and certainly not physically), but it does mean that you can expect understanding and compassion about what you say and do when overwhelmed by your emotions.

This may give the impression that big emotional scenes are normal in talking treatments. A more accurate way of looking at it would be to say that they are not at all unusual, and are neither something to be aimed for nor something of which you should be ashamed.

Why do we always end a session just when we're getting somewhere?

Most kinds of therapy and counselling operate on a timetable. Sessions are booked to last for a specific length of time, and they usually have to end on time so that both client and practitioner can keep to their day's schedule. Occasionally groups have more flexible arrangements, but this is not very common. An individual session is usually an hour in length, but sometimes the talking part of this is only 45 to 50 minutes so that the practitioner can make notes at the end, or prepare for the next client. In psychoanalysis, you will always see your analyst for 50 minutes.

This fixed timetabling can be a worry to clients, who may wish the time could be more flexible. What happens if you have reached an important point in a session when your practitioner brings it to a close? The idea that you may have to leave when you are still feeling upset is very challenging, and it may seem uncaring of the practitioner to expect this. But a skilled practitioner will keep an eye on the clock and should assist clients in managing their sessions safely, by making sure that things are not started unless there is time for them to finish. If you spot your practitioner clock-watching, give him or her the benefit of the doubt. It does not mean that he or she is bored, but instead that he or she is trying to stay conscious of how much more work can be reasonably done in the time allowed.

There is, however, another common problem with time. Many clients realise that they regularly reach a point where some really good things are being achieved, but apparently only within the last few minutes of a session. It can be a major disappointment to have to stop when you are near to taking a big step forward. There are three possibilities as to why this may happen so frequently. First, it may take a lot of time to 'warm up' in a session and start to get close to the root of a problem, with the result that this happens only near the end of the hour. Second, it could be argued that subconsciously – in some part of your mind of which you are not aware – you are anxious about the issue at hand and have mixed feelings about getting too close to the truth. This could lead you to avoid raising points until it is too late to discuss them in detail.

The third possibility is that it may simply be that an hour (or perhaps only 45 minutes) is just not long enough for you to really benefit from a particular kind of talking treatment. Different models of therapy make different demands of people, and we may need more time to work at some therapies than at others. There are practitioners who offer 90-minute or two-hour sessions, and it may be worthwhile seeking them out. Be aware that if you are having private treatment the cost will probably go up accordingly.

Unclear boundaries

Counselling and therapy are organised within 'boundaries': limits that are placed on what should and should not happen between practitioner and client. These boundaries may not be clear unless they are properly discussed. Some are negotiable and will vary between practitioners, but others are not negotiable because any therapist who ignored them would be behaving unprofessionally or unethically. Chapter 9 gives more detail on how such boundaries provide an important safeguard for the client.

Some boundaries are grey areas, not forbidden by codes of conduct but capable of leading to problems anyway. The following questions raise some of these issues, most of which are still being debated within the therapy world at present.

What limits are there on physical contact between clients and practitioners?

The first thing to say is that a sexual relationship between a therapist and a client is expressly forbidden. The codes of conduct of the professional therapy organisations clearly condemn this, and professionals such as doctors, nurses and social workers are likely to lose their jobs if found guilty of this kind of serious offence. (In some circumstances it can even be punishable by a term in prison.) However, few guidelines are used across the board for less intimate kinds of contact. Hugs, briefly holding hands, or even a kiss hello and goodbye are not uncommon with some practitioners. The experience of human warmth and affection may be thought to be very helpful, especially for people who are feeling isolated or abandoned. However, these practitioners would certainly be in the minority. Other counsellors and therapists would see these actions as improper, because they might lead to confusion about the strictly professional nature of the therapeutic relationship.

Another important consideration (sometimes forgotten by those practitioners who like to be more physical) is that not everyone wants to be touched. It can be tempting for a practitioner to see this as a problem in and of itself, but this is a patronising attitude. Some cultures would see such touch as offensive, and many people dislike having their 'body space' invaded. It does not mean that there has to be something wrong with the person who dislikes this kind of intimacy.

It may sound very odd to recommend that you ask a practitioner what his or her beliefs are in this matter. But that may be the only way to ensure that you do not find yourself in an awkward situation later on. Following a discussion, your preference should be clear to both parties. This applies to group therapy sessions as well, where clear guidelines should be discussed for all group members.

Is it all right for my therapist to criticise other practitioners or their ways of working?

Your practitioner should not be doing this, because it is both unprofessional and (probably) a waste of your time. As explained in Chapter 2, there are many different types of talking treatments. The different schools that have emerged since the early 1900s often came into being because people were dissatisfied with whatever school was most popular at the time, and were looking for a new way of doing things. (This also largely explains why you will find different titles: counsellor, therapist, analyst, psychologist; the different terms were chosen to describe different ways of working.) While this guide explains talking treatments from a general perspective, it should not leave you with the impression that all practitioners are basically the same in what they do and what they believe.

Unfortunately, some practitioners are very critical of other types of talking treatments. If they hold strong opinions they may even see it as their responsibility to warn you about what they think are unhelpful types of treatments. Of course, it is understandable that everyone has a preferred way of approaching the work; this preference will have guided each practitioner in the choice of training that he or she decided to do. Some practitioners train in several different approaches and use ideas from more than one school (see the section on 'Eclectic/integrative therapy' in Chapter 2). Others use a distinct approach but still accept that some problems may respond better to another model of therapy.

This criticism of other models is not at all unusual. If this happens during a session, ask yourself whether it is in any way relevant or helpful, and why the therapist is making the criticism (maybe you need to ask the therapist as well). Your time is precious, and spending it listening to a commentary on professional disagreements is not the best use of your time.

However, there is a safety issue here. All practitioners must meet reasonable expectations regarding training, experience and conduct, as outlined in Chapter 9. A practitioner who tells you that another practitioner is ineffective or unethical just because he or she works differently is one thing; but if your practitioner warns you that another therapist is untrained or has been found to be in breach of a code of conduct, that is valuable information that you should take seriously. It is only fair to the accused individual that you ask your therapist for full details of the allegations, and for some clear proof of what he or she is saying.

Are there any circumstances in which a guarantee of confidentiality can be broken?

It is a good idea to discuss the issue of confidentiality with your practitioner at the beginning of your first session. You may feel better if the practitioner can confirm that the intimate details of your life are not going to be divulged to other people, even if you have no major anxieties about this at the time you ask. It also gives you a chance to hear about the exceptions that may be applied to this undertaking; only a very naïve practitioner would guarantee confidentiality in all and any circumstances.

Frequently a client is referred to a therapist by another professional, especially if the client is being seen within the NHS or by another large agency. If you have been referred, it usually means that there will be some feedback from the therapist to the professional who referred you, although this does not necessarily mean that the feedback will be detailed or done after every session. Written or computer notes may also be kept about your sessions, and you may want to know what safeguards exist over these. A responsible practitioner should also be receiving supervision as described in Chapter 5, and this means that he or she may need to discuss your case with his or her supervisor. This is normally done anonymously, with no names or identifying details, and the outcome can be an improvement in the practitioner's understanding of your situation, which should be to your benefit.

Chapter 9 explains the situations in which information that you reveal in a session may be shared among counselling and therapy professionals. Apart from them, there are normally no other reasons why a practitioner would discuss your case with other people. Certainly, your practitioner should never talk about you with people outside his or her working life. He or she should also not reveal any details of your sessions to your family or friends. (One exception to this may be when the client is a child, and parents want to know what progress is being made. However, this is quite a complicated area, because the same guarantees of confidentiality are usually made to children as to adults. If you are a parent or guardian of a child starting therapy it is advisable to come to some agreement on this before the sessions begin.)

Most practitioners do specify, however, that there are situations in which they will not guarantee confidentiality (see Chapter 9). By informing you of this, they are giving you the opportunity to decide for yourself whether you should tell them something or not. Except for the situations listed on pages 189–90, which are considered serious matters of safety, the position varies to some extent from one therapist to another. Practitioners have different viewpoints in the case of 'minor' matters such as the use of illegal drugs or driving offences, but these are very unlikely to be reported.

If you feel that any of these kinds of conflict are likely to arise for you, it would be useful to ask for a clear statement of the practitioner's position on the issue of confidentiality. More information can be obtained from the professional bodies listed in the Resources section at the end of this guide.

'Recovered memory' and other serious misinterpretations

In the last few years, the media have talked a lot about 'recovered memory', and this relates to a bigger difficulty in the field of talking treatments. The experience of therapy and counselling can occasionally bring to mind past experiences and concerns that we may have blocked out of our conscious mind, and have not really been aware of in any clear way. Sometimes these memories are jumbled and confusing, and sometimes they are dreamlike and very disturbing. A skilled practitioner will help you to make sense of these images and recollections, and assist you in working out what they mean.

However, recently practitioners have occasionally used a very unsafe way of doing this. When faced with these kinds of 'memories', some practitioners would automatically relate them to forgotten experiences of sexual abuse, with or without direct evidence to support this conclusion. The process is believed to have happened in the following way: a person would start to recall vague and maybe frightening pictures of being unhappy or anxious as a child; sometimes this would be linked to a sense of having felt out of control; a practitioner might interpret this as a memory of sexual abuse; the practitioner would tell the client that he or she was abused as a child, or at least ask leading questions that made it clear that this was what the practitioner believed; if the client disagreed, the practitioner would convince him or her that this was because he or she was too traumatised by the events to want to think about them. Here the practitioner distorts a vague memory into a very clear one, not by gentle or open-minded questioning, but by forcing an interpretation on the client. The practice, when it came to light, was dubbed the 'recovered memory syndrome'.

This sort of distortion would itself be a terribly abusive experience for the client. There is convincing evidence that both men and women have undergone this kind of serious misinterpretation of their memories. The evidence includes documented cases of young women who were led by their therapists to believe that they had suffered multiple sexual assaults, often by close family members, whereas subsequent medical examination proved that they were still virgins and showed no signs of the physical damage that would have resulted from these events. Yet the therapists involved seemed to have genuinely believed that their interpretation was correct, and the clients became equally convinced by the therapists' suggestions.

Of course, there is a huge difficulty with all of this – namely, that childhood sexual abuse does take place, and it is often hard for survivors to make other people believe that it happened, or even to believe it themselves. It is not uncommon for memories of abuse to emerge slowly and in fragments, and proving beyond a reasonable doubt that it did take place is often very problematic. When the investigation is undertaken many years after the fact, it is equally difficult to prove that abuse did not take place. The cases described above, where clear proof to the contrary was found, are very much the exceptions.

This has led to wide differences of opinion on the recovered memory syndrome. Some among the profession deny that practitioners ever try to convince their clients that something is a real memory when it is not. But most practitioners now seem to agree that there have been at least some examples of therapists making definite mistakes. Even so, there are arguments about how many times mistakes may have occurred, and whether recovered memory is very rare or very common.

From the client's point of view, it is important at least to be aware of how seriously misled you could be by a poorly trained or inexperienced therapist. While you should be open-minded in pondering what your practitioner says, you should also see that he or she can make mistakes. If you think your practitioner may be introducing certain issues too often or too readily into your sessions, discuss this with him or her. The recovered memory syndrome is a particularly disturbing and extreme example of how mistakes can happen, but less serious examples do unfortunately occur. If you believe that your situation is being seriously misinterpreted, your first step should be to discuss this with your therapist, and perhaps ask him or her to discuss it with his or her supervisor. If this does not resolve your concerns, it may be necessary to terminate therapy and depending on how well you feel this matter was handled, could even be grounds for a complaint to a professional body or the organisation for which the practitioner works.

Time to stop?

All talking treatments come to an end. If the decision to stop is not your own, and your experience of therapy has been a good one, this can be a real disappointment and cause a lot of anxiety. Equally, you may be struggling to decide whether to continue or stop because your experience seems to be more negative than positive. Some of the reasons why treatment ends are worth thinking through, because this could help you manage more easily what might be a worrying time.

Why should I continue to see someone when it feels painful? I feel as though I'm stuck and getting nowhere.
Being in therapy is often about challenging yourself, because trying to change your situation and the way that you think about and do things is frequently very difficult indeed. This means that you cannot always expect counselling or therapy to be an easy experience – although neither should you assume that it will definitely be painful or tiring. But if you find it very stressful or depressing, and appear to be receiving no benefits from it, it is reasonable to ask what purpose there would be in continuing.

Clearly there could be many reasons why you are struggling. First and foremost, the model of therapy employed may not be suitable for your problems or may clash with your beliefs. Second, it may not be the correct time to be engaging in a talking treatment – you may be just too tired or over-committed right now. These issues are explored in earlier chapters. A third reason may be that you have reached a natural finishing point, having done as much as you can at present. This does not mean that more progress could not be made later. There is no point in berating yourself for not being able to do more now, and feeling frustrated at what seems a failure.

The sense of feeling 'stuck,' as though you are on the verge of making a big step forward but cannot quite manage it, is in fact quite common in talking treatments. (This is especially true of people who have been in therapy for a long time.) Sometimes the process feels like putting together a jigsaw, making sense of the past and present with the help of interlocking ideas and experiences; it is easy to feel that a piece is missing, and to torture yourself because you cannot find it. It may help to acknowledge this openly, or even to take a holiday from therapy.

Deciding when to rest or even when to give up on a talking treatment is not a precise science. It can be very hard to stop doing something that has helped you. But if the experience has become too negative, it makes no sense to put yourself through suffering just for the sake of it. Therapy may be painful, but it does not have to be – the idea of 'no pain, no gain' may be popular, but it is often a mistake. If you are gaining nothing from a talking treatment, consider whether to change the approach, to take a break, or to stop altogether.

My sessions are full of conflict, and I think that this way of working just isn't for me. My practitioner and I seem to be incompatible.
There is a difference between realising that talking treatments can be a challenging (even painful) experience, and being willing to put up with almost any kind of frustration or discomfort in your sessions in the hope that it is doing you some good. You may be sticking it out because this practitioner is the only person in your area, or someone you had to wait six months to see because you cannot afford private work. Perhaps you are unsure what other alternatives are available. Chapter 11 explores some of the cultural

reasons why you and your therapist may seem incompatible. Whatever the reason for the difficulties, talk to your therapist about your doubts about continuing. It may be worthwhile sticking with the therapy if you are getting at least some benefits from it, even if it has its bad side.

However, if you have tried to discuss this with your practitioner and it has got you nowhere, or if it seems that you cannot do any more good work with the person right now, consider your other options. If you were taking medication that had too many side-effects, you would ask for an alternative, and it is the same with therapy: alternatives are always available. A different approach may be best for you, even if you have to wait. In the meantime, you could try some of the self-help possibilities mentioned in Chapter 1. New models of talking treatments are being developed all the time. A non-talking treatment could be a good alternative, at least for a while (see Chapter 12). You could contact a self-help organisation and see what it can suggest. The Resources section at the end of this book lists self-help manuals and other products, and several self-help organisations.

Staying around just to prove a point or because you do not know what else to do is not a good use of your resources. There is no reason to keep going with something that is not working.

I've been offered a limited number of sessions, but I realise I need many more.

A lot of talking treatments are intended to work only for a fixed number of sessions, because they are based on a clear progression of steps that will take a predictable amount of time. Other approaches run much less to a pattern, and may work best over a long (perhaps a very long) period. But when therapy has been obtained free of charge through the NHS or at a voluntary-sector project, it is usual to have a limit placed on the time available because of the pressure of waiting lists. Clearly this is a poor reason for determining the length of counselling offered to each client. If your model of therapy works according to a fixed number of sessions, this is not a problem. But when the model used would normally be more open-ended, you may feel that the sessions on offer come to an end just when the process is proving to be useful.

Sometimes it is best to see a limited number of sessions as a prepa-ration for longer work, and a way for you to discover whether talking helps you, or at least whether this type of talking helps. On other occasions the limitation may even focus you more determinedly on the difficulties that you are experiencing so that you make sure that your efforts are directed towards the right ends. It is not always helpful to view talking treatments as always being about 'resolving' long-term problems over many years. Therapy may last a long time, or it may be very brief indeed, depending on what you intend to achieve.

If a talking treatment is due to end at a time that feels 'too soon', discuss this with your practitioner. Occasionally the period of support can be extended, or perhaps there are available alternatives that can be recommended. Having longer therapy is always a possibility, but it helps to think through whether it is needed and what your expectations of continuing with it would be.

Why would a therapist decide to stop seeing me?

Sometimes a practitioner will decide that it is best to stop working with you, and this can come as a shock if you believe that you are getting on well. There could be many reasons why this needs to happen. The practitioner may decide that you have a problem about which he or she knows very little, and that it is better to recommend you see someone more skilled in that kind of problem. He or she may feel that his or her particular approach or model does not match your needs or personality. Or he or she may think he or she has given you all the help that he or she usefully can, and that it is time for you to look for a different kind of support.

Any of these situations could make you feel rejected, or even that you are a failure. But in fact knowing when not to continue is a sign of the practitioner's professionalism. Practitioners should not assume that they are all-powerful or can solve all the problems of the world. If your practitioner decides to stop the therapy, the reasons should be made very clear to you, precisely so that any painful misunderstanding is avoided.

Chapter 2 mentions transference and countertransference: the feelings that can develop in a client towards the therapist (transference) and the reciprocal feelings experienced by the therapist (countertransference). These are sometimes acknowledged and sometimes not. It is possible for a client to feel very dependent on his or her therapist, maybe unhealthily so. It also happens that a therapist can start to over-sympathise with a client, or to feel dominated by feelings aroused by work with the client, to the extent that he or she loses his or her balanced view of the person's situation. The practitioner's first move should be to discuss these issues with his or her supervisor so that they may be taken up appropriately and constructively in sessions. However, it may reach the point when feelings in the sessions may be so overwhelming to the client, the therapist, or both, that ending the therapeutic relationship is for the best. In this instance, the practitioner would be responsible for recommending or handing you over to a colleague.

What if my therapist leaves and passes me on to someone else?

In large organisations staff are always coming and going, and practitioners employed by the NHS or large voluntary-sector projects are no exception. Lone practitioners in private practice also go through changes in their private or professional lives. It can be a shock if one day your therapist tells you that he or she is moving away, or is going on maternity leave, or is retiring. A client's first reaction can occasionally be that he or she has made this happen by being too demanding. The reality is that it is normal for people to change jobs or move, or take time off work.

If your therapy is in the public or voluntary sectors, usually a replacement practitioner will be offered from within the same organisation, although staff shortages can sometimes delay this process. Recruiting a new member of staff can take months, although it is very unlikely that this should result in your not being seen for that length of time. If your practitioner works alone in private practice, he or she should still try to find you alternative support or at least make some recommendations about where you can look.

Changing therapists can be stressful, and because no two people work in exactly the same way, you are bound to make comparisons. Talking through the transition can be helpful, and bringing the new practitioner up to date should assist him or her in offering you what you need. Although a change of practitioners is not the same as stopping therapy altogether, it is a difficult process, and your reactions can show you how important the therapy may have become in your daily life.

What if I run out of money before my problems are resolved?

When you are paying for your therapy, finding the money can create a double stress. Few of us are so rich that the cost of therapy makes no impact on our finances, but if you are continuing to pay for it that probably means that you are finding the treatment helpful. So you may be anxious not only about continuing to be able to afford it, but also about what would happen if you had to stop your regular sessions.

A change in financial circumstances can sometimes be managed without too many problems. Many practitioners operate a sliding scale of charges and will accept what you can reasonably afford. This means that what you pay can be negotiated and, if necessary, re-negotiated. It can also be worthwhile thinking about whether you need to attend so regularly. Maybe fortnightly would do instead of weekly, or once every three weeks instead of every fortnight. Your therapist is entitled to have an opinion on this as well; he or she may think that once a fortnight is the minimum attendance for you to work on your difficulties, for instance. But it is always worth discussing the issue to see what arrangements can be made. Occasionally practitioners will allow you to pay them later for therapy received now. This can sound like a good idea but may create debts you cannot discharge. There is no simple answer here, but you can ask your therapist if he or she knows of any alternative sources of support for you.

It is possible to be angry with a practitioner when he or she cannot help you reduce costs, and you may feel your therapist does not care about you or your situation. But practitioners have bills to pay too, and sometimes genuinely cannot meet a client halfway. You will have to judge what the treatment is worth to you in relation to the money you have available. Sometimes it may be worth making sacrifices, but on other occasions your hard-earned cash could be better spent elsewhere. Sometimes it is actually beneficial to take a total break from therapy for a few months, especially if you have been seeing someone for a long time.

Why would a practitioner want to refer me for a mental health assessment?

Sometimes a counsellor or therapist will feel that your problems include elements that go beyond the support he or she is able to give you. This may be because your physical health is affected – for example you are sleeping and eating badly as a result of severe depression. Maybe you have started to suffer from dizzy spells. Or possibly you have told your practitioner that you have recently thought about harming yourself. In any of these situations, and in many others, a practitioner may want you to have a mental health assessment from someone with a training in psychiatry. This is especially true if your practitioner works within the NHS, which is responsible for organising mental health services.

It may feel as though your therapist is trying to tell you that you are too seriously disturbed or that he or she no longer wants to work with you. In fact it is simply an acknowledgement of his or her professional limitations, and a clear message that your problems are complicated and may need a different approach.

Of course, none of us wants to believe that we are 'mentally ill'. This guide refers to 'psychological problems' or 'difficulties' and avoids seeing these normal experiences as 'illness'. After all, many talking treatments are based on the belief that psychological pain and stress are not the same as illness. However, in the NHS the field of mental health covers a very wide range of conditions, including those mentioned in this guide, and others. For NHS employees, mental health covers everything from the smallest episode of stress through to the most serious type of breakdown. A referral for a mental health assessment does not mean that your practitioner assumes that you must have one of the more serious kinds of problem. It means instead that he or she thinks your situation might be best looked at in the context of a 'diagnosis' rather than just as a trauma or problematic behaviour pattern or as a set of difficult experiences; in other words, that the best way to support you may be with a different kind of treatment to his or her own. (See Chapter 1 for a discussion of these different ways of looking at problems, one of which is diagnosis.)

More information on mental health assessments can be found in Chapter 4.

Working with other people

This section deals with difficult situations that can arise in a talking treatment which involves more people than just one client and one practitioner. The presence of even one more person (as in couples work), or perhaps many more (as in large groups), adds a whole new dimension to the experience of therapy. This is what makes these formats effective, but it can also bring new challenges.

Why am I scared to talk in front of the other people?

Talking in front of a group of people, even (or especially) if you know some of them (as in family therapy), can be very nerve-wracking. Any anxieties you may feel about opening up are bound to be multiplied by the number of people present. Perhaps you will be more concerned about confidentiality, or are worried that your problems will seem insignificant compared to those of others. This is especially difficult if the other people involved in your therapy are partners, family members or maybe people with whom you work. Having to deal with them on a daily basis may make it very hard to be honest and open with them during a session. Sometimes certain subjects are 'forbidden' topics within a family or partnership, and it may need great courage to raise and discuss them in detail.

There is no simple solution to this, but it is unquestionable that very little progress can be made without these fears being acknowledged openly. Perhaps this can be achieved by saying something like 'there's a subject I want to discuss, but I'm afraid to talk about it because I don't know how other people are going to react'. This immediately makes the therapist aware of your concerns, and gives everyone the chance to express their own fears. Often it is helpful to know that you are not the only person who is feeling anxious about something.

If a family member or colleague simply refuses to talk about a specific matter, or even refuses to talk at all, your options are very limited. You can ask him or her why he or she is remaining silent, and can tell him or her how it makes you feel, and why you wish he or she would participate in the session. But you cannot force anyone to take an active part, any more than he or she can force you.

However, the problem may simply be that talking in public – and any format that involves more than three or four people can feel very public – is something that you really struggle with under normal circumstances. Group work and other formats are not for everyone, and again there is a trade-off here between challenging yourself to try new things and not putting yourself through pain for the sake of it. Give the approach a chance, and see if the benefits outweigh the difficulties. If not, try something else.

How do I deal with someone who is very loud and overbearing?

It is common in group formats to observe that not everyone says the same amount: some people can be very talkative while others remain silent. There is no reason why everyone should be expected to take an equal share in the proceedings. In any environment, some people are more prone to talking than others, and this is likely to be the same in a group or in family therapy. But sometimes one or more members of the group can talk so much that it seems excessive (even boring), and you may switch off when you hear the sound of their voice. This can be equally true when the person is a member of your family – perhaps this is what he or she does at home, and it just feels like more of the same.

Different practitioners handle this situation in contrasting ways. Some will challenge it very openly, and ask the person why he or she is acting in this way. Others may take a less direct approach, but work hard to make sure that all group members have their say in the course of the session. And some may take no action at all, believing that if necessary these kinds of 'dynamics' can be addressed by any group member, because the practitioners are not there to tell people how much they should or should not say.

In a situation like this, it may be worth thinking through the reasons you are reacting to the talkative person in a certain way. One of the benefits of larger formats is that you have the opportunity to look at your patterns of dealing with other people and discuss these out loud. You may feel apprehensive about speaking out, but the instant feedback you can receive (and give) in a session means that you have the chance to learn a great deal in a short space of time. It could be that the talkative people really do not know the effect they have on others, and will be grateful to have it pointed out. While they are likely to be a little miffed to realise that people don't want to listen to them, they may also accept that it would explain a lot about the way others treat them in the world at large.

Try to approach the issue in a sympathetic and calm way. Remember that you would have mixed feelings about hearing observations like this made to you.

Why don't the therapists take a more active role?

Practitioners working with different approaches may do more, or less, to make a group or family session head in a particular direction. Some see sessions as most likely to be effective if there is a clear structure, and make sure that a specific task is accomplished. Others prefer to allow the group to direct itself, and take more of an observer's role. Some will interpret events within the group and feed them back to the participants.

The upshot of this is that you may feel there is either too little or too much being done to manage the session. If disagreements arise, or boundaries are crossed, participants may look to the practitioners to act as referees and provide a solution. There are some grounds for this – to use a rather dramatic example, it would certainly be the responsibility of the therapists to step in if two people were getting close to exchanging blows. But aside from such highly unlikely events, it may make sense for the group to deal with problems without too much interference. This gives everyone a greater chance to learn about himself or herself, because challenges are overcome without 'experts' stepping in to make things happen. This can feel very empowering.

Very few groups are run by practitioners who are totally passive. But a lot of group and family sessions work with only occasional interventions from the therapists, who perhaps make brief comments about what seems to be happening and invite people to reflect on what has been said. This gives some direction, but still allows the group to follow its own course.

Why does it feel as if the group has split into cliques?

People attending a large group often feel that the participants have split into sub-groups, and that they are closer to some people than others. This can apply in family therapy as well, with some relation-ships appearing very strong and some much less so. In many respects, this is hardly surprising. Put a number of people together, and inevitably some will get on better than others, and friendships will develop. It becomes a problem only if this leads to conflict, or is used to make some people feel isolated.

Thinking about how a situation like this affects you can be instructive in helping you to understand how you relate to people in your daily life. Perhaps you often have the experience of feeling left out, or find it difficult to join in with things and make new friends. Maybe you find it easier to get on with people of your own gender, age, ethnicity or sexuality. Alternatively, you might have frequent problems with people who are somehow different from you, or who represent something that you find challenging or provocative. Seeing this in the splits and cliques that have formed in a group can make these tendencies very clear, and give you the chance to work with them and change whatever you think needs changing. If you feel left out of a session, or perhaps have realised that you are not relating well to another person or persons in the group, it may be beneficial to acknowledge this out loud, and see what responses you get from the therapists or other group members. Making any kind of self-disclosure like this can be nerve-wracking, and take a lot of courage. But it may teach you a lot about other areas of your life.

This is one of the main advantages of larger formats for therapy. You can check out your thoughts and feelings about other people directly, in a way that is pretty much impossible in individual therapy. The group becomes something like a laboratory situation, in which you can test things and examine the results. Providing this is done in a way that is respectful to others, and not seen as an opportunity for dumping negative feelings on people, all members can benefit from this opportunity.

Why does the group go from one extreme of feeling to another?

People new to groups may find that the intensity of feelings expressed can be very strong on some occasions. Perhaps even more confusingly, groups can waver between extremes, with people feeling very confident and positive one moment, and then quite sad soon after. The reason for this is that when a number of people get together in one room, a lot of emotions come with them. If the group begins to focus on one particular feeling, the combined energy of all members together can mean that a very high level of that feeling is on display.

While this probably sounds alarming, it happens sometimes rather than all the time, and is arguably a sign that the group is working well, with people able to listen to each other and share their experiences in an honest way. Finding that you have things, including feelings, in common with other people is often a big relief rather than painful or distressing. Capable practitioners will assist everyone in managing these occasional peaks of emotion, which often have the effect of bringing the group closer together.

Why is the therapist taking sides?

Particularly in couples work, but also in family and group therapy, the practitioner or practitioners should work hard to avoid taking sides. Their role is not to judge the interaction between people, but to point out what happens and allow the individuals themselves to decide whether this is a good or a bad thing. One example is when one person frequently interrupts the other(s). This could be explained as happening because he or she is aggressive and doesn't listen to other people, or because he or she is eager to get a point across and so does not really think through what he or she is doing, or because of many other reasons. The practitioner can communicate this to the person in a helpful and calm fashion, or throw it at the person as a snap judgement that makes clear his or her disapproval of what is taking place.

Any occasion on which you are told that you do something you are not aware of, or which makes things difficult for other people, can feel like an attack. You may respond defensively and refuse to hear what is being said. This is reasonable if you are in fact being criticised, but experienced counsellors and therapists should be able to communicate an observation to you in a way that does not feel damaging. If, despite their best efforts, you feel hurt anyway, it is worth standing back and asking yourself why your reaction is so strong. Sometimes this kind of observation can reinforce the idea that a practitioner sympathises more with someone else than with you, especially if all the problems that are identified seem to be about what you do and none about what others do. Even so, ask yourself if it is possible that the practitioner is right.

But it is also perfectly reasonable to say out loud that the observations seem very one-way, and that you are feeling blamed. At the very least this means that the practitioner should stop and think about his or her comments, and it may even lead to an admission that he or she is not seeing things in as balanced a way as is necessary. Making this challenge to oneself is a necessary and ongoing process for clients and practitioners alike, because any of us can accidentally unload our feelings on a convenient target.

It is always possible that a practitioner can lose impartiality and side with an individual or section of a group against others. This is especially true if the issues being discussed have particular significance for the practitioner. For example, a practitioner who has suffered a recent break-up may find it difficult to discuss relationship issues effectively. These kinds of conflicts should be talked about during professional supervision, but it could happen that the feelings are very strong and start to leak out during work. If you suspect this is happening, point out to the practitioner how you feel, and you may find you get an apology. The experience of therapy is one in which you are given the chance to examine your thoughts and feelings, but it is only fair that practitioners are equally aware of their own emotional and intellectual responses. Usually they will welcome this kind of discussion.

Chapter 9

Safeguards: legal and ethical matters

The strength of the relationship between a practitioner and a client is seen as one of the most important factors in determining the likelihood of a successful outcome to treatment. Sometimes this relationship is referred to as the 'therapeutic alliance'. In many cases this is one of the most intimate types of human contact (in the psychological sense) in which an individual can be involved.

A great deal of trust is involved in a therapeutic relationship. You should be able to trust that:

- your practitioner is adequately trained, competent, and knows the limits of his or her competence
- the practitioner will maintain confidentiality
- your practitioner will obtain your consent before carrying out any investigation or research
- your safety will be of fundamental importance
- your practitioner's personal conduct will be of the highest standard
- there will be no abuse of your vulnerability.

The vast majority of counselling and therapy consultations are conducted by caring people who maintain this trust and go to great lengths to ensure their clients' safety and well-being. In their conduct most of them would go beyond the basic safety matters outlined below. Unfortunately, as in any walk of life, there are a few whose conduct is questionable and could be harmful to their clients. When any trust is broken, it can of course be very damaging, and this is especially true when you are already feeling vulnerable. This chapter is intended to explain how the professions involved in counselling and therapy aim to safeguard you, how you can find out whether these safeguards are in place in the setting of your own therapy, and what steps you can take if you fear these safeguards are not working. It is a good idea to clarify these issues with your practitioner during your first session.

Training

How do you know that the practitioner you plan to consult has been trained and is able to deal with your problem? This is a question of fundamental importance and it is advisable to satisfy yourself with the answer before you proceed with therapy. There are a number of ways of finding out, and the simplest is to ask the practitioner the following questions.

1 Practitioner's profession

Among the many professionals involved in counselling and therapy are:

- psychiatrists
- clinical psychologists
- counselling psychologists
- child psychotherapists.

People belonging to the above professions have had recognised training in talking treatments and are governed in their work by their profession's codes of conduct or guidelines on ethical practice. Other professionals, such as nurses, occupational therapists, social workers and medical doctors, may also be trained practitioners, but they must have completed a second training in counselling or therapy. This is because their basic professional qualifications do not include extended training in talking treatments. Chapter 4 gives more information about what these professionals do in their daily work.

2 Specialisation

Any practitioner of talking treatments who is not a psychiatrist, psychologist or child psychotherapist would be expected to have trained in one of the major approaches outlined in Chapter 2. This does not mean that any given practitioner can carry out all kinds of therapy and counselling – he or she is limited to working with those

approaches in which he or she has been trained. In addition, counsellors and therapists may have experience in working with a particular
problem or a specific group of the population such as children, people
with addictions, and so on. Overall, this combination of professional
standing, training and experience will indicate whether a practitioner is
competent to do the kind of work for which he or she is employed.

3 Membership of a professional body

Does your counsellor or therapist belong to a professional body?
Many of the people listed above will automatically belong to a learned
society such as the Royal College of Psychiatrists, Royal College of
Nursing, or the British Psychological Society.* If your therapist does
not belong to one of these learned societies, he or she should be a
member of a recognised therapy or counselling organisation, usually
the institution with which he or she trained. These organisations
include the British Association for Counselling and Psychotherapy,*
the British Association of Psychotherapists*, and the UK Council for
Psychotherapy.* Members of such organisations are bound by the
codes of conduct that exist for each of these associations.

A practitioner should have information on his or her
membership readily available, for example printed on his or her
business or visiting card, or in his or her leaflet or brochure. It
should be noted that membership of a professional body or society
is not always compulsory – that is to say, it is compulsory for some
professions but not for others. Ask a practitioner about this before
engaging in treatment.

Your practitioner's membership of one of the learned societies or
professional bodies is a safeguard for you, because if you believe that
the practitioner is in breach of that body's code of conduct you can
take your grievance to the organisation and will be able to follow
their established complaints procedure. If the complaint is upheld
the practitioner may be removed from the professional directory
('struck off') or made to pay a penalty.

Competence

Although checking your practitioner's professional status and
training will answer your questions about his or her competence in

general terms, you should also be aware of any limits in his or her ability to deal with your particular case. Your initial assessment session (see Chapter 7) may reveal that you need help with a number of different problems, and some of these may be beyond the practitioner's realm of expertise. A skilled counsellor or therapist would discuss this with you and suggest that you seek treatment from one or more practitioners trained in these areas. However, many clients have gone through quite a struggle to get to see a therapist, and may be reluctant to start the process again, and the practitioner may feel pressure from the client to take him or her on. If this happens, the practitioner could decide to apply the general principles of his or her therapeutic approach to an area with which he or she is not directly familiar or in which he or she does not have special expertise. While this may be acceptable when there is no sound evidence that a particular approach to treatment is more effective than another (see Chapter 6), it could be ethically unsound if there is clear evidence about the best approach and the therapist is not trained to work in this way. In such a case, a poor treatment outcome might mean that the client would be reasonably justified in complaining that the practitioner had acted beyond his or her level of competence.

Another example of a practitioner acting beyond his or her competence is in the use of specific techniques or procedures. However experienced and qualified a practitioner may be, he or she may not be competent to use, for example, specific techniques or procedures such as hypnotherapy or eye movement desensitisation and reprocessing. If any technique is used on you, it is reasonable for you to assume that your practitioner has undergone the specific training and is competent to use it. It may put a strain on the therapeutic relationship to check the limits of your therapist's competence, but you should aim to do so to safeguard yourself against a negative outcome. This means that it is quite reasonable to ask a practitioner – before treatment begins – what training he or she has undergone.

Confidentiality

Discussions with your counsellor or therapist may involve very private matters such as information about your background, difficulties you are experiencing, intimate personal details about yourself, and your doubts about what to do in the future. Often this will be material that you have not shared with anyone before. It is natural to have anxieties about how secure this information will be when you reveal it to your practitioner.

When we share information with someone 'in confidence' this generally means that we trust that individual to keep it completely to himself or herself and not betray us by discussing it with other people. In everyday life, if someone breaks this confidence it is an extremely negative experience for most people. One of the key assumptions that clients have when they enter a therapeutic relationship is that their practitioner will maintain confidentiality, and indeed this is a crucial element in counselling and therapy. However, it is important to be clear about what the counselling and therapy profession understands by the word 'confidentiality'.

Sharing of information

Although counsellors and therapists will adhere to the spirit, or the principle, of our common understanding of confidentiality, it does not necessarily follow that all information remains only within the counselling room. Depending on the setting in which you receive counselling or therapy, your information may be handled in different ways.

Supervision

This process is a safeguard built into any reputable counselling or therapy setting. In supervision (see Chapter 5), your practitioner will discuss his or her work with an experienced colleague (sometimes with a group of colleagues). This may involve talking about your case in terms of any problems the practitioner might be experiencing, or feelings that the work is producing in him or her. The aim of such discussion is for the therapist to receive advice and feedback on the quality of his or her work and on his or her adherence to the model of therapy being used. This process is designed to protect and benefit both the therapist and the client, and is seen as integral to good practice. The same standard of confidentiality that is generally assumed in the counselling room is expected in supervision. Wherever possible, the client is not identified, and facts about his or her circumstances may be disguised to protect his or her identity.

Team settings

Most NHS settings and some voluntary-sector settings now provide many services in multidisciplinary teams. This means that the care may include input from individuals from several different professional backgrounds, such as doctors, nurses, counsellors and psychologists, working together as a team. It also means that for the team to operate effectively, some information about the people under their care has to be shared. This may be done in one-to-one supervision, supervision groups, team meetings or ward rounds. In such settings 'confidentiality' means that information is confidential to the team. In practice, any information shared in supervision and team meetings is a distilled version of discussions in the counselling room, not a detailed replaying of your conversations with the practitioner.

Case notes

It is important for your practitioner to keep notes about your treatment. Some will take notes during a session while others may write notes after. Some practitioners will use the rough notes they take during a session ('process notes') to write up a summary for more formal files, such as hospital records. The practitioner must take responsibility for the security of confidential records by ensuring that notes never fall into the wrong hands. If your treatment is in the public or voluntary sectors you may have the right under the UK Data Protection Act 1998 to see some of your case notes. To comply with the Act, organisations must have a procedure to enable you to do this and you can find out about the procedure by making a formal request.

Audio recordings

Audio recording of sessions is an increasingly routine activity in counselling and therapy. In some treatments, such as in cognitive behavioural therapy, it may be part of the treatment and should be carried out for your direct benefit. In addition, audio recording has become a useful and effective tool in the initial and continuing training of practitioners, and the tapes will be played during teaching or supervision.

As a safeguard, your written permission is needed before sessions can be taped. Find out what the purpose of taping the session is, and who will be listening to the recordings. Professional organisations such as the General Medical Council, NHS Trusts and voluntary-sector organisations have well-developed codes of practice on audio, video and other electronic recordings. If you have concerns about your therapist recording your sessions you should ask to see the code of practice or guidelines produced by his or her professional body. Unauthorised taping of sessions is grounds for complaint.

Video recordings

Some forms of therapy such as family therapy, and cognitive behavioural therapy when used for specific problems such as social phobia, may incorporate video recording as part of the therapy process. Some services may wish to videotape sessions for training purposes. If the tapes are for the practitioner's training, he or she would view them with a supervisor or teacher only. Alternatively, they may be used for research purposes.

No videotaping can take place unless you have signed a consent form giving permission. If you are unhappy about being videotaped you should not feel under any pressure to give your consent: you are perfectly entitled to refuse permission. It is an absolute requirement that if your sessions are being videotaped you understand fully what purposes the tape will be used for, and who will be viewing it. You may also want to know how long any tapes are kept and whether you can have your tape once it has fulfilled its purpose.

Information held in computers

In many settings it is likely that a provider of treatment will hold information about you on computer. Such information has to be protected and the rules for this are set out in the UK Data Protection Act 1998. Increasingly in the NHS and other large organisations, client data are contained in clinical information systems or databases in networked computers. Access to information in networked systems is regulated within and between organisations. If you have any anxieties about who will have access to information about you, contact the organisation's information or communications department and ask for clarification.

Protection of your information

Although your practitioner may share information about you with a supervisor or colleagues in a team providing care, you should expect any professional therapist or counsellor to act with maximum discretion and at all times protect your information from third parties. In particular, under the terms of the professional codes of conduct, or ethical guidelines, of therapy organisations, you should expect:

- that your practitioner will protect all information you have shared from third parties such as the police, newspapers, your employer, insurance companies, your relatives, your friends
- that if your practitioner receives a formal request for information or a report from a third party (for example, your educational establishment if you are at school or college), it is supplied only after you have given your written permission, and that you can read the report before it is sent
- that if the therapist wishes to write about your case in a public document (an article in a journal, or book), or speak about it publicly (in a lecture, for example), in no way should it be possible to identify you by the information the therapist gives.

Breaching confidentiality

Breaching confidentiality in a therapeutic relationship is a serious matter and it is rarely done. Practitioners should never take this step without serious consideration of the ethical and legal issues. In general, confidentiality is broken only in circumstances where it is felt necessary to do this to protect the safety of an individual or the public at large. These are some examples.

- The practitioner has become seriously concerned that you may harm yourself, in view of the thoughts, or clear intention, that you have expressed.
- The therapist is seriously concerned that you may harm someone else because you have made a clear statement to do so (not just expressions of what you might feel like doing), including a plan of how you would do it.
- The practitioner has concerns for public safety, for example because you have said that you have drunk a large quantity of alcohol and that you are going to drive a car.
- The practitioner is sufficiently concerned about existing or potential harm to children either by neglect or by ill-treatment.

In this case the practitioner – along with all employees of health, social work and education departments – is legally bound to break confidentiality under the terms of the Children's Act 1989. (The Act implies that all citizens have to meet this responsibility, but states that certain workers have a definite legal obligation to do so.)

In most cases you would expect the practitioner to discuss with you his or her intention to breach confidentiality, but this may not always be possible.

There are instances where the decision to breach confidentiality is not so clear-cut, but present an ethical and moral dilemma for the therapist. For example, if a client confesses to a serious crime during a session, the therapist has to decide how this information is to be handled within the working relationship. However, the therapist is under no legal obligation to report the client to the police (except in the case of current harm to children, as stated above).

There are some instances where the practitioner and client will both agree that the practitioner should resist a request for information from an interested party (such as the police) to breach confidentiality. An example might be where the practitioner is asked to provide a report to support a legal case, but chooses not to do so. However, the practitioner may be compelled to breach confidentiality if the interested party gets a court order for information to be divulged (a subpoena). In law, the therapist is then obliged to give evidence in court or allow the court to see your case notes. Even so, there are some therapists who might contest this, and would look for the legal backing of their professional body in opposing an enforced breach of confidentiality. Some professional bodies have legal contingency funds to contest injunctions and court orders through a barrister.

Safety

When you engage in a therapeutic relationship you trust that the counsellor or therapist will at all times work towards ensuring your safety. The single most important factor in ensuring this is the therapist's professional competence, as discussed earlier in this chapter. There are at least two further matters that are important for your security and you should be able to feel that your practitioner is addressing these matters.

Your state of mind

A competent and experienced therapist will conduct therapy in a way that makes your safety his or her prime consideration. For example, he or she should always ensure that you are in a fit state to explore difficult material, and that you are not so troubled by the work done in a session that you feel at risk of harming yourself. The therapy process inevitably involves looking at difficult material at times, and you might have preferred to avoid this because of the pain it brings. If you are feeling vulnerable you should be able to rely on your therapist to talk your anxieties through with you, to check the kinds of support that you have in place and the steps you can take to ensure your safety. This could include advice to contact your GP or go to the accident and emergency clinic at your local hospital, especially if you are really afraid you might harm yourself. If you feel your practitioner does not show enough concern for your safety and well-being, or you are left repeatedly feeling unsafe after sessions, this could be grounds for a complaint (see 'Taking action', below).

The therapy environment

Practitioners must also ensure their clients' security in terms of the environment in which they are seen. Counselling rooms that are not properly sound-proofed, or where people keep intruding or interrupting, are not secure enough settings for therapy.

Boundaries and codes of conduct

It is important for anyone engaging in counselling or therapy to understand the concept of 'boundaries': limits on what can be said and done by both parties in the therapeutic relationship. Staying within boundaries is another major factor in ensuring the safety of the client; conversely, inadequate or inappropriate observance of boundaries can make therapy unsafe or damaging to the client.

Chapter 8 explains how a misunderstanding of any of the common boundaries may make you feel that your therapist is uncaring. Remember that a good therapeutic relationship is a very intimate kind of interaction. This is only possible if it is contained within certain boundaries: for example, having no other kind of relationship with your therapist outside the therapy room.

The most stringent form of 'boundary maintenance' is practised in psychoanalysis and analytical psychotherapies. Here, the therapeutic space (the sessions, the consulting room) can be likened to a 'sterile environment'; the therapist becomes a 'blank screen' and gives virtually nothing away about himself or herself. These rigid boundaries are in keeping with the theoretical perspective in psychoanalysis and are aimed at enhancing 'transference' (see Chapter 2).

Physical contact

Shaking hands would often be the limit of physical contact for many therapists. Most forms of therapy would not consider hugging or kissing as acceptable conduct between practitioner and client, although there are exceptions to this. There should be no other form of physical contact between clients and therapists in a talking therapy.

Gifts

A client who has benefited from therapy may feel an enormous debt of gratitude and may want to show this by giving the therapist a gift. Although technically this may constitute a breach of boundaries, a small token or a card at Christmas may be appreciated, or at least accepted, by most practitioners. Anything more substantial is potentially problematic and such a seemingly innocuous gesture would need to be taken up by the practitioner in the course of therapy. Of course, all this has the potential to cause much embarrassment and could be damaging to the therapeutic relationship if your therapy is ongoing. A gift from a practitioner to a client (apart from material such as a book that is relevant to therapy) is highly unusual and would raise serious questions about conduct. The simple rule is not to offer gifts. Therapy is a professional relationship. However well-intentioned, gifts only serve to 'muddy the waters'.

Socialising

Observance of the therapeutic boundaries means that there is simply no place for socialising between clients and therapists. Having dinner (or even coffee) with your therapist would create a parallel relationship that would inevitably be damaging to the thera-peutic relationship. In circumstances where the therapy has finished and there is no probability of your re-entering therapy with the same practitioner, there may occasionally be scope for friendship much later, but you should not feel offended if the practitioner prefers not to start a friendship with you.

Accidentally meeting your counsellor or therapist may some-times be inevitable, and particularly in rural and small communities it would be very common. If this is likely to happen often, it is best for you to come to an agreement with your practitioner on the way to handle such occasions. For example, if you happen to meet in a public place (a pub, say) it may be agreed that the practitioner will show no signs of recognising you unless you show that you know him or her first; you will both say hello and move on, with neither party attempting to strike up a conversation with the other or buying him or her a drink.

Self-disclosure by the therapist

'Self-disclosure' is your practitioner volunteering information about himself or herself, for example by referring to similar experi-ences in his or her own life to something you describe during a session. Some therapists, particularly those from a humanist orien-tation, may do this to show empathy or to make the client feel at ease. However, research shows that self-disclosure by practitioners does not lead to a better outcome and may be unhelpful. If the client hears about the practitioner's own problems this can have the effect of leaving the client feeling unable to burden the practitioner with his or her own difficulties. Alternatively, it can cause the client to question the practitioner's ability to help him or her, and could thereby seriously undermine confidence in the practitioner. You may want to question your practitioner if this happens.

On the other hand, there are notable exceptions to this position, particularly in the area of addictions. Many therapy settings and rehabilitation centres employ recovering or ex-addicts as coun-sellors because these individuals may generate greater confidence in the client group; such clients tend to express the belief that these counsellors have greater understanding and empathy for their situation.

Abuse of client's vulnerability

More serious transgressions of boundaries will fall into this category. The intimacy of the therapeutic relationship often generates strong feelings both in the client and the therapist. This phenomenon, labelled transference and countertransference, is described in Chapter 2. The boundaries described above are crucial in containing these feelings and preventing either party from acting on them. If the boundaries are transgressed, it often leads to serious consequences.

One example of this is the therapist having a 'primary relationship' (physical and sexual) with a client. The status of the therapist and the information that he or she holds would invariably place him or her in too powerful a situation, so that such a relationship could never be a relationship between equals. In other words, it is more likely to be exploitative, an abuse of power. If a transgression of this nature is proven to have happened, any practitioner belonging to a profession or reputable therapy organisation will be disciplined, and this usually means he or she is removed from the register ('struck off'). Some professions and therapy organisations specify a period of time, following the end of the therapy, after which such a relationship will be allowed without disciplinary consequences. The specified period could be as long as five years.

Other examples of exploitation of a client's vulnerability would include therapists taking money from clients (outside of the agreed fee) or requesting favours. Again, such action is against practitioners' codes of conduct and if proven will result in the practitioner having to face disciplinary action.

In the USA, reported instance of such abuse by practitioners seems to be common and much is written about it. Two books that explore the issue are *Against Therapy*★ by Jeffrey Masson and *Staying Sane*★ by Raj Persaud. No good research on this matter exists regarding practitioners in the UK.

Taking action

Terminating the therapy

The most common step taken by clients following a breach of trust is to drop out of therapy without making a complaint. This is understandable, but it is often a very unsatisfactory solution and may be unhelpful to the client in a number of ways. His or her loss of faith in talking treatments may mean that he or she is less likely to seek help in the future. In cases of abuse, particularly sexual exploitation, the consequences of the abuse may be even worse than the original problem, or greatly worsen the client's situation. Not taking action may also lead to guilt and anxiety because other people may still be exposed to the practitioner's abuse. Simply dropping out like this could leave things so unresolved that the damage done might remain for a long time.

Taking action may not seem easy, particularly if you are feeling vulnerable and shocked. There may be a number of options open to you. One method is to confront your practitioner, but you may understandably be reluctant to do this. If you do want to address the situation directly with the practitioner you could do this with help, perhaps with a friend or family member. Alternatively, you can get advice and support regarding this from organisations such as MIND* (the National Association of Mental Health).

Making a complaint

You can complain to the practitioner's professional body or therapy organisation. These bodies exist to maintain the highest standards of professional conduct and to protect the rights and well-being of clients. In circumstances of serious professional misconduct or abuse they are there to bring the therapist to account and to investigate your complaint. Complaints have to be made in writing and the organisation will require you to identify yourself (you cannot make an anonymous complaint). You can either write a letter, or ask if the organisation has a standard form that you can fill out. If writing such a letter would be difficult for you, you can get help from your local Citizens Advice Bureau or an organisation such as MIND.* The organisation POPAN* is a registered charity that offers support to people who have been abused by healthcare and social care professionals, including practitioners of talking treatments. If you have any documents that support your case or any other forms of evidence, send copies of these together with your complaint. Most organisations will keep you informed of the progress of their investigations. You will be informed of the outcome and given advice on any further courses of action open to you.

Disciplinary procedures vary from one professional organisation to another. Most will provide you with information about their procedure when you wish to make a complaint. Further information is also available on the websites of these organisations.

If the therapist commits a criminal act, such as theft or physical abuse, you must go to the police straight away.

Chapter 10

Specialist areas of counselling and therapy

This chapter looks at some areas of counselling and psychotherapy that require specialist skills and expertise, and for which practitioners require added knowledge or training.

Children and adolescents

Special skills and expertise are often required when providing psychological help for children and adolescents. Young people commonly suffer from the same problems as adults: depression, low mood, insomnia, anxiety, eating disorders. However, in addition, there are problems specific to children and adolescents, such as attention deficit and hyperactivity disorder (ADHD), refusal to go to school, truancy, specific learning difficulties and behavioural problems. Psychotherapy may also be used with children who have learning disabilities (see below) like autism and Asperger's Syndrome, or if they are severely physically ill. Parents and guardians should talk to the practitioner about issues surrounding confidentiality.

Public sector

The NHS provides Child and Adolescent Mental Health Services for children in special treatment centres. These centres have multi-disciplinary teams that include child psychiatrists, clinical psychologists, child psychotherapists, family therapists, remedial teachers, doctors, nurses and counsellors. The centres have been set up to provide expert assessments and treatment using the most appropriate professionals in each case. Assessments often take several sessions and sometimes also involve parents and other members of the family. The therapy sessions themselves may or may not involve family members. Practitioners of many approaches used with young people in these settings prefer to see the child or adolescent without parents or carers present.

A lot of psychological work with children has an emphasis on systemic or family therapy as described in Chapter 3, and psychodynamic approaches and cognitive behavioural therapies are very commonly used. However, child therapists and counsellors may work within any of the main schools of therapy. Their special expertise is in adapting their model of therapy to working with children and their parents.

Sessions often involve play therapy as mentioned in Chapter 12 (especially for very young children), or the acting out of feelings, and the therapists are trained to be sensitive to signals provided by the child's behaviour. Practitioners will also work with school teachers and other care staff in helping them understand and cope with disturbed behaviour in children in their care.

Information on your local Child and Adolescent Mental Health Service can be obtained from your GP, local school, or local library. You can sometimes receive helpful information or advice by contacting the service by telephone, or alternatively an assessment can be arranged. To access the service you need a referral from your GP or from the school your child attends. These services, like most services in the NHS, operate within strict catchment areas, and in some areas there may be lengthy waiting lists.

People designated as child psychotherapists may have originally trained for professions such as teaching, social work, nursing or psychology, and will have undergone a minimum of four years' postgraduate specialist training in psychotherapy for children and adolescents. They must be registered with the Association of Child Psychotherapists* in order to work in the NHS. There are currently only about 400 trained child psychotherapists registered with the association, and provision of child psychotherapy in the NHS is mainly in London and the south east of England, with extremely limited provision elsewhere in the UK. Child psychotherapy is not currently available in all health authorities, and not all Child and Adolescent Mental Health Services will have this kind of support available.

The Tavistock Clinic★ in London is one of the few clinics in the NHS that operates as a national service, and if you can get to London easily this would be an alternative to your local service. You would still require a referral by your GP or consultant to be assessed by the Tavistock Clinic.

Voluntary sector

In some areas of the UK there is provision within the voluntary sector for counselling and therapy to be provided to young people. Sometimes local projects that offer talking treatments may also work with children and adolescents as well as adults, or on some occasions even work exclusively with a younger age group. Often there will be a strict policy on what ages are catered for. Your GP or school may be able to help you find any services of this kind that exist near to you. The self-help agencies who offer support to children listed below are also a good source of information about local voluntary projects.

The Child Psychotherapy Trust★ is a charitable organisation dedicated to increasing and improving the provision of child psychotherapy. It publishes booklets and leaflets about children's psychological problems and the support available, and is a useful source of information and advice.

Private sector

The Tavistock Clinic, the Anna Freud Centre★ and the British Association of Psychotherapists★ offer child and adolescent psychotherapy in the private sector. Many other practitioners of talking treatments also see young people privately, although as always it is advisable to check on qualifications and experience. You have to locate a suitable practitioner and negotiate fees, the kind of support needed and length of treatment offered on behalf of your child or adolescent in the same way that you would for yourself.

Self-help

There are several national self-help agencies which offer support and advice to children, adolescents and their parents and carers. Childline★ is a free 24-hour helpline for young people in trouble or in danger and offers confidential help to callers. Childwatch★ offers free and confidential telephone counselling to children who have suffered or are suffering any kind of physical, sexual or emotional abuse. Parentline★ gives support to parents and all other people who have responsibility for caring for children including foster parents and grandparents.

YoungMinds★ is a national charity devoted to improving the mental health of young people. It provides information and support to parents and also operates a confidential helpline. The Family Welfare Association★ helps family members of all ages with practical problems and offers social work support and charitable grants for essential household needs.

Addictions

This specialist area is mainly concerned with people who have problems related to the misuse of alcohol and drugs. However, people with other addictive behaviours, such as gambling or compulsive sex, may also be able to obtain specialised help.

Alcohol and drugs

For a number of years it was believed that individuals who were addicted to substances were not suitable for engaging in talking treatments. This often meant that people whose primary problem was seen as an addiction were told to overcome that problem and remain abstinent for a while, sometimes as long as two years, before commencing any significant kind of counselling or therapy. Since the early 1970s, however, drug and alcohol counselling services have been developed throughout the UK both in the public sector (NHS) and in the voluntary sector. Today there are alcohol and drugs counselling services in every part of the country.

In the public sector these services are generally carried out by multidisciplinary teams made up of professionals such as psychiatrists, general medical practitioners, nurses, psychologists, pharmacists, social workers and counsellors. A range of services is provided by these teams, depending on the type of professionals working within them. The centres may offer specialised assessments, physical investigations, detoxification, substitute prescriptions, and counselling and therapy (both one-to-one and in groups).

Voluntary-sector projects generally employ counsellors, although some may also employ health-service professionals like nurses and psychologists. In general they offer a narrower range of services than the public sector. Because voluntary-sector working practices are less rigidly dictated by the Department of Health, they can sometimes operate in a more flexible and responsive manner and be more easily accessible to people seeking help for their substance-use problems.

The most important factor in providing this kind of specialist service is ensuring that the people who work within them are experienced in dealing with substance-using individuals. These kind of addictions often carry a great deal of stigma, and heavy drinkers and drug users may find themselves treated like social outcasts in their daily lives. This means that staff must be more accepting and sympathetic towards this client group than are some non-specialist agencies and practitioners. The talking treatments offered in these centres span almost the entire range of approaches mentioned in Chapter 2, with a preference for eclectic and integrative work, and cognitive behavioural therapy. These include specialised interventions such as motivational interviewing – a counselling approach that helps an individual to resolve his or her ambivalence about the addiction – and relapse prevention, a cognitive behavioural technique aimed at the promotion and maintenance of positive changes in behaviour. These kinds of talking approaches to addiction are also available privately from experienced practitioners.

If you would like specialist treatment for an addiction you have a number of options. Most services operate on a self-referral basis: you can find out the nearest or most conveniently located service and contact it on the phone, or drop in for an assessment. You can locate services by looking in *Yellow Pages*, the front pages of your local phone directory, or at your local library. Or you can contact Alcohol Concern★ or Drugs Scope★; these are national organisations which can tell you what services are available to you locally. You can also discuss your problems with your GP and ask for a referral to your local alcohol or drugs service.

Self-help
The best-known self-help group in this field, Alcoholics Anonymous,★ was founded in 1935 and since the 1950s this kind of

self-help has probably been the biggest source of psychosocial help for addicted individuals the world over, including in the UK. The helpline numbers and website addresses for Alcoholics Anonymous, Narcotics Anonymous,★ and Cocaine Anonymous★ can be found in the Resources section of this guide. These three organisations offer you the chance to attend local support meetings at which confidentiality is assured, as the names imply. If you are nervous about attending for the first time, a group member (male or female, as you wish) can meet with you and accompany you to your first meeting. The membership of the group is entirely made up of people with the same problem as yourself, and you are not required to speak unless you feel ready to do so. Meetings take place at lots of different locations and (if preferred) there are also separate meetings for men, for women, for various ethnic and cultural groups, and for gay men and lesbians. A list of meetings is available from each of the three organisations listed above.

Several of these self-help organisations have a separate offshoot to support the family and friends of the addicted individual: for example, Al-Alon★ is the offshoot of Alcoholics Anonymous. Support and advice for the children of alcoholics (including people who are now adults themselves) are offered by the National Association for Children of Alcoholics★. For general advice on abuse of drugs and solvents, you can contact the National Drugs Helpline.★

Residential facilities

Addicted people sometimes seek help for their problems at a stage when their addictions have got completely out of hand. The severity of the addiction, their psychological and emotional problems and their lifestyles are such that they require more intensive, longer-term residential treatment to overcome their difficulties. Residential facilities that cater for this need are invariably run by the voluntary sector. These are commonly known as 'rehabs' – rehabilitation houses.

Because the different rehabilitation houses have different philosophies they are sometimes referred to as 'concept houses'. Many rehabs are run according to a philosophy based on the Twelve-Step Model of Alcoholics Anonymous, which is sometimes called the 'Minnesota Model'. Residents are expected to spend six months to one year (sometimes longer) in the 'rehab' and undergo intensive group and individual therapy. Much of this therapy may be based on psychodynamic and humanistic models and, to a lesser extent, the cognitive behavioural approach. Rehabilitation houses are mainly staffed by counsellors and therapists, although some employ health-service professionals such as psychiatrists and psychologists. Most also have a policy of employing recovering addicts who have undergone training in counselling.

To gain admission to a rehab, first of all you have to be alcohol- or drug-free. In other words, if your dependence is severe you have to undergo detoxification before you can gain admission. Since rehabs operate in the voluntary sector, funding is also an issue. If you don't have private finances to pay for your stay there are some alternative funding possibilities. Private healthcare insurance is one such option. In the absence of insurance you can approach your local authority, or social services. Funding assessments are usually carried out by social work staff attached to NHS drug and alcohol treatment centres, and this is your best point of access if you are interested in this kind of treatment. Funding is discretionary, meaning that a decision is made by the assessor as to whether a detox or rehab are the best option for you at this time.

Gambling and other addictive behaviours

There are fewer services for people with other addictive behaviours. Gamblers Anonymous★ is a self-help group for people addicted to gambling and Gam-Anon★ is its offshoot for the family and friends. These give people the opportunity to meet and talk with other sufferers using the same model of support as Alcoholics and Narcotics Anonymous. GamCare★ is another organisation which offers support to people addicted to gambling. Sexaholics Anonymous★ offers help to people who compulsively have sex and feel that they are unable to control their sexual behaviours.

All kinds of addiction can be discussed in private counselling and therapy with a suitably experienced person. The methods for locating the right practitioner for your needs described in Chapter 3 can be used to look for someone with these specialist skills if desired or needed.

Learning disabilities

Degree of disability

People with learning disabilities are another group who require specialist skills when receiving talking treatments. Disability may be labelled as being mild, moderate or severe, and the level of severity is based upon an estimation both of IQ and of the extent of the individual's abilities to communicate and process information. It is assumed that 'emotional intelligence' (the capacity to process feelings) is present however severe the disability, and that a skilled and experienced practitioner will be able to communicate with people despite the presence of a learning disability.

People with **mild** learning disabilities may be able to access and use the counselling and therapy services outlined elsewhere in this guide, provided the therapist is capable and is aware of the person's disabilities. However, because most counsellors and therapists will not generally have the opportunity to gain much experience of working with this client group (or have specialist supervision for their work) appropriate help is more likely to be found in specialist centres.

People with **moderate** learning disabilities may have less ability to think and talk about abstract things like feelings, beliefs and dreams, and so the skill and experience of the practitioners becomes more crucially important. Therapy may be more useful if it is conducted using pictures and drawings or music as aids. Even greater skill is required of the therapist when it comes to working with people with **severe** and **profound** learning disabilities, and often families need to be involved in any ongoing work.

Fluent communication with this client group can be very difficult, especially if disability is so severe that the individual is unable to use spoken or written language. This can sometimes lead to abuses of the client's right to determine his or her future – once a person is identified as having learning disabilities, his or her decisions may be undermined by society's assumptions that he or she is completely incapable of making choices.

Getting help

Specialist services in learning disabilities are largely provided by the public sector, although in some areas of the UK there may also be support (including talking treatments) in the voluntary sector. The public-sector services are provided by local authority multidisciplinary 'community teams'. These comprise psychiatrists, nurses, psychologists, social workers and counsellors, and can provide specialised assessments and recommendations, in addition to comprehensive packages of care depending on the individual's needs. They will identify emotional problems and provide appropriate therapy for these. Your GP can help you access this kind of help. Situated in London, the Tavistock Clinic★ provides a national service offering assessment and therapy to individuals as an NHS treatment, including those with learning disabilities.

The national charity Mencap★ gives information (including advice on how to locate appropriate talking treatments) to people with all kinds of learning disabilities, their families and their carers. The National Autistic Society★ provides similar support for people diagnosed with autistic disorders and Asperger's Syndrome. The Down's Syndrome Association★ offers help to people with Down's Syndrome and their families and carers. All of these organisations have extensive websites listed in the Resources section of this guide.

Sexual problems

While most counsellors and therapists will be willing to discuss any sexual problems that you may have, they generally do not attempt to treat such problems unless they have specialist training. If they have not completed this kind of training, they are more likely to recommend that you see a specialist, often known as a sex therapist. Some sexual problems may have a purely physical basis, but it is generally considered that many (or even most) have a large psychological component. Sex therapists use psychological techniques to try to help you to overcome these difficulties. If you have a regular or permanent sexual partner, he or she will usually be asked to accompany you to the sessions.

Common problems include difficulties with achieving or maintaining an erection and premature ejaculation in men; tightness of the vagina or pain during intercourse in women; and difficulties with orgasm, feelings of inadequacy and loss of sexual urges in both men and women. The talking treatments used are mainly from the psychodynamic and cognitive behavioural schools. Sex therapy may also include physical therapies such as medication (for example, Viagra), intravascular injections, prostheses and surgical procedures.

Getting help

As with most problems, it is recommended that your first step in getting help is to talk to your GP. However, some people find it embarrassing to ask their GP about sexual problems. You can contact specialist NHS clinics direct: departments of genito-urinary medicine (GUM clinics), family planning clinics and infertility clinics are among those that offer sex therapy as part of their service, and should be listed in the phone book or advertised at your local medical centre.

Assistance can also be obtained from the voluntary and private sectors. Organisations such as RELATE★ employ trained sex therapists and they may be the most accessible voluntary-sector organisation for most people. The British Association of Sexual and Relationship Therapy★ is also a good source of information when finding private help. RELATE (www.relate.org.uk/pst_home.html) and the BBC health website (www.bbc.co.uk/health/sex/enjsex_sextherapy.shtml) have extensive information about sexual therapy.

Sexually transmitted diseases including HIV/AIDS

Since the 1980s sexually transmitted diseases (STD) clinics have become a specialised area for providing counselling and psychotherapy. The HIV epidemic was largely responsible for this growth. The psychological impact of AIDS and other STDs required therapists with special sensitivity and skill to help individuals cope. HIV infection was met with a kind of disapproval from most of society that was very intense and widely reported in the media. This, combined with the fear that the virus would lead to AIDS and unpleasant (and probably fatal) health complications, made many infected people extremely depressed and agitated. Although this kind of social isolation is no longer the norm, and negative attitudes to HIV have changed in many ways, there is still a lot of stigma and a 'serves-them-right thinking' attached to all kinds of STDs.

Because of this a lot of psychological support is available from sexual health clinics. 'Health advisors' are a new profession in this area, and are people who train in giving both advice and counselling regarding all aspects of sexual health. Other professions involved in this kind of work include psychiatrists, psychologists, nurses and social workers. Training and experience help develop the specialist expertise to provide talking treatments for people suffering from the psychological consequences of these diseases.

Getting help

STD clinics, also known as genito-urinary medicine (GUM) clinics, are found in most large hospitals, and you can walk into these without referral. A physical assessment will be carried out and as well as practical advice and medical treatment, psychological support will usually be offered where needed. GUM clinics are unique in that medical records have an extra layer of legal protection, and cannot be communicated to your GP without permission or unless he or she referred you initially (which, as stated above, is not necessary unless you wish it). Many people use an alias at GUM clinics and this is seen as acceptable.

Information about all aspects of sexual disease is available online from the Society of Health Advisers in STDs at www.shastd.org.uk/. The Terrence Higgins Trust* offers support and information about HIV and AIDS, including how to access psychological support.

Chapter 11

Talking treatments, culture and difference

Talking treatments are not like most other methods for relieving pain and distress. If someone has a broken leg, no one is surprised to hear that it hurts, and that putting a cast or splint on the fracture and taking painkillers helps. But psychological and social problems are not always so easy to define or label, and therefore the 'cure' that is needed is not always obvious either. Even when a technique has been found to work well for a certain problem, it can be hard to understand why it is successful. This is because what goes on in people's minds is basically 'invisible', so even experts are left having to guess both what the problem is and what the solution might be. It would be convenient if we could always say out loud what is troubling us and why. But most of us are not that insightful, and even when we are, we usually have no clear idea of what would make the problem go away. (If we did, we wouldn't have the problem for very long.)

This basic difficulty – the near-impossibility of proving what makes an individual 'tick' – is behind much disagreement on how the mind works, and is what has led to the development of different schools of psychology and their approaches to therapy and counselling. It is also a complicating factor in researching what kind of therapy is best for each kind of problem (see Chapter 6). Comparisons are possible only if you assume that ten people receiving ten different types of counselling all have the same problem to begin with; otherwise, it is hard to make any justifiable research conclusions. And while we may frequently use labels such as 'depression' or 'anxiety' to describe personal difficulties, the reality is that everyone experiences these kinds of problems differently. Human beings are not all the same, and we do not all react in the same way, even to identical events or situations. So how useful is it to compare the treatment of ten people simply because they are all labelled as being 'depressed'?

Having things in common but being different

Acknowledging 'difference' is an ongoing priority when looking at human experience. Consider some of the following personal attributes:

- **physical ability** – presence or lack of disability, size and strength, co-ordination and dexterity
- **intellectual capacity** – intelligence, quality of memory, speed of thought, effective reasoning skills, creativity and artistic ability
- **social advantages** – self-confidence, sense of humour, being conventionally 'attractive', economic and financial stability.

These are simply examples of the ways people differ. It is obvious that not everyone has the same mixture of the above, and this is true also for the many other factors involved in making each of us unique. This being so, it seems (at best) optimistic to expect that we will all need the same kind of talking approach when we are suffering. More than that, it is naïve to think that the same things will cause us all to suffer in the first place – what is a problem to one person may not be to someone else. We have different expectations of life and of other people, different attitudes and beliefs, and different motivations and reasons for doing what we do.

How important are cultural differences?

Talking treatments have not always acknowledged the issue of difference to the degree that most practitioners would now believe is necessary. In the past, people were often perceived as acting and reacting in ways that could largely be predicted or understood in terms of a personal development that was broadly identical for all of us – a kind of 'determinism'. Such a philosophy assumes that the unique attributes that we possess or acquire in our lives are of minor importance in shaping personality or character, in comparison to the underlying psychological patterns that are common to all of us.

However, these universal 'patterns' are themselves open to debate. Most recognised schools of therapy and counselling have developed from within the Western scientific tradition, and were the creation of middle-class academics (usually white and usually male). It can reasonably be argued that attempts to identify psychological patterns common to humanity are inevitably heavily influenced by the bias of the people doing the work. This means that these (usually white and usually male) middle-class academics from the Western scientific tradition, having analysed their own patterns of development, could be accused of assuming that the rest of humanity must experience these same patterns as well.

If this is an accurate criticism, it leaves us with two possibilities regarding many of the ideas that underpin the practice of talking treatments. First, that even if our development is 'determined' by common psychological patterns, much of what has been written about these patterns may be of questionable use, because we can never really know whether the underpinning theories are really applicable to *all* people, or just to a certain kind of person growing up in a certain kind of place. Second, that it is just as likely that the 'determinist' theory is wrong, and that personal development is in fact unique for each individual. Since we all end up being different, what evidence is there that we have all passed through similar stages of development? The theories of the Western thinkers may be true for everyone; or they may be true for only a minority of people in the world (namely those who fall into the same category as these thinkers); or they may simply represent the attitudes and prejudices of those thinkers. In this respect they could be no more 'scientific' than religious faith or political dogma.

This may be an unfairly negative view of how talking treatments emerged and of the people who developed the different approaches. Even if largely true, it does not mean that the current approaches to psychological treatment are in no way useful or effective. Many practitioners can justifiably argue that their therapeutic model has been around for many years and has helped a lot of people, so there must be something solid about it and the ideas behind it. However, the debate is not simply theoretical. It may significantly affect your experience of a talking treatment if you and your practitioner do not share the same worldview and your practitioner is not sufficiently aware of the implications. This is a matter of vital importance in the current delivery and future development of talking treatments.

Culture and expectations

'Culture' is sometimes thought of as meaning the same thing as 'race' or 'ethnicity', but it properly refers to many different aspects of individual experience. The culture of the Western thinkers mentioned above was not limited to their nationality. In fact, if you were trying to analyse the cultural background of the pioneers in talking treatments to see what they had in common, nationality would probably be one of the less important factors in determining their views of the world. This is because they came from many countries in Middle and Western Europe as well as North America, so that no single nationality dominated the ideas that emerged.

Our view of the world

An individual's cultural perceptions are probably made up of all the following factors, and perhaps others too:

- age and experience
- ethnic heritage
- gender
- language
- physical ability or disability
- political situation
- profession and educational background
- religious and spiritual beliefs
- sexuality
- social and economic class or status
- wealth and practical resources.

All these factors have significant impact on how we see the world and how we deal with other people. Some of them are more apparent – others less so – to us as features of our daily lives. The extent to which we are aware of these factors will depend on whether we are in a minority or majority group for each characteristic, and on whether we belong to the more, or the less, privileged group. (For example, a heterosexual person is usually less aware of being heterosexual than a homosexual is aware of being homosexual; and an old person is usually more aware of being old than a young person is aware of being young.) These different 'identifiers' may be the cause of mistaken assumptions being made about us, or excessive curiosity or hostility from others. They may give us a sense of belonging and shared experience, or may lead to feelings of isolation and confusion. Being 'different', not being accepted because of our cultural identity, can itself be a major cause of personal distress and suffering.

Our expectations of life

Cultural factors also give rise to expectations. Our view of our life, and what we reasonably hope to gain or experience from it, is greatly affected by our cultural identity. Some sections of society have stronger family ties than others. Some prize academic achievement and professional status whereas others value wealth or physical comfort. For some people religion and spiritual beliefs are central to their daily routines, but in other cases they are a minor consideration or entirely absent. Each client and each practitioner brings these expectations to their counselling and therapy sessions, and it can become a problem if they are not aware of it.

For instance, as a representative of contemporary European culture, a counsellor may think that women should look for equal opportunities in education and employment, and choose their own romantic partners, the clothes that they wear, and when to have children. But women born in some parts of the world (or to parents from those places) might believe that wanting to make these choices for themselves is disrespectful of their parents or future husband. A practitioner might also question why his or her client is not interested in engaging in a talking treatment and might see this as 'resistance' or lack of motivation. But perhaps, in the client's social circle, therapy is seen as self-indulgent or a sign of failure, and so cannot be engaged in without criticism or even contempt from other people. Another therapist might encourage a client to openly explore his or her belief that he or she is gay or lesbian, but if the client is from a strict religious background, this may be impossible because some orthodox beliefs hold that a person cannot be gay and still be faithful to his or her religion.

These are simple descriptions of what are often much more complex situations. But it is a good idea for both counsellor and client to talk about such matters in simple words so that each party involved in the therapeutic relationship can be confident that no mistaken assumptions will be made. Your practitioner is responsible for trying to see the world through your eyes, and not assuming that his or her own beliefs are shared by all clients. You, too, need to be aware that the practitioner is unlikely to be an expert on the needs and norms of all cultures. If your practitioner is open to the different perspectives of other individuals, then you can express yourself without fear of being judged. You will also be reassured that no attempts will be made to force you to adopt your practitioner's cultural position.

Cultural perceptions of personal distress

One of the major underlying factors in this kind of miscommunication between practitioner and client is a difference in what they think has led to the problems the client has brought to the counselling session. Chapter 1 looked at some of the possible causes of personal distress and outlined various models for approaching these in the table 'Five ways of looking at our experiences' (see page 28).

A significant 'culture gap'

M, a young person, is soon to start university and must leave the home he shares with his parents. He tells his GP that he is feeling unbearably agitated, and is referred to a local therapy service. The practitioner believes that M is worried both about the academic work he will be doing and about taking on new responsibilities. M is excited by the academic challenges ahead but believes that he will not be able to manage without his parents' daily advice. The practitioner thinks that M's main problem is that he has unresolved issues about parental control, dating from early childhood. M is convinced that the panic attacks he is experiencing are no less than what he deserves for questioning the career path that his parents have chosen for him. The practitioner thinks that a brief course of cognitive analytical therapy will help to give a clearer perspective on what is going on. M thinks that medication will control his anxiety and believes that talking about the family behind their back would be an insult to them and a betrayal of their trust.

Often the assumptions of the practitioner and the client about what has led to a given problem are quite at odds with each other. This is true not only where there is a significant cultural gap between people, and can in fact happen at any time. But it is even more likely when a significant cultural difference does exist.

Imagine the therapeutic relationship between 'M' and his practitioner (see box). Between them, these two people have introduced a number of possible explanations for M's agitation. In fact, when considered together these explanations cover pretty much all the possible causes of distress that are described in the table in Chapter 1 – unwanted and distressing feelings, problems to do with a change in daily routine, past experience, current events, and questions about major personal beliefs. But the client and practitioner have not agreed once about where the main emphasis lies, where some overlap between their ideas may be taking place, or what should be done. Are either or both of them wrong? It may be tempting to take sides, but the real problem here is that no useful communication is taking place. The two people in this relationship have brought very different beliefs and expectations into the room, and the counsellor has not acknowledged or managed this situation in any helpful way. Perhaps they are not suited to working together, and alternative arrangements should be made. More productively, the counsellor should work harder to acknowledge the client's perspectives.

Cultural sensitivity

It is to be hoped that nowadays most counsellors and therapists are aware of the significance of culture in the work that they do. But there is a difference between being aware of the issue and being able to address it by offering a more flexible way of working. Not all practitioners have achieved this. Even more significantly, some counsellors and therapists remain convinced that cultural difference should have relatively little impact on how they work. It may be worth asking a practitioner what his or her views are on this issue when you are first getting to know him or her.

Are some approaches more adaptable than others?

It has been argued that some models of counselling and therapy are more adaptable to different cultural needs. Humanistic practitioners often work with a greater sense that individual ways of looking at the world are unique and cannot be taken for granted. This sounds like a better starting point for dealing with people from widely varying backgrounds, and frequently it is. But humanistic therapy still makes assumptions about the potential for growth and the basic needs of the individual that may not be consistent with all social, political and spiritual ways of thinking. Most humanistic practitioners try to avoid telling people what to do, yet clients from some cultures would think it entirely pointless to go and see a skilled professional who refuses to offer advice and share his or her learning. A similar problem could easily occur with cognitive behavioural techniques: if someone believes in fate or predestination, it will be of little help to discuss with him or her how he or she can take control of his or her life by active decision-making. Equally, someone whose cultural beliefs demand that he or she is forward-looking and should concentrate on the present and the future may struggle with a psychodynamic approach that appears to expect him or her to focus on the past and examine early childhood.

These are only simplified examples, and should not be seen as blanket statements about how different schools of therapy and counselling deal with issues of difference. But they do serve to illustrate the kind of problems that could develop if those issues are not considered. Most practitioners are willing to adapt their way of working, within certain limits. They will also recognise that their own methods will not suit everyone, and that recommending a different approach may sometimes be the best option.

Cultural differences in the therapeutic relationship

Sometimes a practitioner may not recognise his or her incompatibility with a particular client. At worst, a practitioner may even want to change the client's views on something by persuasion or confrontation. This could be done with the best intentions, perhaps from an inappropriate desire to 'enlighten' the client: the practitioner may question the client's belief out of conviction that it is the belief that is troubling the person. However, if this belief is central to the client's cultural identity, it needs to be respected rather than contradicted.

At the extreme, it is even possible to see an attitude or belief that is fundamentally different to your own as immoral, as a symptom of severe disturbance or mental illness, or even as criminal. In the past, having a child outside marriage was referred to as 'moral insanity', and unmarried mothers and their babies often found themselves in Victorian asylums. Lesbians and gay men were subjected to behaviour therapy to try to convert their sexual preferences to the opposite sex. (Some practitioners still carry out these kinds of interventions on willing clients who are unhappy about their sexuality; most of the therapy world would see this as unnecessary and perhaps even as unethical.) More recently it has been observed that, in the UK, people from overseas or from outside mainstream British culture are more likely to be diagnosed as being seriously mentally ill. One reason for this appears to be that their different behaviours and cultural beliefs somehow get misinterpreted as evidence of mental illness. It is easy to see the unfamiliar as unacceptable, even when it leads to no harm or hurt to anyone, but this can be an extremely dangerous position.

No one can be knowledgeable about every culture or every possible combination of cultural attitudes, and of course cultures change. But therapists and counsellors need to be especially aware of their own prejudices, assumptions and beliefs, and how these might cloud their understanding of their clients' world and needs. As a client, it is important to be mindful of the possibility of this kind of clash between your own beliefs and expectations and those of your practitioner. Recognising the possibility can prevent misunderstandings and help you get the most from your sessions, but if you are convinced that there is a significant cultural clash in the relationship, you may need to talk to your practitioner about it. If this does not resolve the situation, you will probably need to find another kind of support.

Feeling out of place

Problems arising from cultural differences are, of course, an issue for society as a whole. These problems can in themselves be the cause of many kinds of personal difficulty, or at least contribute to the difficulty. It is worth considering whether this may apply in your own situation. The effects of cultural identification (and intolerance) may take many forms, but the following are some of the more obvious.

- **'Culture shock'** – the struggle to readjust in an unfamiliar environment or when having to deal with situations that are completely new to us. This could happen to people newly arrived in a country where the way of life is unfamiliar. It could also happen to anyone after a significant change in their life, or a move to a new environment: even settling into a new workplace can be a disturbing experience. The process will be made easier or harder by the level of support and welcome offered by other people within the new environment.
- **Encountering prejudice and bigotry** – dealing with insulting or aggressive attitudes and beliefs because of difference or minority status. This can include racism, sexism, homophobia, religious intolerance, and many other forms of discrimination. Prejudice may be experienced from individuals, or from larger structures and institutions, including society itself.
- **Isolation** – where you are so attacked or culturally deprived as to feel completely isolated and unsupported. The belief that no one values your lifestyle choices, heritage or needs can lead to despair. It is not only individuals who may feel isolated; whole sections of society can feel marginalised and devalued in this way.
- **Scape-goating** – where minority groups are blamed for the problems of the population as a whole. This makes communication between different cultures or people with other perspectives even more difficult.

Where any of these or other types of similar hardship are consistently experienced, they are likely to lead to high levels of stress and personal suffering. Sometimes an individual's cultural identity may prevent him or her from choosing a talking treatment to try and address this pain. But for anyone who does look to counselling or therapy for help, it essential that he or she obtains sensitive treatment, because any insensitivity towards his or her cultural identity will inevitably reinforce the feeling of distress.

Finding the right practitioner

A practitioner familiar with your culture

Many clients try to reduce the risks of having to deal with a culture clash by looking for a practitioner who shares some aspects of their background, and perhaps is from the same minority group or groups. Often this is achievable: it may not be difficult to find someone of the same gender, sexuality or nationality. But this depends on how much choice you have in the first place. If you are able to pay for private therapy, your options are wide. If you have approached your GP and asked to be referred to the practice counsellor, it is a matter of chance whether that person will be at all familiar with your personal or cultural background. Even a large voluntary-sector agency with dozens of practitioners may not be able to match your needs. Ideally the therapy world should be more representative of society as a whole, but there is still a shortage of trained practitioners from many minority groups within the UK. Specialist organisations exist to offer talking treatments to people from specific ethnic backgrounds, sexual orientations and other identified types of difference. A few are included in the Resources section. These services may have limited funding and are usually located in urban areas, although telephone support may also be available.

Although it may be an illusion to expect to find someone who is like you in every way, it is reasonable to want to find someone with whom you have at least a few things in common. It is up to you whether you are willing to try to work with a practitioner whom you see as being very different from yourself. It may be worth asking yourself how important issues of cultural identity are in relation to the matters that you want to discuss. Perhaps this means considering what is unique about yourself, and what you feel has to be understood by anyone offering you support. This may in fact help you in openly stating to a practitioner what your needs are, and could be a way to ensure that you can work towards the same aims.

Occasionally clients want the exact opposite of a practitioner from their own background: some minority communities in the UK are very small, and clients from those groups may fear – because of a different understanding of the concepts of confidentiality and privacy – that anything they say to another member of that community will become known to the community as a whole. This is a good example of how even a supposedly culturally sensitive reading of a situation can be completely wrong. In this case a client would be less, not more, likely to confide in a practitioner from a similar background.

Even where there are similarities between you and your practitioner, and you think this will be of benefit, it is important to check that you have a shared understanding of key issues. Just because you both have parents from the same part of the world or have comparable educational backgrounds or share a religion does not mean that you will see eye to eye on everything.

The transcultural approach

Of course, it is practitioners who are the professionals within the therapeutic relationship, and who should therefore take responsibility for meeting the challenge of cultural differences. It is they who should be fully aware of the possibility of a cultural clash and its effects. A capable practitioner does not take anything for granted, but asks questions, learns and improves over time. The willingness to understand other viewpoints (perhaps without agreeing with them), and being able to see a situation from the perspective of other people, are key abilities for any counsellor or therapist.

Practitioners who have these skills and are able to put aside their own assumptions and prejudices when engaged with a client who has very different cultural needs to themselves are sometimes said to be using a 'transcultural' approach. Their expectations of the client, and their understanding of the client's situation, need to be very flexible. Although these practitioners would probably not abandon the theories of their own school of therapy, they appreciate that a client may not view his or her personal distress in a way that is consistent with those theories. Perhaps the client wants advice rather than a discussion; he or she may see the issue as more likely to be resolved by intellectual problem-solving than by emotional release. If so, the client might see the practitioner as an authority figure rather than as someone providing support. His or her entire worldview could differ significantly from the therapist's, because he or she has different beliefs about family, personal morality, social justice and spiritual enlightenment.

Transcultural work assumes that the client's worldview is always likely to be different from the practitioner's, not just that it may occasionally be so. The practitioner accepts the limitations of his or her own knowledge, and uses these as a strength, rather than allowing them to become a weakness. By admitting that he or she does not fully appreciate or understand the client's experiences and beliefs, the practitioner becomes willing to learn about them and to incorporate this into the way that he or she provides counselling or therapy. This is more than just being aware that culture has an impact on talking treatments. It is a question of basing the delivery of the talking treatment upon that awareness.

The transcultural approach is an attitude rather than a specific model of working, and could be applied to any school of practice. This does not mean that all practitioners will share this attitude or that it should be expected of any agency or individual that you encounter within the therapy world. How important it is to seek out a transcultural perspective will vary from client to client. It is to be hoped that in the future counselling and therapy will become increasingly sensitive to culture and difference and that this will broaden the choices available.

Chapter 12

Non-talking treatments

This chapter outlines some of the alternatives to talking approaches, ranging from orthodox medical approaches to some less familiar methods. The approaches included here are all commonly used in the UK today, either as a specific way of managing personal difficulties, or as treatments for more general health problems that might have the additional benefit of promoting peace of mind.

Trying these approaches may not be entirely without risk, any more than trying talking approaches is without risk. It is sensible to research any treatment closely before you get involved, and to be wary of extravagant claims of 'miracle cures'. For each form of treatment, it is strongly recommended that you contact a reputable organisation that can give you more information about the method and can recommend skilled practitioners in your area. All these bodies have codes of conduct governing their members' activities. You will find details of such organisations in the Resources section. If you contact a practitioner direct, ask about experience, formal training and supervision, and think very carefully before committing yourself to treatment with anyone who says that these are not necessary for some reason.

Medication

Concerns about using medication

To many people, the idea of taking tablets to manage unhappiness or anxiety seems a very bad idea. You should be very suspicious of anyone who tells you that a tablet is going to take away all your psychological problems, because obviously no tablet can change your environment or your social situation, or transform your personal relationships. But when your difficulties have become chronic and your physical health is suffering, medication may offer considerable or even vital help and give you the chance to look for some practical answers. Often this will mean starting a talking treatment as well.

Warning

Always tell a prescribing doctor if you are pregnant or breast-feeding, or are trying for a baby. Many drugs should be avoided in these situations. Also mention any past history of epilepsy or convulsions.

Taking medication while you are seeing a counsellor

Be aware that some counsellors and therapists think that taking medication is a bad idea while you are engaged in counselling or therapy. This is because those practitioners believe that the medication will suppress or 'flatten' too many of your emotions, and so could limit the usefulness of a talking approach. Discuss this with your counsellor or therapist, and with your doctor, where necessary.

Names of medicines

All medicines come with at least two names. First, there is an approved or 'generic' name, used worldwide to give the medication a unique pharmacological identification: for example, diazepam, amitriptyline, fluoxetine. Second, there are brand names, used by the manufacturers to indicate that this is their version of the drug in question: Valium is one of the brands of diazepam, for example, and Prozac is a brand of fluoxetine. Because some popular drugs are made in many countries and by many different drug companies, some medications may have literally dozens of different brand names worldwide. Any brand should also list the approved name on the packet, often in the wording 'Each tablet contains ...' or 'Active ingredient ...'. For simplicity, **approved names** will be used in this section.

Medicines for depression or anxiety

There are three main types of medicines that are commonly prescribed for anxiety and depression. These medicines affect the central nervous system and may alter mood. New medications are appearing all the time.

Seeking advice

All queries about medications used in treating mental health problems must be discussed with a medical doctor or pharmacist. Further information is available from the organisations listed under 'General information' in the Resources section.

Antidepressants

Antidepressants are believed to work by altering imbalances in certain essential chemicals found in the brain. However, there is something of a chicken-and-egg problem with severe depression. Feeling low, and eating or sleeping badly as a result of this, can lead to changes in the chemistry of your body and brain which in turn can push the mood further down. Equally, a shift in brain chemistry can lower the mood and lead to poor sleep and appetite. Which comes first? Often it is difficult to say, but in either event anti-depressants are thought to correct any chemical imbalance and help to stabilise mood. The two most widely used types are the *tricyclic* antidepressants (amitriptyline, dothiepin, imipramine and others) and the *selective serotonin re-uptake inhibitors* (SSRIs) (including fluoxetine, paroxetine, citalopram).

Research suggests that neither type is much better than the other. Tricyclics are mildly sedating, and are best taken last thing at night so that by the time you awake next morning this side-effect has largely worn off. SSRIs, on the other hand, are mildly stimulating, so they are best taken first thing in the morning so that sleep is not inter-rupted. Neither the sedative nor the stimulating effect is very strong, but it can help to determine which type is prescribed: depression can make you sleep either more or less than normal, so a tablet which has the opposite effect may be better, in theory, than one that will make it worse.

People do not always realise that antidepressants will not work immediately. The positive effect builds up very slowly, usually over two to three weeks, and it can be anything from two to four weeks before any real benefits are experienced. The dose must be taken every day. Missing a tablet because you feel better on that day will reduce the level of the drug in your system, which has to be kept at a certain amount to be effective. Often a dose is increased gradually over time until an effective 'therapeutic' level is reached. As with many kinds of medication, side-effects are common. Discuss this with your prescribing doctor before starting a tablet for the first time.

It is usually recommended that once started, a dose is maintained for at least six to eight months and perhaps much longer. Any reduction of tablets should be achieved over the space of a few weeks with your doctor's help before stopping altogether, or your mood may fall rather suddenly and you can experience unpleasant withdrawal side-effects. Always plan any reduction with your doctor rather than suddenly deciding to stop taking your medication.

Stronger medicines such as lithium carbonate and carbamazepine are used to regulate moods in less common conditions like manic depression, which is covered in more detail below. This is quite different to short-lived depression caused by loss or traumatic events.

Anxiolytics

These are anti-anxiety drugs, and are used to help people manage panic attacks and other symptoms of agitation. Previously the most common drugs used for this purpose were *benzodiazepines* such as diazepam and lorazepam. It is now clear that there can be major problems with these drugs because of the development of what is called 'tolerance' to the drug. When tolerance develops, the low dose that was effective at first no longer works, so that after a period of a few weeks or months a bigger dose is needed to have the same effect. This may lead to a person needing an extremely big dose to experience any positive benefits, by which stage they might be said to be dependent upon (or even addicted to) the medication.

Because of this, benzodiazepines are now seen as an unsuitable treatment for anxiety except, occasionally, for very short-term use (no more than four weeks) to help someone cope with a crisis and high levels of anxiety. A small dose, given for a short time, is usually safe because it is not long enough for tolerance to become a major problem. Even so, a small dose can still be strong enough to make operating machinery or driving very hazardous and it is recommended that you avoid both while you are taking the medication. The effect of benzodiazepines is also increased, perhaps dangerously, if alcohol is taken on top of the medication. A sudden large reduction in intake or abruptly stopping the use of benzodiazepines can be very dangerous and lead to convulsions. Talk with your prescribing doctor before making any reductions.

Alternatively, longer-term anxiolytics are available, in the form of SSRIs such as citalopram (usually used for depression, see above). They may be given in smaller doses to treat panic attacks and some other forms of anxiety (such as phobias). Tolerance is much less of a problem with SSRIs but there is increasing evidence that stopping an SSRI can cause unpleasant withdrawal problems which may be mistaken for a return of anxiety or panic symptoms; severe problems have been reported in some people. As with antidepressants, the positive effect can be slow to develop, but sudden withdrawal of the tablet should be avoided. A gradual reduction is much less uncomfortable and much safer, and should be discussed with your doctor before any decision is made.

'Beta-blockers' such as atenolol and propanolol, usually given for high blood pressure, can also be effective in controlling agitation. They have a more immediate effect, but do not lift the mood as SSRIs do.

Hypnotics

Despite the term used here, these drugs have nothing to do with going into a trance, but are used to treat poor sleep. Many hypnotics are chemically very similar to anxiolytics, but instead of having just a calming effect, they make the user feel drowsy. This can be effective for short-term use, but in the longer term it is much better to find out what is causing the interrupted sleep and to try to deal with that. This is particularly important because most hypnotics quite commonly lead to the tolerance problems explained under 'Anxiolytics' above: benzodiazepines such as temazepam are effective at helping people to sleep, but soon wear off unless bigger doses are taken and can become addictive. Non-benzodiazepine medications such as zopiclone also carry risks if they are taken for too long. Most doctors and pharmacists agree that, as with benzodiazepine anxiolytics, anything more than three to four weeks of taking these medications is not advisable.

Medicines for manic depression and schizophrenia

As mentioned in Chapter 4, both schizophrenia and manic depression (as well as endogenous depression) are considered to be major mental health disorders with complex and perhaps multiple causes. People with manic depression are often prescribed lithium carbonate or carbamazepine to regulate mood, and there is a very wide range of different medications used to treat schizophrenia. None of these medications should be reduced or discontinued without consulting the prescribing doctor because this may lead to sudden and severe worsening of symptoms.

Creative therapies

In addition to talking approaches, some counsellors and psycho-therapists also use methods based around creative activities. Sometimes the activity itself is the end product, a way for people to divert their attention and stop focusing on painful things. On other occasions the activities are analysed after they are finished, with the practitioner offering interpretations or ideas about what the clients are experiencing. Alternatively, the setting can be an opportunity for clients to express themselves and reflect on their own thoughts and feelings.

Most artistic and creative actions can be used as a basis for this kind of work. Sessions can be held between one client and one prac-titioner, or as a group with many clients and several practitioners. Although some of the time may be spent in conversation, especially when feeding back experiences at the end of the time allowed, most of the session will be devoted to the activity itself rather than analysing what is going on. Practitioners of these approaches should have received training and should also have supervision or the opportunity to discuss their work with other qualified staff. These techniques may be used by people from any of the major schools of counselling and therapy. Creative therapies may sound a little unusual to many people, but they are seen as 'mainstream' approaches and have been practised for a long time.

Drama therapy

Drama therapy uses the acting-out of scenes to explore the reactions of the person or persons involved. This can include role-play, when people pretend to be someone (or somewhere) else to see how it makes them feel, or psychodrama, when important scenes from someone's past are re-enacted to help them come to terms with those experiences. Other methods involve puppetry or the wearing of masks to help people feel a little more distanced from what is happening and make the scenes being portrayed less threatening. This does not require any acting ability. The intention is to be open to yourself rather than to give a good performance.

Drama therapy is usually carried out by practitioners with training in therapy and counselling as well as theatre and acting skills. It is not always easily obtained within the NHS, but workshops and one-off sessions are sometimes available in the private sector at reasonable costs. Some talking approaches such as Gestalt therapy are particularly suitable for this kind of work, but most schools of practice may make use of these techniques.

Art therapy

Art therapy is based on the concept of expressing ideas through drawings, paintings and sculptures, especially when someone finds it hard to use words to explain how they are feeling. A lot of people see art as an alternative to talking, and find it to be a more inspiring way to identify their needs and wants.

A trained art therapist may suggest a topic for clients to base their work upon, such as family or home, and then discuss with them the image that they produce. On other occasions a particular medium – clay, charcoal or mosaic, for instance – may be used as a starting point. This may take the client back to childhood experiences, because that was the last time they used this medium, or because the chance to be messy is a kind of fun usually denied to them. No artistic skill is needed or expected. The finished product may be discussed and interpreted by the client, the therapist, or both. Sometimes groups work together to produce a larger piece of work.

Practitioners may work privately or in the NHS. Like most creative approaches, it is not well funded in many areas.

Music therapy

Music therapy is very similar to art therapy except that it uses sound rather than images to express thoughts and feelings. Musical instruments and the human voice can be used to create harmony or even disharmony. This can be very empowering when it may be otherwise difficult to voice anything or make yourself heard. Afterwards people may choose to describe the experience, or they may allow the music to speak for itself. No familiarity with singing or instruments is expected.

Like other creative approaches, music therapy is very suitable for work with children, and also people with learning difficulties. Again, it is available on the NHS only in a limited fashion. There has been a lot of interest recently in applying this kind of work to music from different parts of the world and relating the approach to matters of cultural identity (see Chapter 11).

Dance therapy

Dance therapy uses movement as a tool in helping the client to gain a greater sense of himself or herself physically and mentally. Mood and emotional problems can often make us feel low in energy and lead us to abandon our interests and ways of passing the time. Dance can be a way to lift the spirits of the individual by encouraging physical activity and responses to music or rhythm. Skill is not required, just enthusiasm!

Dance therapy is more commonly available in the voluntary sector or as a private service, with workshops and courses being popular ways to promote this kind of approach. Traditional dance styles from many different countries, as well as classical Western dance, may be used. Often the focus is on individual self-expression rather than keeping to a particular style. Dancing in groups can be a fun way to promote a sense of community and sharing.

Play therapy

Play therapy is most often used with children, although it can also be pleasurable for adults to indulge in playing with toys. The therapist keeps a stock of games and play objects from which clients can choose, and sometimes encourages clients to reflect on the particular activities that they perform. The process can help the person to relax, and can also be a way to assist them to get in touch with their leisure and creative needs. This can be very important if tiredness or agitation is making it difficult to engage in any enjoyable or stimulating pursuits on a regular basis.

Play therapy may involve interpretation of the client's feelings as they arise in response to what they are doing. This can seem a lot less threatening than approaching issues directly, especially for children. Play therapy is commonly used in child and adolescent services as provided in the UK by the NHS and the education system.

Complementary therapies

Many different complementary and alternative therapies can be used to help people with emotional problems or mental illnesses. They include acupuncture, aromatherapy, Ayurvedic medicine, biofeedback, flower remedies, healing such as reiki, shiatsu and many other types of massage, herbal remedies, homeopathy, hypnotherapy, reflexology and some personal disciplines like yoga and tai chi.

Some complementary and alternative methods may include talking as part of the overall package, even when it is not the main aim of the work being carried out. This is because holistic thinking is based on the belief that physical pain or discomfort may be related to psychological or emotional difficulties, and this may also be seen as part of a bigger spiritual issue. Some practitioners of these approaches may be trained in talking treatments, although most are not. A lot of practitioners will not use talking in their work because they do not see themselves as experts in counselling or therapy. Much effort is being made to integrate these therapies with talking treatments, with scientific and medical thinking, and with each other. The intention is that if this is successful clients will be able to get the best of several worlds when they need help.

All these approaches can be used to help people encountering negative thoughts and emotions, including problems that have been given a clear medical diagnosis. Doctors and nurses sometimes train in one or more of these methods, and many of them are becoming widely used within the NHS. Research has been carried out into most complementary and alternative therapies. To find out what evidence there is for a particular therapy, see *The Which? Guide to Complementary Medicine*. Professional bodies exist for all the above techniques, and recognised training and supervision are provided. Some of these are listed in the Resources section and will be able to help you locate a practitioner in your area, whether NHS or private.

The need for professional regulation and evidence-based practice is now being emphasised not only for counsellors and therapists, but also for the practitioners of many of the non-talking approaches mentioned above. It is possible that some people are unhappy at the prospect of training, supervision and practice becoming too rigid. However, the need for accountability (a clear structure for complaints and safeguards) and for formal and continuing professional education and development will probably lead to clearer organisation and the government overseeing of professional bodies, with the introduction of nationally recognised qualifications like those found in the medical world (where these do not already exist).

A number of hospitals and clinics now provide complementary therapies to NHS patients, and this is likely to grow in the future. It should be understood that all these treatments are specialised approaches that are safest and most effective in the hands of experts.

The following is only a very brief list of some popular products and types of preparation. It is not in any sense meant to be a comprehensive guide to what is available, and concentrates on remedies that may help you with depression or anxiety.

Aromatherapy

Essential oils are preparations of plant oils that have healing properties. Many are recommended for psychological problems, and there is some good research indicating that oils such as camomile, ylang ylang and lavender have a calming effect. Oils such as geranium may help to lift the mood. A systematic review of six randomised controlled trials (RCTs) has found that aromatherapy helps in mild anxiety.

Essential oils should never be taken by mouth. They are either diluted and applied to the skin, or inhaled. To inhale the oils, you can heat them in a special vessel (by candle or electric source) so that their vapour spreads around a room, or simply place a few drops on a handkerchief or tissue.

Most oils are quite strong in their undiluted form. Great care should be taken to avoid contact with the skin unless they have been diluted in a base (neutral) oil such as grapeseed oil or almond oil. Do not put undiluted essential oils in the bath, since they will not diffuse properly in water and may irritate your skin. Look for information about how to safely use essential oils before trying anything yourself.

A trained aromatherapist may also use essential oils for a light form of massage. Ensure that the practitioner has a professional qualification in aromatherapy, because the properties of the oils are complex and their effects can be strong. Some oils that are safe in most cases should not be used if you are pregnant or have particular physical or psychological conditions. Particular caution is needed with some oils that tend to irritate or sensitise the skin more than most.

Biofeedback

Biofeedback is a training technique that teaches a person to self-regulate biological functions that are not normally controlled voluntarily by the conscious mind. Its aim is to help people improve their health and well-being. This is achieved by using electronic machines to observe how certain functions, such as blood pressure, heart rate or muscle tension, change in different circumstances. The idea is that once you learn to use biofeedback to affect bodily functions, you can use it in times of stress to help relieve stress-related problems such as high blood pressure or irritable bowel syndrome, or avoid the physical effects of stress or anxiety such as palpitations and breathlessness.

Biofeedback is most commonly used to treat:

- problems that may be helped by a reduction in stress and tension, such as anxiety, insomnia and asthma
- disorders that may be affected by an alteration in a biological function such as high blood pressure and irritable bowel syndrome
- conditions that are associated with muscle tension, such as chronic pain and tension headaches.

Biofeedback is used in many hospitals around the UK, with 'stress management' instruments most often found in psychology departments, and electromyograph instruments in physiotherapy and occupational therapy departments. Many independent practitioners also use biofeedback equipment and techniques with their patients.

Research has conclusively shown that we can alter our involuntary biological responses by being 'fed back' information about what is occurring in our bodies. There have also been a lot of clinical trials and observational studies carried out looking at the effectiveness of biofeedback. Systematic reviews of such research into biofeedback for tension headaches and migraine suggest that it is more effective than relaxation alone and that the combination of biofeedback and relaxation is more effective than either therapy alone. Controlled trials have shown that it can be used to relax shoulder muscles and relieve muscle tension in the lower back. Other studies have shown that it can help people with panic and anxiety control these states to the point that they no longer interfere with daily life.

Flower remedies

These are a collection of 38 different tinctures based on flower products and developed by Dr Edward Bach in the 1930s. Very small amounts of the flower are preserved in brandy and taken either neat (a few drops at a time) on in a glass of water. They are not used for treating physical illness, but are intended to manage a wide variety of stresses and psychological problems. This includes not only different types of anxiety and depression, but also negative thinking and phobias. Combinations of the different remedies can also be used (usually no more than five or six at a time). One of these mixtures is called 'Rescue Remedy', and contains cherry plum, impatiens, rock rose, clematis and Star of Bethlehem extracts. This is said to be very effective at times of extreme panic or shock, and is a non-addictive tonic that many people use to help control panic attacks.

Bach remedies are extremely popular, but their effects are anecdotal and have not been scientifically researched. However, people have been using them for decades without apparent ill-effect and with many reports of positive benefits. Side-effects seem to be very rare, although mild rashes have been reported.

Herbal remedies

Herbal remedies are often seen as more gentle alternatives to neuroleptic medications. The idea is that because these are naturally occurring substances, and not the product of a laboratory, they will cause less disruption to the individual's body chemistry. However, herbal remedies can have unwanted side-effects.

Some of these remedies are sufficiently well thought of today as to be recommended by GPs and nurses, and they are often sold by larger chemists. Take care to read any accompanying instructions. As always, caution is recommended. Buying lots of items and mixing them together is no more safe or advisable than taking half a dozen medications bought over the counter at a pharmacy and trying them all at the same time. If you are interested in these preparations, learn as much about the subject as you can before trying anything. If you have severe or long-standing problems, it is probably better to approach a skilled professional (herbalist, homeopath or aromatherapist) than to try to treat yourself. In all cases, it is a good idea to discuss the use of these treatments with your doctor or pharmacist. Particular care should be exercised if you are pregnant or breast-feeding.

St John's Wort

St John's Wort (hypericum) is a herbal preparation that has been used for mild to moderate depression. It should *not* be taken if you are taking a prescribed antidepressant medication, nor if you are pregnant or experience photosensitivity. Some research suggests that it may be as effective as prescription antidepressants for milder forms of depression and may have fewer side-effects. However, like conventional medicines it is not effective for everyone and can be slow to start working (up to six weeks in some cases). Although hypericum can be bought at most chemists without a prescription, and St John's Wort is on sale at health food shops as a herbal tea, it is advisable to ask your doctor or herbalist whether taking it is a good idea for you. It may not be suitable for people with certain medical histories. It is very important to realise that hypericum works (just as antidepressants do) because of its active chemical ingredients. As with any other drug, you can take too much and it may interreact with other medicines your doctor may be prescribing for you.

Herbal teas

Herbal teas ('tisanes') are often taken as tonics and for their curative properties as well as for their unusual tastes. Preparations such as fennel, peppermint and rosehip have been used for centuries to relieve minor physical symptoms and other teas for mood problems and to boost energy levels. Camomile is often recommended as a sedative for people when they are anxious or have difficulty in sleeping. Although many teas used for physical illnesses have been proven to have at least some beneficial effect, the success of tisanes in promoting mental well-being needs confirming. Herbal teas are usually mild and are unlikely to have significant side-effects. Not everyone likes the tastes, however, and sweetening with honey or sugar is usually acceptable.

Homeopathy

Homeopathy, which is a complete therapy in its own right, uses very dilute preparations called remedies, made from plant, mineral, metal or insect sources, to treat illness. It is not known 'scientifically' how homeopathy works, but homeopaths believe that the remedies stimulate the body's own healing powers, known as the 'vital force'. Homeopathy emphasises the importance of treating the whole person – mind, body and spirit – and not just the localised symptoms of the illness. Because it is claimed to be holistic, it is used to deal with almost any disorder. It is most commonly used to treat chronic or relapsing conditions, such as eczema and other skin problems, asthma, allergies, rheumatoid arthritis, menstrual and menopausal problems, pregnancy problems such as morning sickness, and mental disorders such as anxiety and shock. Homeopathy is a very popular way of treating similar conditions in children.

A growing number of double-blind randomised controlled trials have shown that people treated with homeopathy have significant benefits compared with those treated with just a placebo (dummy treatment). Studies combining the results of these clinical trials suggest that it is more than twice as effective as a placebo. However, overall, it is not possible to say reliably which disorders are best treated with homeopathy, except perhaps hay fever.

Hypnotherapy

Hypnotherapy is the practice of achieving deep relaxation in which people are in an increased state of awareness, and can focus entirely on the voice of the therapist without other thoughts and concerns becoming distractions. If a trusting relationship is established, the hypnotic state can be used to explore even very deep-rooted fears and anxieties. Contrary to what many people think, the person in this state remains fully aware of what is going on around him or her, and cannot be made to do anything that he or she does not want to do. The use of hypnosis for entertainment on television and in the theatre has led to mistaken impressions about this.

There is some disagreement on what makes hypnotherapy effective, but more evidence exists from RCTs of hypnotherapy than of any other complementary therapy. Many clients report very positive results in the treatment of addictions and in controlling long-standing phobias or unreasoning fears. Detailed research has been carried out into methods and the application of hypnotherapy for different kinds of problems.

The use of hypnosis for medical purposes has been recognised in the UK for many decades, and clinical psychologists are often trained in some of these techniques. However, hypnotherapy has had a bad press in recent years because it has often been practised by people with little or no real training. There have been a number of cases where people who have attended no more than a weekend course in basic hypnotherapy have then presented themselves as fully qualified practitioners. This kind of misrepresentation is not unique to hypnotherapists and, as repeated often in this guide, the practitioners of all kinds of therapy should be questioned on their experience and qualifications.

Relaxation therapy and meditation

Relaxation techniques and meditation are used by a wide range of people, for many different reasons. Some people meditate for spiritual reasons, others to relieve stress and improve well-being. Relaxation techniques and meditation are also used to treat specific conditions, particularly those that are triggered or made worse by stress. Healthcare professionals are increasingly recognising the value of relaxation techniques and meditation, which are often taught in NHS hospitals, for example in psychiatric units and in health centres. Many complementary practitioners also use relaxation methods and meditation with their patients, as do psychotherapists and clinical psychologists.

There are several techniques that can help you relax, such as meditation, deep breathing and muscle relaxation. True relaxation occurs when the mind is still, the muscles deeply relaxed and the breathing regular and slow. Breathing is automatic and we do not usually exert any control over it. However, we can do so, and consciously controlling our breathing can form a useful bridge between our bodies and our minds. When we are under stress, the muscles become tense, which can result in pain and fatigue. Consciously trying to relax your muscles is an effective way of relaxing the body which will also calm the mind. Meditation can be broadly defined as any activity that keeps the mind calm, clear of all thoughts and focused on the present. It essentially involves either focusing on something such as your breath, a mantra (a continuously repeated word or phrase, e.g. 'Om') or an object (e.g. a candle flame), or being aware of your thoughts but not engaging in them.

Muscle relaxation has been shown scientifically to normalise blood supply to the muscles, reduce oxygen use, slow the heartbeat and breathing, and reduce muscle activity. It also increases alpha brain waves and skin resistance, which are a sign of relaxation. Other relaxation techniques have been shown to be effective in reducing muscle tension. Meditation also leads to the production of alpha brain waves and changes in muscle tone and skin resistance.

A lot of good scientific evidence exists to show that relaxation therapies can help reduce anxiety. RCTs have shown that relaxation can also help with agoraphobia, panic disorder and anxiety associated with serious medical conditions such as cancer. Most of the studies attesting to the benefits of meditation relate to a type of meditation called transcendental meditation (TM). Some 500 scientific studies on TM have been published since the mid-1970s, all testifying to the effectiveness of this form of meditation in the treatment of anxiety, mild depression, insomnia, tension headaches, migraine, high blood pressure, irritable bowel syndrome, post-natal depression and a number of stress-related conditions. The few studies comparing TM with other forms of meditation have conflicting results.

Clinical diagnosis of psychological problems

This appendix aims to describe how psychological problems can be categorised according to one of two current diagnostic systems.

The concept of 'diagnosis' is crucial to the medical world, which has grappled with sorting psychological problems into diagnostic categories since the 1950s. Exactly what problem constitutes a psychiatric or mental illness in the diagnostic world is arrived at by consensus and sometimes by political decision. For example, not so long ago being homosexual was classified as a mental illness that was seen as treatable. Those who argue the case for having diagnostic categories state that a diagnosis helps focus and target interventions, that it helps to have specific approaches for specific problems. They also argue that it enables evaluation of the effectiveness of treatment, determining what approach works best for what problem. The view is that unless problems are clearly defined it is not possible to assess the sufferer's improvement or deterioration. On the other side, those opposed to the use of diagnosis for psychological problems argue that these problems are so complex, and affect the sufferer in so many ways, that a system used for physical problems cannot serve any useful purpose in the area of mental health. They argue that instead of being useful, diagnoses have a negative effect by labelling people and stigmatising them.

Diagnostic systems

There are two accepted diagnostic systems in the West:

- the system established under the World Health Organisation's International Classification of Diseases (ICD)
- the system in the American *Diagnostic and Statistical Manual of Mental Disorders* (DSM).

The current ICD system is the tenth revision and is referred to in short as 'ICD 10 (1992)'; it is less commonly used in the UK than the DSM system and, since the two are broadly similar, especially in the most recent versions, it is not covered here. The current DSM system is the fourth version and is known as 'DSM IV (1994)'. Publication details of both systems are given at the end of this appendix.

Decisions about diagnostic categories are reached by committees after they have looked at research evidence and the clusters of symptoms and responses to treatment interventions. The committees specify the criteria (for example: number of symptoms, intensity, duration) under which a problem qualifies for a diagnosis. When new evidence becomes available, the criteria may be changed, and the disease categories (diagnosis) may be changed too.

However, the difficulty in fitting psychological symptoms (or clusters of symptoms) into neat categories is that symptoms don't fit nicely into boxes. Human emotions and behaviours are complex and, unlike physical symptoms, they defy rigid classification. We seem to function at different levels at the same time, which makes classification very difficult. One solution to this is now provided by the DSM and is called the 'multi-axial system of classification'. This means that a person is assessed in five different ways at the same time in order to arrive at a comprehensive diagnosis.

DSM system of diagnosis
DSM IV uses these five different assessments in reaching a diagnosis:

- main clinical problems
- personality disorders and mental retardation (learning disabilities)
- medical conditions
- psychosocial and environmental problems
- global assessment of functioning (GAF).

1 Main clinical problems
These are the main diagnostic categories in the older systems, such as depression, anxiety disorder, and so on.

2 Personality disorders and mental retardation (learning disabilities)

DSM IV specifies ten personality disorders, characterised by enduring qualities of a client's personality that can be traced back to adolescence or early adulthood. The ten disorders, and the ways they are characterised, are as follows:

- **antisocial** – disregard for (and violation of) the rights of others, failure to conform, violence
- **avoidant** – social inhibition, feelings of inadequacy, hypersensitivity to criticism
- **borderline** – instability in interpersonal relationships, in self-image and mood, marked impulsivity
- **dependent** – excessive need to be taken care of, being 'clingy' and submissive
- **histrionic** – excessive emotionality and attention-seeking
- **narcissistic** – pattern of grandiosity, need for admiration, lack of empathy
- **obsessive compulsive** – preoccupation with orderliness, lack of flexibility, perfectionism, desire to control
- **paranoid** – distrust of others, suspiciousness, interpreting others' actions as invariably having harmful intent
- **schizoid** – avoidance of social relationships (including family relationships), showing restricted range of emotions, difficulty in taking pleasure
- **schizotypal** – cognitive or perceptual distortions, eccentricities of behaviour, 'magical' thinking, reduced capacity to make close relationships.

The above examples of characteristics are only a brief guide, and to meet the criteria for a diagnosis of a personality disorder an individual has to satisfy a much larger number of criteria and conditions. Even if you recognise some of your own qualities in the list above, don't attempt a self-diagnosis. The full list of criteria and conditions is printed in the DSM IV manual or pocket guide. Learning disabilities and other kinds of impairment are also considered in this assessment.

3 Medical conditions

The DSM system recognises that medical conditions – past or present – can have a profound influence on mental health, mood, thought and behaviour, and therefore requires the recording of any such illnesses. The acknowledgement that physical and mental illness are interconnected is seen as an important development in the field of diagnosis. The medical conditions that are most commonly noted when making a diagnosis of mental illness include AIDS, cancer, cardiac disease, chronic pain, dermatological problems, diabetes, endocrine (hormone) problems, gastric problems, genito-urinary diseases, neurological diseases and respiratory problems.

4 Psychosocial and environmental problems

At this level in the DSM system, recognition is given to environmental stress factors that may affect the individual's mental health. This enables a person's difficulties to be put into context. The DSM system suggests nine categories to list these problems:

- problems with the primary support group – e.g. death of a family member, separation, divorce, estrangement, sexual or physical abuse
- problems related to the social environment – e.g. death or loss of a friend, inadequate social support, isolation
- educational problems – e.g. difficulties in reading and writing, problems with teachers
- occupational problems – e.g. unemployment, threat of unemployment, workload, conflict with manager
- housing problems – e.g. homelessness, inadequate housing, problems with neighbours, unsafe neighbourhood
- economic problems – e.g. poverty, debt, benefit problems
- problems with access to healthcare services – e.g. being on a long waiting list, transport difficulties
- legal problems – e.g. being in trouble with the law, being involved in litigation, being a victim of crime
- other psychosocial and environmental problems that do not fall into the above categories – e.g. disasters, war.

Some of these stress factors trigger the problems for which people commonly seek counselling or therapy. This indicates that people use talking therapies to a significant degree when they are trying to mitigate stress factors that contribute to mental illness, or to find ways of coping with them.

5 Global assessment of functioning (GAF)

This assessment has been developed in the DSM system in order for the clinician to be able to make a judgement of the individual's overall level of functioning. In order to minimise errors of judgement between clinicians, a ten-item scale – the GAF scale – has been developed to rate individuals. People with severe mental illness score 0 and those with no problem score 100; the higher the score the better the level of functioning. The GAF scale is also useful in making judgements about the outcome of treatment.

Who can diagnose?

Diagnosis not only requires the professional to look for signs and symptoms and judge whether they meet the agreed criteria for a particular disorder, but also to rule out other possible disorders that may share the same symptoms. Diagnosis also has to take into consideration the person's social and cultural context and belief systems. In the UK only a few kinds of professionals are believed to have the necessary training to make them legally qualified to diagnose psychological problems. These include medical practitioners, psychiatrists and clinical psychologists.

Use of diagnosis in counselling and therapy

The therapy and counselling world is divided on the issue of diagnosis. Although some therapists reject diagnosis completely and prefer to see all psychological problems as problems of living, others may take a more flexible approach. Counsellors and therapists who engage in longer-term work often place greater emphasis on dealing with the core personality issues (how someone perceives the world and how they typically respond to events) and lesser emphasis on symptoms which form the basis of diagnostic categories. Those who feel strongly against diagnosis argue that it serves only to imply that human distress and problems of living are a form of disease, and that it serves no useful purpose. Those practitioners who work within a cognitive behavioural framework (see Chapter 2) may show a preference for diagnosis because different techniques have been developed which have proven efficacy for specific conditions.

It is beyond the scope of this guide to provide information to aid self-diagnosis, and many people seeking counselling and therapy would not have problems that would merit a diagnosis. Nevertheless, if you want to research the effectiveness of talking treatments for a particular kind of problem, it is helpful to have the problem labelled so that it can be categorised. The table below provides a list of problems for which people commonly seek counselling and therapy, and shows whether there is an ICD 10 or DSM IV method of diagnosis for that problem. In addition, the table shows whether – according to the ICD 10 or DSM IV evaluations – that kind of problem is helped by talking treatments. The problems are listed alphabetically.

Types of problem: Does a diagnosis exist, and are talking treatments useful?

Problem	Diagnosis (ICD 10 or DSM IV)	Helped by talking treatments
Academic problems (study difficulties)	No	Yes
Addictions (dependence and misuse, e.g. alcohol dependence, gambling, numerous other activities)	Yes (not all)	Yes
Age-related cognitive decline (e.g. loss of memory, Alzheimer's disease, other forms of dementia)	Yes	No
Anxiety problems (e.g. phobias: agoraphobia, social phobia; panic disorder; generalised anxiety disorder; post-traumatic stress disorder; obsessive compulsive disorder)	Yes	Yes
Assault, rape and abuse (could include acute stress reactions and other psychological reactions)	No	Yes
Bereavement and loss, problems with mourning	No	Yes
Bipolar disorders (sufferer experiences mood swings, e.g. manic depression)	Yes	Yes (in combination with other treatments)

Problem	Diagnosis (ICD 10 or DSM IV)	Helped by talking treatments
Body image	Yes (in extreme cases)	Yes
Communication difficulties	No	Yes
Depression	Yes	Yes (sometimes in combination with medication)
Disorders of childhood and adolescence (e.g. sleep and behavioural problems, attention deficit and hyperactivity, school avoidance, bullying, bedwetting, etc.)	Some	Yes
Eating disorders (e.g. anorexia, bulimia)	Yes	Yes
Identity problems (e.g. gender identity, race)	In some cases relating to gender	Yes
Insomnia (sleep difficulties and disturbances)	No	Yes
Medical condition – psychological impact of (e.g. chronic pain, chronic fatigue)	No	Yes (for psychological component)
Obsessive compulsive disorder	Yes	Yes
Personality disorders	Yes	Yes
Post-traumatic stress (but see also assault, rape and abuse)	Yes	Yes
Psychosis, including schizophrenia	Yes	In combination with other therapies
Relationship problems (e.g. parent-child, between couples and partners, between work colleagues)	No	Yes
Sexual abuse	No	Yes
Sexual problems	Some	Yes, sometimes in combination with other therapies
Work-related problems (stress at work, performance worries)	No	Yes

References

DSM-IV (1994) *Diagnostic and Statistical Manual for Mental Disorders.* 4th edn, American Psychiatric Association, Washington DC.

ICD-10 (1992) *The ICD-10 Classification of Mental and Behavioural Disorders: Clinical Descriptions and Diagnostic Guidelines.* 10th edn, World Health Organisation, Geneva.

Opinions about psychological problems: Questionnaires

The following questionnaire was referred to in Chapter 3. It contains two self-report forms that were developed to measure how people view the causes of and treatments for psychological problems. This may help you to decide what kind of talking treatment will best suit you.

Information about research validation of the questionnaire is available from:

Dr Chris Barker
Sub-Department of Clinical Health Psychology
University College London
Gower St
London WC1E 6BT
Email: c.barker@ucl.ac.uk.

This questionnaire has two parts. The first asks about how you view the *causes* of your problems; the second asks how you think these problems can be *helped*. The key for interpreting these question-naires follows in Appendix III.

Causes of psychological problems

People have different views about what causes psychological problems. The following questions ask for your opinion of the causes of your *own* problems. There are no right or wrong answers: your own opinion is what counts. Please indicate how much you agree or disagree with each statement by using the following scale. Circle one number for each statement.

My problems are caused by:	Disagree strongly	Disagree moderately	Disagree mildly	Agree mildly	Agree moderately	Agree strongly
1. Feelings that are buried out of sight	−3	−2	−1	+1	+2	+3
2. Illogical beliefs	−3	−2	−1	+1	+2	+3
3. Other people not accepting me for who I am	−3	−2	−1	+1	+2	+3
4. Becoming too anxious in certain situations	−3	−2	−1	+1	+2	+3
5. A disorder of the brain or nervous system	−3	−2	−1	+1	+2	+3
6. Worrying too much about what other people think of me	−3	−2	−1	+1	+2	+3
7. Exaggerating the importance of things that may happen	−3	−2	−1	+1	+2	+3
8. Unemployment or an unsatisfactory job	−3	−2	−1	+1	+2	+3
9. Events that happened in childhood	−3	−2	−1	+1	+2	+3
10. Having learnt bad habits over the years	−3	−2	−1	+1	+2	+3
11. An inherited physical cause	−3	−2	−1	+1	+2	+3
12. Repeating old patterns in relationships with other people	−3	−2	−1	+1	+2	+3
13. Hiding feelings from friends or family	−3	−2	−1	+1	+2	+3
14. Lack of money	−3	−2	−1	+1	+2	+3
15. Running away from responsibilities	−3	−2	−1	+1	+2	+3
16. Repressing basic human impulses	−3	−2	−1	+1	+2	+3
17. Thinking about myself too much	−3	−2	−1	+1	+2	+3
18. Having learnt the wrong reactions to certain situations	−3	−2	−1	+1	+2	+3
19. Unsatisfactory means of transport	−3	−2	−1	+1	+2	+3
20. Not paying attention to my feelings	−3	−2	−1	+1	+2	+3
21. Making harsh judgements of myself	−3	−2	−1	+1	+2	+3
22. A lack of will power	−3	−2	−1	+1	+2	+3
23. Not accepting myself for who I am	−3	−2	−1	+1	+2	+3
24. Conflicting feelings about my parents when I was young	−3	−2	−1	+1	+2	+3
25. Dissatisfaction with the community I live in	−3	−2	−1	+1	+2	+3

	Disagree strongly	Disagree moderately	Disagree mildly	Agree mildly	Agree moderately	Agree strongly
26. Not having a realistic view of the good and the bad things that have happened	−3	−2	−1	+1	+2	+3
27. Conflicts in my unconscious mind	−3	−2	−1	+1	+2	+3
28. Illness, such as colds or 'flu	−3	−2	−1	+1	+2	+3
29. The state of the economy	−3	−2	−1	+1	+2	+3
30. Unrealistic thinking	−3	−2	−1	+1	+2	+3
31. Rewards or punishments received in the past	−3	−2	−1	+1	+2	+3
32. A conscience that won't let me alone	−3	−2	−1	+1	+2	+3
33. Not liking myself	−3	−2	−1	+1	+2	+3
34. Having unrealistic expectations	−3	−2	−1	+1	+2	+3
35. Something going wrong with my body	−3	−2	−1	+1	+2	+3
36. Not understanding what I really feel inside	−3	−2	−1	+1	+2	+3
37. Laziness	−3	−2	−1	+1	+2	+3
38. Not having learnt the right ways to cope with certain situations	−3	−2	−1	+1	+2	+3
39. Not being true to myself	−3	−2	−1	+1	+2	+3
40. Other people being unreasonable	−3	−2	−1	+1	+2	+3
41. Putting myself down for no reason	−3	−2	−1	+1	+2	+3
42. Poor housing	−3	−2	−1	+1	+2	+3
43. The wrong balance of chemicals in my body	−3	−2	−1	+1	+2	+3
44. Bad luck or fate	−3	−2	−1	+1	+2	+3
45. Having learnt wrong ways of doing things from someone else	−3	−2	−1	+1	+2	+3
46. Unsatisfactory relationships with other people	−3	−2	−1	+1	+2	+3
47. It's impossible to explain the cause of my problems	−3	−2	−1	+1	+2	+3

If you think there are other important causes not listed above, please add them here:

Help for psychological problems

People have different views about what may help psychological problems. The following questions ask for your opinion of how your *own* problems could be helped. There are no right or wrong answers: your own opinion is what counts. Please indicate how much you agree or disagree with each statement by using the following scale. Circle one number for each statement.

A good way to help my problems would be:	Disagree strongly	Disagree moderately	Disagree mildly	Agree mildly	Agree moderately	Agree strongly
1. Taking the attitude that I should count my blessings, rather than looking on the dark side of things	-3	-2	-1	+1	+2	+3
2. Having an expert show me how to think in a more logical way	-3	-2	-1	+1	+2	+3
3. Getting tablets to regulate my mood	-3	-2	-1	+1	+2	+3
4. Learning to pay attention to my feelings	-3	-2	-1	+1	+2	+3
5. Discussing the problems with someone in an honest, person-to-person way	-3	-2	-1	+1	+2	+3
6. Understanding the childhood origins of the problems	-3	-2	-1	+1	+2	+3
7. Having an expert teach me better ways of reacting to certain situations	-3	-2	-1	+1	+2	+3
8. Getting medication	-3	-2	-1	+1	+2	+3
9. Better housing	-3	-2	-1	+1	+2	+3
10. Having an expert point out the meaning of my dreams and fantasies	-3	-2	-1	+1	+2	+3
11. An improvement in the economy	-3	-2	-1	+1	+2	+3
12. Examining, with an expert, what situations make the problems better or worse	-3	-2	-1	+1	+2	+3
13. Talking to an expert about my relationship with my parents when I was young	-3	-2	-1	+1	+2	+3
14. Having someone listen to my feelings without giving advice	-3	-2	-1	+1	+2	+3
15. Worrying less about what other people think of me	-3	-2	-1	+1	+2	+3

	Disagree strongly	Disagree moderately	Disagree mildly	Agree mildly	Agree moderately	Agree strongly
16. Learning to live with the problems rather than trying to change them	−3	−2	−1	+1	+2	+3
17. Being shown by an expert how to change my outlook on the problems	−3	−2	−1	+1	+2	+3
18. Learning to accept myself for who I am	−3	−2	−1	+1	+2	+3
19. Taking my mind off myself	−3	−2	−1	+1	+2	+3
20. Having medical treatment to put the chemicals of my body back into balance	−3	−2	−1	+1	+2	+3
21. A better community to live in	−3	−2	−1	+1	+2	+3
22. Learning the skills needed in difficult situations	−3	−2	−1	+1	+2	+3
23. Putting my bad feelings aside, so I can feel more cheerful	−3	−2	−1	+1	+2	+3
24. Tackling the problems in a planned, step-by-step way	−3	−2	−1	+1	+2	+3
25. Learning to think more realistically	−3	−2	−1	+1	+2	+3
26. Having other people change, rather than changing myself	−3	−2	−1	+1	+2	+3
27. Having an expert teach me specific ways to change my behaviour	−3	−2	−1	+1	+2	+3
28. Discovering what I really feel inside	−3	−2	−1	+1	+2	+3
29. Deciding to 'keep a stiff upper lip'	−3	−2	−1	+1	+2	+3
30. Talking about my feelings to someone I trust	−3	−2	−1	+1	+2	+3
31. Learning to think differently about the problems	−3	−2	−1	+1	+2	+3
32. Having an expert analyse my unconscious reasons for doing things	−3	−2	−1	+1	+2	+3
33. Keeping busy, so as not to think about the problems	−3	−2	−1	+1	+2	+3
34. Hearing from other people that I am doing well or trying hard	−3	−2	−1	+1	+2	+3
35. Getting a satisfactory job	−3	−2	−1	+1	+2	+3
36. Learning to judge myself less harshly	−3	−2	−1	+1	+2	+3
37. Talking to someone who listens closely to what I'm really saying	−3	−2	−1	+1	+2	+3

	Disagree strongly	Disagree moderately	Disagree mildly	Agree mildly	Agree moderately	Agree strongly
38. Realising how I repeat old patterns in relationships with other people	−3	−2	−1	+1	+2	+3
39. Deciding to 'grin and bear it'	−3	−2	−1	+1	+2	+3
40. Getting tablets	−3	−2	−1	+1	+2	+3
41. Getting physically fit and healthy	−3	−2	−1	+1	+2	+3
42. Having an expert point out how I think about myself can sometimes be wrong	−3	−2	−1	+1	+2	+3
43. Better means of transport	−3	−2	−1	+1	+2	+3
44. Coming to understand feelings or impulses that I'm not aware of	−3	−2	−1	+1	+2	+3
45. Having more money	−3	−2	−1	+1	+2	+3
46. Using will power to overcome the problems	−3	−2	−1	+1	+2	+3
47. There's nothing that can be done to help my problems	−3	−2	−1	+1	+2	+3

If you think there are other ways in which your problems could be helped, please add them here:

Opinions about psychological problems: Key to interpreting results

In the key below the questions in Appendix II have been grouped according to the forms of therapy and other causes/sources of treatment of people's problems. For each section below add up the scores from your answers to the numbered questions. For example, under 'Psychodynamic' there are seven questions: 1, 9, 12, 16, 24, 27 and 32. Add up your scores for these questions. Repeat this exercise for each section. The section with the highest score indicates what is closest to your thinking. Note that the results of the cause ('etiology') part may not match your results in the help ('treatment' part). Only the first four sections below indicate forms of talking treatments. The last three are non-talking approaches. It is hoped that this exercise will point you in the direction of the help that your beliefs indicate is most appropriate for you.

© Chris Barker, Nancy Pistrang and David A. Shapiro, 1983

Etiology section

My problems are caused by:

Psychodynamic
  1. Feelings that are buried out of sight.
  9. Events that happened in childhood.
  12. Repeating old patterns in relationships with other people.
  16. Repressing basic human impulses.
  24. Conflicting feelings about my parents when I was young.
  27. Conflicts in my unconscious mind.
  32. A conscience that won't let me alone.

Humanistic/Interpersonal
3. Other people not accepting me for who I am.
13. Hiding feelings from friends or family.
20. Not paying attention to my feelings.
23. Not accepting myself for who I am.
33. Not liking myself.
36. Not understanding what I really feel inside.
39. Not being true to myself.
46. Unsatisfactory relationships with other people.

Behavioural
4. Becoming too anxious in certain situations.
10. Having learnt bad habits over the years.
18. Having learnt the wrong reactions to certain situations.
31. Rewards or punishments received in the past.
38. Not having learnt the right ways to cope with certain situations.
45. Having learnt wrong ways of doing things from someone else.

Cognitive
2. Illogical beliefs.
6. Worrying too much about what other people think of me.
7. Exaggerating the importance of things that may happen.
21. Making harsh judgements of myself.
26. Not having a realistic view of the good and the bad things that have happened.
30. Unrealistic thinking.
34. Having unrealistic expectations.
41. Putting myself down for no reason.

Organic
5. A disorder of the brain or nervous system.
11. An inherited physical cause.
28. Illness, such as colds or 'flu.
35. Something going wrong with my body.
43. The wrong balance of chemicals in my body.

Social/Economic
8. Unemployment or an unsatisfactory job.
14. Lack of money.

19. Unsatisfactory means of transport.
25. Dissatisfaction with the community I live in.
29. The state of the economy.
42. Poor housing.

Naïve
15. Running away from responsibilities.
17. Thinking about myself too much.
22. A lack of will power.
37. Laziness.
40. Other people being unreasonable.
44. Bad luck or fate.
47. It's impossible to explain the cause of my problems.

Treatment section

A good way to help my problems would be:

Psychodynamic
6. Understanding the childhood origins of the problems.
10. Having an expert point out the meaning of my dreams and fantasies.
13. Talking to an expert about my relationship with my parents when I was young.
32. Having an expert analyse my unconscious reasons for doing things.
38. Realising how I repeat old patterns in relationships with other people.
44. Coming to understand feelings or impulses that I'm not aware of.

Humanistic/Interpersonal
4. Learning to pay attention to my feelings.
5. Discussing the problems with someone in an honest, person-to-person way.
14. Having someone listen to my feelings, without giving advice.
18. Learning to accept myself for who I am.
28. Discovering what I really feel inside.
30. Talking about my feelings to someone I trust.
37. Talking to someone who listens closely to what I'm really saying.

Behavioural

7. Having an expert teach me better ways of reacting to certain situations.
12. Examining, with an expert, what situations make the problems better or worse.
22. Learning the skills needed in difficult situations.
24. Tackling the problems in a planned, step-by-step way.
27. Having an expert teach me specific ways to change my behaviour.
34. Hearing from other people that I am doing well or trying hard.

Cognitive

2. Having an expert show me how to think in a more logical way.
15. Worrying less about what other people think of me.
17. Being shown by an expert how to change my outlook on the problems.
25. Learning to think more realistically.
31. Learning to think differently about the problems.
36. Learning to judge myself less harshly.
42. Having an expert point out that how I think about myself can sometimes be wrong.

Organic

3. Getting tablets to regulate my mood.
8. Getting medication.
20. Having medical treatment to put the chemicals of my body back into balance.
40. Getting tablets.
41. Getting physically fit and healthy.

Social/Economic

9. Better housing.
11. An improvement in the economy.
21. A better community to live in.
35. Getting a satisfactory job.
43. Better means of transport.
45. Having more money.

Naïve

1. Taking the attitude that I should count my blessings, rather than looking on the dark side of things.
16. Learning to live with the problems, rather than trying to change them.
19. Taking my mind off myself.
23. Putting my bad feelings aside, so I can feel more cheerful.
26. Having other people change, rather than changing myself.
29. Deciding to 'keep a stiff upper lip'.
33. Keeping busy, so as not to think about the problems.
39. Deciding to 'grin and bear it'.
46. Using will power to overcome the problems.
47. There's nothing that can be done to help my problems.

Resources

This part of the guide aims to provide a starting point for finding the kind of psychological help that you need and want.

There is overlap between the different sections – an organisation may provide books and leaflets, host a telephone helpline and also have a website. You may have to look in more than one section to find what you want. Telephone numbers and addresses change quickly, books go out of print, and web addresses change. Try not to be disheartened if you have to work a little harder at chasing down the advice or assistance that you need.

The inclusion of details in this Resources section does not necessarily mean that the authors or Which? Books personally recommend the publication or organisation, but it does mean that they have at least had positive feedback about it. However, no responsibility can be taken for advice given or services offered by anyone listed here. It is strongly recommended that you exercise caution in all dealings with advice workers and with practitioners of talking treatments and other therapies. Be aware of the limitations of the help on offer, the level of training and experience of the staff with whom you deal, professional and organisational safeguards within the services used, and of your own vulnerability when seeking help.

Bibliography

Books and leaflets

There is an endless amount in print about talking treatments and mental health issues, but most of it is written for practitioners rather than clients. The following publications are either specifically written for lay people or provide a lot of useful information that should be accessible to the casual reader.

Talking treatments

Baker, P. (1999) *Talking Cures: A Guide to the Psychotherapies*. Nursing Times Books.

Berne, Eric (1971) *A Layman's Guide to Psychiatry and Psychoanalysis*. Penguin.

Child Psychotherapy Trust (1998) *With Children in Mind: How Child Psychotherapy Contributes to Services for Children and Young People* and *Is Child Psychotherapy Effective for Children and Young People?: A Summary of the Research*. Two booklets.

Department of Health (2001) *Treatment Choice in Psychological Therapies and Counselling: Evidence-based Clinical Practice Guideline*. Department of Health Publications. Available also on www.doh.gov.uk/mentalhealth/treatmentguideline

Dryden, Windy (ed.) (2002) *Handbook of Individual Therapy*. Sage Publications.

Dryden, Windy (ed.) *Counselling in Action*. Sage Publications. (Each book in this series deals with a specific type of talking treatment or a major associated issue.)

Garfield, Sol and Bergin, Allen (1995) *Handbook of Psychotherapy and Behavior Change*. John Wiley & Sons, New York.

Masson, Jerry. (1994) *Against Therapy*. Common Courage Press, USA.

MIND (2000) *Talking Treatments*. In the *Understanding* ... series. MIND.

Nathan, P.E., Gorman, J.M. and Salkind, N.J. (2000) *Treating Mental Disorders: A guide to what works*. Oxford University Press.

Yalom, Irvin D. (1995) *Theory and Practice of Group Psychotherapy*. Basic Books, USA.

Particular problems

Corry, M. and Tubridy, A. (2001) *Going Mad? Understanding mental illness*. Newleaf.

Farrell, E. (1997) *The Complete Guide to Mental Health*. MIND/ Vermilion.

Greener, M. (2003) *The Which? Guide to Managing Stress*. Which? Books

MIND Books in the *Understanding* ... series, including: *Anxiety*; *Attention Deficit Hyperactive Disorder*; *Autism in Children and Adolescents*; *Bereavement*; *Borderline Personality Disorder*; *Childhood Distress*; *Dementia*; *Depression*; *Dual Diagnosis*; *Eating Distress*; *Gender Dysphoria*; *Learning Disabilities*; *Manic Depression*; *Mental Illness*; *Obsessive Compulsive Disorder*; *Paranoia*; *Personality Disorder*; *Phobias*; *Postnatal Depression*; *Post-Traumatic Stress Disorder*; *Premenstrual Syndrome*; *The Psychological Effects of Street Drugs*; *Schizophrenia*; *Seasonal Affective Disorder*; *Self-harm*. MIND. (An award-winning series of leaflets about a wide range of mental health issues.)

Rachman, Stanley and De Silva, Padmal (1996) *Panic Disorder: The Facts*. Oxford University Press, Oxford.

Self-help guides

Atkinson, S. (1993) *Climbing out of Depression: A Practical Guide for Sufferers*. Lion Publishing.

Butler, G. and Hope, T. (1995) *Manage Your Mind: The Mental Health Fitness Guide*. Oxford University Press, Oxford.

Butler, G. (1999) *Overcoming Social Anxiety and Shyness: A Self-Help Guide Using Cognitive-Behavioural Techniques*. Robinson.

George, M. (2000) *Learn to Relax*. Duncan Baird.

Herbert, C. and Wetmore, A. (1999) *Overcoming Traumatic Stress: A Self-Help Guide Using Cognitive-Behavioural Techniques*. Robinson.

Kennerley, H. (1997) *Overcoming Anxiety*. Robinson.

Kennerley, H. (2000) *Overcoming Childhood Trauma: A Self-Help Guide Using Cognitive-Behavioural Techniques*. Robinson.

Lynch, T. (2001) *Beyond Prozac: Healing Mental Suffering Without Drugs*. Marino Books.

McKay, M. and Rogers, P. (2000) *The Anger Control Workbook*. New Harbinger Press, USA.

Parkinson, F. (2000) *Coping with Post-Traumatic Stress*. Sheldon Press.

Persaud, R. (2001) *Staying Sane*. Bantam.

Rowe, D. (1996) *Depression: The way out of your prison*. Routledge.

Smail, David J. (1998) *The Nature of Unhappiness*. Robinson.

Smail, David J. (2001) *Why Therapy Doesn't Work and What We Should Do About It*. Robinson

Trickett, S. (1997) *Coping with Anxiety and Depression*. Sheldon Press.

Important issues in mental health, counselling and therapy

Barnett, H. (2002) *The Which? Guide to Complementary Therapies*. Which? Books

Cordess, C. (2000) *Confidentiality and Mental Health*. Jessica Kingsley Publishers.

D'Ardenne, Patricia and Mahtani, Aruna (1999) *Transcultural Counselling in Action*. Sage Publications.

Fernando, S. (2002) *Mental Health, Race and Culture*. Routledge, London.

Kuipers, E. and Bebbington, P. (1997) *Living with Mental Illness: A book for Relatives and Friends*. Souvenir Press.

MIND Leaflets in the *Making sense of ...* series, including: *Antidepressants*; *Cognitive Behaviour Therapy*; *ECT*; *Herbal Remedies*; *Homeopathy*; *Lithium*; *Major Tranquillizers*; *Sleeping Pills*; *Traditional Chinese Medicine*. MIND. (A series explaining treatment options.)

Papatola, Kathleen J. (1997) *The Therapy Answer Book: Getting the Most Out of Counselling*. Fairview Press, Minneapolis.

Ramsay, R., Gerada, C., Mars, S. and Szmukler, G. (2001) *Mental Illness: A Handbook for Carers*. Jessica Kingsley Publishers.

Yalom, Irvin and Elkin, Ginny (1990) *Every Day Gets A Little Closer: A Twice-told Therapy*. Basic Books. (A book that relates the events of a specific episode of a talking treatment from the perspectives of both the practitioner and the client.)

Audiocassettes and CDs

This market changes rapidly and it is very difficult to make specific recommendations. You can ask the organisations listed under

'General information' in the Address list for assistance in finding an appropriate product for your needs.

CD-ROMs

Beating the Blues. For depression. Institute of Psychiatry (Kings College London, De Crespigny Park, London SE5 8AF; tel: 020-7836 5454; website: www.iop.kcl.ac.uk)

Restoring the Balance. For mild to moderate anxiety and depression. Mental Health Foundation (see 'General information', in the Address list, for address)

Addresses and websites

General information

These voluntary-sector organisations offer a wide range of information about all kinds of personal problems, and are a very good place to start when looking for support. They are national organisations, but can put you in touch with more local services.

Mental Health Foundation
7th Floor, 83 Victoria Street
London SW1H 0HW
Tel: 020-7802 0300
Fax: 020-7802 0301
Website: www.mentalhealth.org.uk
Email: mhf@mhf.org.uk

MIND (National Association for Mental Health)
Granta House
15–19 Broadway
Stratford
London E15 4BQ
Tel: 020-8519 2122
Fax: 020-8522 1725
Website: www.mind.org.uk
Email: contact@mind.org.uk

POPAN
2 Wyvil Court
Wyvil Road
London SW8 2TG
Tel: 020-7622 6334
Fax: 020-7622 9788
Website: www.popan.org.uk
Email: info@popan.org.uk
Offers support to people who have been abused by health and social care professionals, including practitioners of talking treatments

Rethink
28 Castle Street
Kingston upon Thames
Surrey KT1 1SS
Tel: 020-8547 3937
Fax: 020-8547 3862
Website: www.rethink.org
Email: info@rethink.org

Rethink (Scotland)
Claremont House
130 East Claremont Street
Edinburgh EH7 4LB
Tel: 0131-557 8969
Fax: 0131-557 8698
Website: www.nsfscot.org.uk
Email: info@nsfscot.org.uk

SANE
First Floor
Cityside House
40 Adler Street
London E1 1EE
Tel: 020-7375 1002
Fax: 020-7375 2162
Website: www.sane.org.uk
Email: info@sane.org.uk

Specialist and self-help organisations

Some of these organisations provide telephone counselling, and offer face-to-face counselling for sufferers and often for their family and friends. Others provide only advice and information, but they may be able to help you find local counsellors or therapists, or practitioners of non-talking treatments.

Alcoholics Anonymous
General Service Office
PO Box 1
Stonebow House
Stonebow
York YO1 7NJ
Tel: (01904) 644026
Fax: (01904) 629091
Website:
www.alcoholics-anonymous.org.uk

Anna Freud Centre
21 Maresfield Gardens
London NW3 5SD
Tel: 020-7794 2313
Fax: 020-7794 6506
Website: www.annafreudcentre.org/
Email: info@annafreud.org
Dedicated to child psychotherapy

Association for Postnatal Illness
145 Dawes Road
Fulham
London SW6 7EB
Tel: 020-7386 0868
Fax: 020-7386 8885
Website: www.apni.org
Email: info@apni.org

British Association for Sexual and Relationship Therapy
Tel/Fax: 020-8543 2707
Website: www.basrt.org.uk

ChildLine
Studd Street
London N1 0QW
Tel: 020-7239 1000
Fax: 020-7239 1001
Website: www.childline.org.uk
Email: info@childline.org.uk

Child Psychotherapy Trust
Star House
104–108 Grafton Road
London NW5 4BD
Tel: 020-7284 1355
Fax: 020-7284 2755
Website:
www.childpsychotherapytrust.org.uk
Email: cpt@globalnet.co.uk

Cocaine Anonymous
Tel: 020-7284 1123 (10am-10pm)
Website: www.cauk.org.uk
Email: info@cauk.org.uk
Support groups for people who use cocaine

CRUSE Bereavement Care
CRUSE House
126 Sheen Road
Richmond
Surrey TW9 1UR
Tel: 020-8939 9530
Fax: 020-8940 7638
Website:
www.crusebereavementcare.org.uk
Email:
helpline@crusebereavementcare.org.uk
info@crusebereavementcare.org.uk

Depression Alliance
35 Westminster Bridge Road
London SE1 7JB
Tel: 020-7633 0557
Fax: 020-7633 0559
Website: www.depressionalliance.org
Email:
information@depressionalliance.org

Drugscope
32-36 Lohan Street
London SE1 0EE
Tel: 020-7928 1211
Fax: 020-7928 1771
Website: www.drugscope.org.uk
Email: services@drugscope.org.uk

Eating Disorders Association
1st Floor, Wensum House
103 Prince of Wales Road
Norwich NR1 1DW
Tel: 0870-770 3256
Fax: (01603) 664915
Website: www.edauk.com
Email: info@edauk.com

Enable (Scotland)
6th Floor, 7 Buchanan Street
Glasgow G1 3HL
Tel: 0141-226 4541
Fax: 0141-204 4398
Website: www.enable.org.uk
Email: enable@enable.org.uk
*Scottish-based help for people with learning
disabilities and their families and carers*

Family Welfare Association
501-505 Kingsland Road
London E8 4AU
Tel: 020-7254 6251
Fax: 020-7249 5443
Website: www.fwa.org.uk
Email: fwa.headoffice@fwa.org.uk

Gamblers Anonymous
PO Box 88
London SW10 0EU
Tel: 0870-050 8880
Website:
www.gamblersanonymous.org.uk/
*Information about support groups for
people who engage in compulsive gambling*

GamCare
2&3 Baden Place
Crosby Row
London SE1 1YW
Tel: 020-7378 5200
Fax: 020-7378 5233
Website: www.gamcare.org.uk
Email: direct@gamcare.org.uk
Advice and support about all aspects of problem gambling

Institute of Psychosexual Medicine
12 Chandos Street
Cavendish Square
London W1G 9DR
Tel: 020-7580 0631
Fax: 020-7436 2786
Website: www.ipm.org.uk
Email: ipm@telinco.co.uk

Manic Depression Fellowship England
Castle Works
21 St George's Road
London SE1 6ES
Tel: 020-7793 2600
Fax: 020-7793 2639
Website: www.mdf.org.uk
Email: mdf@mdf.org.uk

Mencap (England)
123 Golden Lane
London EC1Y 0RT
Tel: 020-7454 0454
Fax: 020-7696 5540
Website: www.mencap.org.uk

Mencap (Northern Ireland)
Segal House
4 Annadale Avenue
Belfast BT7 3JH
Tel: 028-9069 1351
Fax: 028-9064 0121
Website: www.mencap.org.uk
Email: mencapni@mencap.org.uk

Mencap (Wales)
31 Lambourne Crescent
Cardiff Business Park
Llanishen
Cardiff CF14 5GF
Tel: 029-2074 7588
Fax: 029-2074 7550
Website: www.mencap.org.uk
Email: information.wales@mencap.org.uk

Nafsiyat Inter-Cultural Therapy Centre
262 Holloway Road
London N7 6NE
Tel: 020-7686 8666
Fax: 020-7686 8666
Offers counselling and therapy to people from ethnic and cultural minorities

National Association for Premenstrual Syndrome
41 Old Road
East Peckham
Kent TN12 5AP
Tel/Fax: 0870-772 2178
Website: www.pms.org.uk
Email: contact@pms.org.uk

National Autistic Society
393 City Road
London EC1V 1NG
Tel: 020-7833 2299
Fax: 020-7833 9666
Website: www.nas.org.uk/
Support for people diagnosed with autism and Asperger's Syndrome

National Phobics Society
Zion Community Resource Centre
339 Stretford Road
Hulme
Manchester M15 4ZY
Tel: 0870-770 0456
Fax: 0161-227 9862
Website: www.phobics-society.org.uk
Email: natphob.soc@good.co.uk

Rape Crisis Federation
7 Mansfield Road
Nottingham NG1 3FB
Tel: 0115-900 3560
Fax: 0115-934 8470
Website: www.rapecrisis.co.uk

RELATE
Herbert Gray College
Little Church Street
Rugby
Warwickshire CV21 3AP
Tel: (01788) 573241
Fax: (01788) 535007
Website: www.relate.org.uk
Provides counselling for couples
throughout the UK

RELATE (Northern Ireland)
74–76 Dublin Road
Belfast BT2 7HP
Tel: 028-9032 3454
Fax: 028-9031 5298
Web: www.relateni.org/infopage.htm
Email: office@relateni.org

Scottish Child Psychotherapy Trust
13 Park Terrace
Glasgow G3 6BY
Tel: 0141-353 3399
Fax: 0141-332 3999
Email: Catriona@scpt.fsnet.co.uk

Sexaholics Anonymous
Website: www.sauk.org
Tel: 0700-0725463
Information about support groups for
people who engage in compulsive sex

Society Of Health Advisers In
Sexually Transmitted Diseases
(SHASTD)
Website: www.shastd.org.uk

The Tavistock Clinic
The Tavistock Centre
120 Belsize Lane
London NW3 5BA
Tel: 020-7435 7111
Fax: 020-7447 3709
Websites: www.tavi-port.org
www.tavistocksociety.org
Email: chiefexecutive@tavi-port.org

Terrence Higgins Trust
52-54 Grays Inn Road
London WC1X 8JU
Tel: 020-7831 0330
Fax: 020-7242 0121
Website: www.tht.org.uk
Email: info@tht.org.uk
Information for people affected by HIV
and AIDS

Triumph Over Phobia
PO Box 1831
Bath BA2 4YW
Tel: (01225) 330353
Fax: (01225) 469212
Website:
www.triumphoverphobia.com
Email:
triumphoverphobia@compuserve.com

YoungMinds
102-108 Clerkenwell Road
London EC1M 5SA
Tel: 020-7336 8445
Fax: 020-7336 8446

Website: www.youngminds.org.uk
Email:
enquiries@youngminds.org.uk
Advice and information about the mental health of young people

Professional bodies: counselling and therapy

These organisations represent practitioners who work with a broad range of approaches to counselling and therapy. They can provide information about the kinds of talking treatment on offer and can usually give you details of practitioners working near you. Professional bodies also give advice on their codes of conduct, complaints procedures, and what to expect from practitioners.

Association of Child Psychotherapy
120 West Heath Road
London NW3 7TU
Tel: 020-8458 1609
Fax: 020-8458 1482
Website: www.all4kidsuk.com
Email: acp@dial.pipex.com

British Association for Counselling and Psychotherapy
BACP House
35-37 Albert Street
Rugby
Warwickshire CV21 2SG
Tel: 0870-443 5252
Fax: 0870-443 5160
Website: www.bacp.co.uk
Email: bacp@bacp.co.uk

British Association of Psychotherapists
37 Mapesbury Road
London NW2 4HJ
Tel: 020-8452 9823
Fax: 020-8452 5182
Website: www.bap-psychotherapy.org
Email: mail@bap-psychotherapy.org

British Association for Sexual and Relationship Therapy
Tel/Fax: 020-8543 2707
Website: www.basrt.org.uk
Email: info@basrt.org.uk

British Confederation of Psychotherapists
37 Mapesbury Road
London NW2 4HJ
Tel: 020-8830 5173
Fax: 020-8452 3684
Website: www.bcp.org.uk
Email: mail@bcp.org.uk

British Psychological Society
St Andrews House
48 Princess Road East
Leicester LE1 7DR
Tel: 0116-254 9568
Fax: 0116-247 0787
Website: www.bps.org.uk
Email: mail@bps.org.uk

Independent Practitioners Network
86 Burley Wood Crescent
Leeds LS4 2QL
Tel: 0113-278 0230
Website: www.ipnosis.postle.net/
PDFS/IPNBriefing07.pdf
An alternative network for practitioners of
a variety of talking treatments

The Tavistock Society of
Psychotherapists
The Tavistock Centre
120 Belsize Lane
London NW3 5BA
Tel: 020-7435 7111
Fax: 020-7447 3709
Websites: www.tavi-port.org
www.tavistocksociety.org
Email: chiefexecutive@tavi-port.org

United Kingdom Council for
Psychotherapy
167–169 Great Portland Street
London W1N 5FB
Tel: 020-7436 3002
Fax: 020-7436 3013
Website: www.psychotherapy.org.uk
Email: ukcp@psychotherapy.org.uk

Professional bodies: non-talking treatments

These organisations represent practitioners working in a range of non-talking treatments (see Chapter 12). They can give the same kind of information about their particular treatments as the professional bodies listed above can give about counselling and therapy. Some of these non-talking treatments are commonly used within the NHS, others are not. It is advisable to obtain as much information as possible before engaging in any of these treatments.

Aromatherapy Organisations Council
PO Box 19834
London SE25 6WF
Tel: 0870-774 3477
Website: www.aocuk.net
Email: info@aocuk.net

Association of Professional Music
Therapists
26 Hamlyn Road
Glastonbury
Somerset BA6 8HT
Tel/Fax: (01458) 834919
Website: www.apmt.org.uk
Email: APMToffice@aol.com

Association of Reflexologists
27 Old Gloucester Street
London WC1N 3XX
Tel: 0870-567 3320
Fax: (01989) 567676
Website: www.aor.org.uk
Email: aor@reflexology.org

Biofeedback Foundation of Europe
PO Box 75416
1070 AK Amsterdam
The Netherlands
Tel: (00 31) 20 44 22 631
Website: www.bfe.org

British Acupuncture Council
63 Jeddo Road
London W12 9HQ
Tel: 020-8735 0400
Fax: 020-8735 0404
Website: www.acupuncture.org.uk
Email: info@acupuncture.org.uk

British Association of Art Therapists
Mary Ward House
5 Tavistock Place
London WC1H 9SN
Tel: 020-7383 3774
Fax: 020-7387 5513
Website: www.baat.org/
Email: baat@ukgateway.net

British Association of Drama Therapists
4 Sunnydale Villas
Durlston Road
Swanage BN19 2HY

British Association of Play Therapists
31 Cedar Drive
Keynsham
Bristol BS31 2TY
Tel/ Fax: 0117-986 0390
Website: www.bapt.uk.com/
Email: info@bapt.uk.com

British Massage Therapy Council
17 Rymers Lane
Oxford OX4 3JU
Tel: (01865) 774123
Website: www.bmtc.co.uk

British Reflexology Association
Monks Orchard
Whitbourne
Worcester WR6 5RB
Tel: (01886) 821207
Website: www.britreflex.co.uk

Dr Edward Bach Centre
Mount Vernon
Sotwell
Wallingford OX10 0PZ
Tel: (01491) 834678
Website: www.bachcentre.com

Faculty of Homeopathy and British Homeopathic Association
15 Clerkenwell Close
London EC1R 0AA
Tel: 020-7566 7800
Fax: 020-7566 7815
Website: www.trusthomeopathy.org
Email: info@trusthomeopathy.org

*National Federation of Spiritual
Healers*
Old Manor Farm Studio
Church Street
Sunbury-on-Thames
Middlesex TW16 6RG
Tel: (01932) 783164
Fax: (01932) 779648
Website: www.nfsh.org.uk
Email: office@nfsh.org.uk

*National Institute of Medical
Herbalists*
56 Longbrook Street
Exeter
Devon EX4 6AH
Tel: (01392) 426022
Fax: (01392) 498963
Website: www.nimh.org.uk
Email:
nimh@ukexeter.freeserve.co.uk

*National Register of Hypnotherapists
and Psychotherapists*
Suite B
12 Cross Street
Nelson
Lancashire BB9 7EN
Tel: (01282) 716839
Fax: (01282) 698633
Freephone: 0800 1613823
Website: www.nrhp.co.uk
Email: nrhp@btconnect.com

*Professional Association for Dance
Movement Therapy*
C/o Quaker Meeting House
Wedmore Vale
Bristol BS3 5HX
Website: www.admt.org.uk
Email: query@admt.org.uk

School of Meditation
158 Holland Park Avenue
London W11 4UH
Tel: 020-7603 6116

Society of Homeopaths
4a Artizan Road
Northampton NN1 4HU
Tel: (01604) 621400
Website: www.homeopathy-soh.org

Websites for general information

The Internet contains many useful sites but even more that are of very questionable value. The following web pages contain a lot of helpful and practical information, although they may express opinions different to that of the authors. These are mainly large sites offering general advice.

The Therapy Index
www.therapyindex.com

UK Therapists
www.uktherapists.com/directory/search/choose.asp
Both these sites provide online listings of counsellors, therapists and other practitioners across the UK

Your Health
www.bbc.co.uk/health/mental
An excellent guide to common psychological problems. Also see the web pages of MIND, Rethink and SANE for other comprehensive guides to a wide variety of personal issues

Natural Health Web
www.naturalhealthweb.com

Self-help UK
www.self-help.org.uk
Two sites that link to information about many types of healing including talking treatments

Royal College of Psychiatrists
www.rcpsych.ac.uk
Information about the practice of psychiatry and the use of diagnosis

British National Formulary
bnf.vhn.net/home
An online guide to all medications available in the UK

Your Guide to the NHS
www.nhs.uk/nhsguide

Department of Health
www.doh.gov.uk
Information about legal and statutory issues affecting health care and public planning

Telephone helplines

Telephone helplines are often a first point of contact for people looking for support.

Hours: Not all helplines operate all day long or every day. The hours listed may have changed since publication of this guide. Be prepared to check hours of availability and to have to call back.

Help offered: Some of these services offer advice and information only, others offer telephone counselling, and still others can arrange for face-to-face counselling or therapy. Many also offer support for the family and friends of people affected by specific problems.

Cost: Some helplines can be contacted free of charge, others can be called at reduced rates. All 0800 numbers are free and 0845 numbers are charged at the local call rate. For other numbers, it is advisable to check what you will be charged if you are likely to be on the phone for a long time.

Confidentiality: The large majority of helpline services offer complete confidentiality, and you do not have to give your name. However, if you call from your own home, any number other than an 0800 number may later be listed on your phone bill. You can avoid this by calling from a public phone box or a friend's house. You may wish to take steps to conceal your own telephone number from any service that you call.

Abuse, violence and crime

Family Matters
01474 537 392 (times vary)
Advice and telephone counselling regarding abuse, for adults and children aged eight and upwards

Refuge
0870 599 5443 (24 hrs)
Telephone counselling, advice and information about accommodation, for women and children escaping domestic violence

Victim Supportline
0845 303 0900 (Mon–Fri, 9am–9pm;
Sat & Sun, 9am–7pm)
*Advice and information for people affected
by crime*

Alcohol

Al-Anon Family Groups
020-7403 0888 (10am–10pm)
*Runs local support groups for family and
friends of people with alcohol problems*

Alcoholics Anonymous
020-7833 0022 (10am–10pm)
*Runs local support groups for people with
drink problems*

DrinkLine England and Wales
0800 917 8282 (Mon–Fri, 9am–
11pm; Sat & Sun, 6pm–11pm)
*Advice and information on all aspects of
problematic alcohol use*

**National Association for Children of
Alcoholics**
0800 358 3456 (Mon–Fri,
10am–7pm)
*Advice and support for the children, of any
age, of people with alcohol problems*

Anxiety, depression and stress

ASSIST
01788 560 800 (Mon–Fri,
10am–4pm)
*Information, telephone counselling and
referrals for face-to-face counselling for
people suffering from traumatic stress*

First Steps To Freedom
01926 851 608 (10am–10pm)
*Advice, information and telephone
counselling for sufferers of phobia, anxiety,
panic attacks and eating disorders*

**National Association for
Premenstrual Syndrome**
08707 772177 (times vary)
*Advice, information and support for people
affected by PMS, and for their families
and friends*

No Panic
0800 783 1531 (10am–10pm)
*Advice, telephone counselling and referrals
for sufferers of all kinds of panic and
anxiety*

Samaritans
0845 790 9090 (24 hrs)
*Telephone counselling for people who are
severely depressed, in crisis, and
considering suicide*

Bereavement

Compassionate Friends
0117-953 9639 (10am–4pm,
6.30pm–10.30pm)
*Support and telephone counselling for
families coping with the death of children
of any age*

CRUSE Bereavement Care
0845 7585 565 (Mon–Fri, 5pm–9pm,
Sat 3pm–5pm, Sun 3pm–7pm)
*Information, telephone counselling and
referrals for anyone dealing with recent or
past bereavements*

Lesbian and Gay Bereavement Project
020-8455 8894 (Mon, Tue & Thurs,
7.30–10.30pm)
*Advice, telephone counselling and
appointments for individual counselling,
for people affected by the death of a same-
sex partner*

Stillbirth and Neonatal Death Society
020-7403 5969 (weekdays,
10am–4pm)
*Information, telephone counselling and
local support groups for people who have
experienced the death of a baby*

Children

Childline
0800 1111 (24 hrs)
*Telephone counselling and advice for
children and young people up to the age of
18. Can make referrals to support
agencies. Help with many kinds of
problems, including all forms of abuse*

Childwatch
01482 325 552 (Mon–Fri, 9am–5pm)
*Telephone and face-to-face counselling for
adults who were abused as children*

NSPCC Child Protection Line
0800 800 500 (24 hrs)

Drugs

Cocaine Anonymous
020-7284 1123 (10am–10pm)
Support groups for people who use cocaine

Narcotics Anonymous
020-7730 0009 (10am10pm)
Self-help groups for narcotic abusers

National Drugs Helpline
0800 776 600 (24 hrs)
*Advice and information for anyone
concerned about drugs and solvent abuse*

Eating

Eating Disorders Association (adults)
0845 634 1414 (8.30am–8.30pm)
Eating Disorders Association (youth)
0845 634 7650 (4–6.30pm)
*Advice and information on all aspects of
eating disorders, plus referrals to local
support groups*

Elderly people

Age Concern (England and Wales)
0800 009 966 (7am–7pm)
Age Concern (Northern Ireland)
028-9024 5729 (Mon–Thur,
9am–5pm, Fri, 9am-4pm)
Age Concern (Scotland)
0131-220 3345 (Mon–Fri, 9am–5pm)
*Gives advice and information for older
people and all aspects of caring for the elderly*

Gambling

Gam-Anon
0870 0508 880 (24 hrs)
*Support and encouragement for families
and friends of compulsive gamblers*

Gamblers Anonymous
020-7384 3040 (24 hrs)
*Local support groups for people with
addictions to gambling*

GamCare
0845 6000 133
*Confidential counselling, advice and
information for anyone affected by a
gambling dependency*

Health and mental health

Alzheimer's Helpline
0845 300 0336 (Mon–Fri,
8.30am–6.30pm)
Advice and information about Alzheimer's disease and other dementias

Manic Depression Fellowship (England)
020-7793 2600 (Mon–Fri,
9am–5pm)

Manic Depression Fellowship (Wales)
01633 244 244 (Mon–Fri,
9.30am–4.30pm)
Advice and information for people diagnosed with manic depression and their friends, families and carers

MIND Info Line
0845 766 0163 (Mon–Fri,
9.15am–5.15pm)
Information and advice on all aspects of mental health and support services

NHS Direct
0845 4647 (24 hrs)
Information and advice about all aspects of health, physical and mental

National Women and Mental Health Information Line
0845 300 0911 (Mon & Wed,
10am–12 noon; Mon–Thur,
2pm–5pm)
Information for women with mental health problems

Rethink
020-8974 6814 (Mon, Wed & Fri,
10am–3pm; Tue & Thur, 10am–1pm)
Advice, information and telephone counselling regarding schizophrenia and other severe mental illness

Saneline
0845 767 8000 (12 noon–2am)
Information, telephone counselling and referrals for people affected by mental health problems

Schizophrenia Association of Great Britain
01248 354 048 (Mon–Fri,
9.30am–4pm)
Information and support for people diagnosed with schizophrenia and their carers

Terrence Higgins Trust
0845 122 1200 (Mon–Fri,
10am–10pm, Sat–Sun 12–6pm)
Advice, information and telephone counselling regarding HIV and AIDS

Lesbians and gay men

Lesbian and Gay Switchboard
020-7837 7324 (24 hrs)
Support and information on all aspects of gay and lesbian lifestyles

Parents

Gingerbread (England and Wales)
0800 018 4318 (Mon–Fri, 9am–5pm)
Gingerbread (Northern Ireland)
028-90 234 568 (Mon–Fri,
9.30am–4.30pm)
*Telephone counselling and information for
lone parents*

Parentline Plus
0808 800 2222 (24 hrs)
*Support and information for parents and
other carers of children*

Sexual addiction

Sexaholics Anonymous
07000 725463 (24 hrs)
*Support groups for people who engage in
compulsive sex*

Index

Abrahams, Karl 51
academic problems 242
active listening 161
addictions 76, 193, 200–3, 242
  alcohol and drugs 25, 62, 76, 86,
    159, 160, 200–3, 273, 274
  compulsive sexual behaviour 76,
    203
  gambling 76, 203, 274
addresses and websites 262–71
adjustment reaction 27
advice-giving 33, 157–8, 215, 219
age-related cognitive decline 242
agitated depression 24
agoraphobia 143
alcohol-related problems 25, 62, 76,
    86, 159, 160, 200–3, 273
Alcoholics Anonymous (AA) 18, 82,
    201–2, 263, 273
Alternatives to counselling and
    psychotherapy 17–21
  see also non-talking treatments
Alzheimer's disease 108, 275
amitriptyline 222, 223
analytical psychology 32, 52–3
analytical psychotherapy 145, 192
anger 25, 162
Anna Freud Centre 199, 263
anorexia nervosa 105
anthropology 39
antidepressants 153, 223–4
  selective serotonin re-uptake
    inhibitors (SSRIs) 223, 225

tricyclics 223
anxiety 24, 42, 104, 242
  effective therapies 143, 231, 232
  generalised anxiety disorder 143
  health-related problems 24
  medication 223–6
  telephone helplines 273
anxiolytics 224–5
appointments
  evening appointments 122
  missed appointments 120–1
  session length 121, 162–3
approved social workers (ASWs)
    100
aromatherapy 20, 230–1
art therapy 227
Asperger's Syndrome 197, 205
assault, rape and abuse 242, 272–3
assessment session 148–55, 185
  assessment of the practitioner
    153–4
  describing your problems 149–51
  expectations and goals 154–5
  pre-assessment questionnaire 149,
    245–55
  providing information 150–3
Association of Child
    Psychotherapists 198, 267
atenolol 225
attention deficit and hyperactivity
    disorder (ADHD) 197
audio recordings of sessions 187–8
autism 108, 197, 205

autogenic training 56
aversion therapy 45

Bach remedies 232
Baker Miller, Jean 64
Balint, Michael 52
Beck, Aaron T. 45, 54
behaviourism 43–5, 46, 48, 53–6
    cognitive analytical therapy (CAT)
        55, 101, 144
    cognitive behavioural therapy
        (CBT) 45, 53, 54, 75, 101,
        142, 143–4, 188, 198, 201,
        215, 242
    cognitive behaviourism 34, 48
    coping strategies 55
    interpersonal therapy (IPT) 55–6,
        101, 143, 144
    rational emotive behavioural
        therapy (REBT) 54–5
behaviours, problematic 25, 28
    see also addictions
benzodiazepines 224–5
bereavement 242
bereavement counselling 130, 273–4
Berg, Insoo Kim 62
Berne, Eric 61
beta-blockers 225
bibliotherapy see self-help guides and
    manuals
biofeedback 56, 231–2
Bion, Wilfred 52
bipolar disorders 242
    see also manic depression
body image 243
boundaries 191–3
    boundary maintenance 192
    gifts 192
    physical contact 116, 164–5, 192
    professional disagreements 165–6
    recovered memory syndrome
        167–8, 169
    socialising 192–3
    therapist's self-disclosure 193
    unclear boundaries 163–9

uncomfortable issues 159–60, 176
    see also confidentiality
breakdown 16, 103
brief solution-focused therapy 61–2
British Association for Counselling
    and Psychotherapy 33, 82, 157,
    184, 267
British Association of
    Psychotherapists 82, 184, 199,
    267
British Association for Sexual and
    Relationship Therapy 206, 263,
    267
British Psychological Society 184,
    268
Brown, Laura S. 64
bulimia nervosa 105

carbamazepine 224, 226
case notes 166, 187
causes of illness 95, 96, 97
    interpersonal 96
    intra-psychic 96
    medical 96
    socio-political 96
    spiritual 96
child psychotherapists 183, 198
Child Psychotherapy Trust 199, 264
child/adolescent problems 243
    attention deficit and hyperactivity
        disorder (ADHD) 197
    childhood sexual abuse 167–8
    learning disabilities 197
    school refusal 197
child/adolescent therapy 72, 197–200
    confidentiality 166–7, 189–90
    NHS provision 76, 197–9
    play therapy 228–9
    private sector 85, 199
    self-help agencies 199–200
    telephone helplines 199–200, 274
    voluntary sector 199
childcare, arranging 121–2
Childline 78, 199, 263, 274
Children's Act 1989 190

Childwatch 199–200, 274
citalopram 223, 225
Clark, David 54
client characteristics 145
clinical psychologists 34, 75, 100–1, 183
clinics 98
    private 85–6
Cocaine Anonymous 202, 264, 274
cognitive analytical therapy (CAT) 55, 101, 144
cognitive behavioural therapy (CBT) 45, 53, 54, 75, 101, 188, 198, 201, 215, 242
    effectiveness 142, 143–4
cognitive behaviourism 34, 44–5, 48
cognitive psychology 45
cognitive triad 45, 54
collective unconscious 53
communication difficulties 115, 204, 243
communication failures 156–63
    advice-giving 33, 157–8, 215, 219
    apparent resistance to change 158–9
    'culture gap' 213, 214
    emotional display issues 161–2
    silence, discomforting 161
    therapist's own agenda 160–1
    timetabling issues 162–3
    uncomfortable issues 159–60, 176
community leaders and elders 18
community mental health teams (CMHTs) 98, 99, 103, 187, 205
company-sponsored counselling 86–7
complaints and grievances 153, 160, 169, 188, 195–6
complementary therapies 20, 229–36
    aromatherapy 20, 230–1
    biofeedback 56, 231–2
    flower remedies 232
    herbal remedies 232–4
    homeopathy 234
    hypnotherapy 185, 234–5
    NHS provision 230
    professional associations 229–30
    relaxation therapy and meditation 19, 232, 235–6
    research evidence 229
conditioning 44, 46
confidentiality 154, 166–7, 182, 185–90
    audio recordings 187–8
    breaching 166–7, 189–90
    case notes 166, 187
    child/adolescent therapy 166–7, 189–90
    court orders and 190
    data protection 187, 188–9
    networked information 188
    protection of your information 188–9
    sharing information 166, 186–8
    in supervision 127, 166, 186
    in team settings 187
    telephone helplines 272
    video recordings 188
confiding in a stranger 124–5
congruence 57, 126
control, notion of 133
controlled trials 140
'coping' notion 114
costs 119–20, 173–4
    hidden costs 120
    missed appointments 120–1
    payment difficulties 173–4
    private sector therapy 83–4, 87, 119–20
    public sector therapy 87
    sliding scale 119, 174
    voluntary sector therapy 87
counselling 17
    professional discipline 33
    and psychotherapy distinguished 33–4
    term explained 32–3
counselling psychologists 101, 183
counsellors 34, 35, 81
    term explained 33
    see also practitioners

countertransference 43, 172–3, 194
couples therapy 67, 68, 70, 72, 85, 143, 179
creative therapies 226–9
    art therapy 227
    dance therapy 228
    drama therapy 227
    music therapy 228
    play therapy 198, 228–9
critical incident debriefing 146
CRUSE Bereavement Care 78, 264, 273
cultural issues 153, 162, 208–20
    cultural differences 209–10
    cultural identification and intolerance 216–17
    cultural sensitivity 214–17
    'culture gap' 213, 214
    finding the right practitioner 217–20
    perceptions and expectations 211–14
    transcultural perspective 219–20

dance therapy 228
Data Protection Act 1998 187, 188
De Shazer, Steve 62
delays in starting therapy 118–19
delusions 106
Department of Health website 90, 141, 271
depression 23, 54, 104, 143, 243
    agitated depression 24
    effective therapies 143, 232
    endogenous depression 106
    health-related problems 24
    herbal remedy 233
    manic depression 106, 226
    medication 223–6
    telephone helplines 273
detoxification 200, 203
diagnosis 23–4, 28, 110, 237–44
    diagnostic systems 237–41
    global assessment of functioning (GAF) 241

psychiatric diagnosis 104–8
    qualified persons 241
    self-diagnosis 242
    use in counselling and therapy 241–3
diagnostic systems 237–41
    DSM system 237, 238–41
    ICD system 237, 238
dialectical behaviour therapy 56, 144
diary keeping and note taking 53, 148
diazepam 222, 224
difference
    acknowledging 209
    cultural differences 209–10
    see also cultural issues
difficulties, dealing with 156–81
    communication failures 156–63
    ending treatment 169–75
    group therapy 175–81
    unclear boundaries 163–9
dothiepin 223
Down's Syndrome 108, 205
drama therapy 227
dream analysis 53
drug-related problems 76, 86, 200–3, 274
Drugscope 201, 264
Dryden, Windy 55
duration of treatment see open-ended therapies; time-limited therapies

e-therapy 20
early-life experiences 26, 41, 46, 51, 55
eating disorders 76, 105, 243, 274
    anorexia nervosa 105
    bulimia nervosa 105
    effective therapies 144
eclectic/integrative therapies 34, 47, 48, 49, 61–4, 165, 201
    brief solution-focused therapy 61–2
    feminist therapy 63–4
    multimodal therapy (MMT) 62–3

effectiveness of treatment 138–47,
        242–3
    client's belief in 131, 136–7
    contraindications 146
    equivalence paradox 142–3
    evidence-based practice 138, 140,
        147
    factors affecting good outcomes
        144–6
    research evidence 139–41, 146–7
    for specific problems 142–4
ego 42
ego states 60
elderly people 114, 242, 274
Ellis, Albert 55
empathy 57, 153
Employee Assistance Programmes
        (EAPs) 86–7
employment see work
ending treatment 169–75
    breach of trust 194–5
    changing therapists 173
    client–therapist incompatibility
        170–1
    cost issues 173–4
    natural finishing point 170
    negative experience of treatment
        169–71
    referral for mental health
        assessment 174–5
    therapist's decision 172–3
    time-limited treatment 66, 119,
        123, 145, 154, 155, 171–2
evidence-based practice 138, 140,
        147
examining the problem 21–30,
        149–51, 245–50, 251–5
    diagnosis 23–4, 28, 237–44, 267
    problematic behaviours 25, 28
    psychological development 25–6,
        28
    spiritual beliefs 27–8
    trauma 26–7, 28
existential therapy 58–9
existentialism 46, 58

extrovert and introvert personalities
        53
eye movement desensitisation and
        reprocessing (EMDR) 56, 143,
        185
Eysenck, Hans 139

Fairbairn, Ronald 52
family and friends 15, 17–18, 128–9,
        152
family therapy 67–8, 70, 72, 143, 144,
        177, 178, 188, 198
    'forbidden' topics 176
    NHS provision 75–6
    private sector provision 85
    therapist's role 179–80
Family Welfare Association 200, 264
feminist therapy 63–4
Ferenczi, Sandor 51
finding appropriate help 88–90
    GP and other primary care
        services 88
    Internet 20, 69, 90
    library information 89
    personal recommendations 90
    publications 89
    telephone directories 88–9
    see also professional associations;
        self-help groups and
        organisations
fixation 41
flower remedies 232
fluoxetine 222, 223
Fordham, Michael 53
formats 65–71
    see also couples therapy; family
        therapy; group therapy;
        individual face-to-face
        therapy; self-help groups and
        organisations; telephone
        counselling
free association 41, 49–50, 51, 53
Freud, Anna 51
Freud, Sigmund 40–1, 46, 51, 52
Fromm, Erich 51

gambling addiction 76, 203, 274
genetic factors 95, 105–6
genito-urinary medicine (GUM)
    clinics 206, 207
Gestalt therapy 59–60, 227
gifts between client and therapist 192
global assessment of functioning
    (GAF) 241
goals of therapy 154–5
GPs 73–4, 183
    practice counsellors 74
    referrals 88
group therapy 60, 66–7, 69, 70, 72,
    165
    anxieties about 127–8
    difficulties 175–81
    disagreements 178
    emotional swings 179
    fear of talking in front of others 176
    'forbidden' topics 176
    group dynamics 176–7, 178, 179,
      180
    private sector 85
    session rules 128
    sub-groups and cliques 178–9
    talkative people 176–7, 180
    therapist's role 177–8, 179–81
guilt 52

hallucinations 106
herbal remedies 232–4
herbal teas 233–4
HIV/AIDS 206
holistic approach to healthcare 73, 229
homeopathy 234
Horney, Karen 51
hospitals
    day hospitals 99
    hospital-based care 98–9, 103
humanistic therapies 34, 45–7, 48,
    56–61, 142, 143, 193, 214–15
    existential therapy 58–9
    Gestalt therapy 59–60, 227
    person-centred therapy 57–8
    transactional analysis (TA) 60–1

hypnotherapy 185, 234–5
hypnotics 225–6

id 41
identity problems 243
illness
    causes 95, 96, 97
    definitions of 94–5
    mental illness 95
    physical illness 94
    social 'illness' 95
imipramine 223
independent sector see private sector
    provision
individual face-to-face therapy 65–6,
    68, 70, 72, 84–5
insomnia 243
integrative therapies see
    eclectic/integrative therapies
Internet 20, 69, 90
    e-therapy 20
    see also addresses and websites
interpersonal therapy (IPT) 55–6,
    101, 143, 144
irritable bowel syndrome 231
isolation 217

Jung, Carl 42, 46, 52–3

Klein, Melanie 51–2
Klerman, Gerald 56

Lazarus, Arnold 63
learning disabilities 108, 197, 204–5,
    239
learnt helplessness 13
lesbians and gay men 202, 216, 274,
    275
library information 89
life changes, making 135–6
lithium carbonate 224, 226
lorazepam 224

manic depression 106, 110, 226, 275
Maslow, Abraham 46

massage 20, 231
May, Rollo 59
media-influenced ideas about
    counselling and therapy 116,
    135
medicalisation of problems 92
medication 20, 153, 221–6
    antidepressants 153, 223–4
    anxiolytics 224–5
    approved names and brand names
        222
    hypnotics 225–6
    side-effects 171, 224
    while engaging in counselling or
        therapy 222
meditation 235, 236
Mencap 205, 265
mental health assessment 74, 98–9,
    102–3, 174–5
mental health, definition of 93–4
mental health legislation 108–10
    Mental Health Act 1983 109
    Mental Health Act (Scotland)
        1984 109
    Mental Health (Northern Ireland)
        Order 1986 109
    'sectioning' arrangements 109–10
mental health professionals 99–102
    approved social workers (ASWs)
        100
    clinical psychologists 34, 75,
        100–1, 183
    counselling psychologists 101, 183
    occupational therapists 101, 183
    psychiatric nurses 100
    psychiatrists 99–100, 103, 104, 183
    psychotherapists 34, 35, 101
mental health services
    community mental health teams
        (CMHTs) 98, 99, 103, 187,
        205
    day hospitals 99
    hospital-based services 98–9, 103
    learning disabilities 108
    legislation 108–10

mental health assessment 74, 98–9,
    102–3, 174–5
National Health Service (NHS)
    92–111
    specialist services 98
    staffing 99–102
    structure 97–9
mental illness 30
    breakdown 16, 103
    cultural issues 216
    neuroses 104–5
    perceptions of 110–11
    personality disorders 107–8
    psychoses 105–7, 243
    telephone helplines 275
    types of 103–8
MIND (National Association of
    Mental Health) 195, 262, 275
motivational interviewing 201
multimodal therapy (MMT) 62–3
music therapy 228

Narcotics Anonymous 202, 274
National Health Service (NHS) 72,
    73
    child and adolescent services 76,
        197–9
    clinical psychology services 75
    complementary therapies 230
    family therapy 75–6
    GPs 73–4, 183
    mental health services 92–111
    psychotherapy 75
    self-referral 75
    specialist help 74–6
    substance-misuse services 76
needs, prioritising your own 114–15,
    125–6
negative experiences of therapy 117,
    160, 169–71
negative thoughts and behaviours 26,
    54, 55, 61
neuroses 104–5

see also anxiety; depression; eating disorders; obsessive compulsive disorder; phobias
non-talking treatments 171, 221–36, 269–70
  complementary therapies 20, 229–36
  creative therapies 226–9
  medication 221–6
nurses 183
  psychiatric nurses 100
  registered mental nurses (RMNs) 100

object relations theory 51–2
obsessive compulsive disorder 24, 105, 143, 239, 243
occupational therapists 101, 183
Oedipus complex 41, 51
open-ended therapies 66, 119, 123, 145, 154–5, 172
Orbach, Susie 64

panic disorder 24, 104, 143, 145
  effective therapies 143, 232
  panic attacks 16, 123, 224, 225
Parentline 200, 276
paroxetine 223
pastoral care 18
Pavlov, Ivan 43–4
peak experience 58
Perls, Fritz 60
Perls, Laura 60
person-centred therapy 57–8
personal insight 35–7, 43
personal resources and strengths 14–16, 134, 153
personality development 25–6, 28
personality disorders 107–8, 239, 243
  effective therapies 144
phenomenology 46, 59
phobias 24, 104–5, 145, 225
physical contact between clients and practitioners 116, 164–5, 192, 194

play therapy 198, 228–9
POPAN 195, 262
post-traumatic stress disorder 26, 143, 243
power map 14, 15
practitioners
  accountability 82, 230
  bad practitioners 57, 117, 126, 135, 182
  client's assessment of 153–4
  client–therapist incompatibility 170–1
  communication failures 156–63
  competence 184–5, 190
  confidentiality 127, 185–90
  cultural issues 212–20
  disciplinary action against 194, 195–6
  emotional responses 126–7
  professional membership 153, 184
  professional supervision 127, 161, 166, 186
  registration 35
  self-disclosure 193
  specialisation 183–4
  training and experience 80–1, 145, 183–4
prejudice and bigotry 216, 217
private health insurance 83, 86, 87, 203
private sector provision 82–7
  child/adolescent therapy 85, 199
  company-sponsored counselling 86–7
  costs 83–4, 119–20
  couples therapy 85
  family therapy 85
  group therapy 85
  individual therapy 84–5
  public sector funding 83, 86
  residential programmes 85–6
problems
  causes of 245–7, 251–3
  chronic problems 30
  core issues 29–30, 132

differing cultural perceptions of
213–14
examining 21–30, 149–51, 245–50,
251–5
examples 21–2
living with 134–5, 136
responses to 23
scale of 29–30, 131–3, 150–1
surface issues 29, 30
see also diagnosis
professional associations 82–3, 88,
89, 153, 184, 229–30, 267–70
propanolol 225
Prozac 222
psychiatric nurses 100
psychiatrists 99–100, 103, 104, 183
psychiatry 93
psychoanalysis 32, 40–3, 50, 75, 144,
162, 192
psychoanalysts 34, 50
psychoanalytic psychotherapists 50
psychodrama 227
psychodynamic therapies 34, 40–3,
46, 48, 49–53, 75, 101, 142, 143,
144, 198
psychologists
clinical psychologists 34, 75,
100–1, 183
counselling psychologists 101, 183
psychology 38–9
analytical psychology 32, 52–3
behaviourism 43–5, 46, 48, 53–6
cognitive psychology 45
eclectic/integrative therapy 34, 47,
48, 49, 61–4, 165, 201
humanistic therapy 34, 45–7, 48,
56–61, 142, 143, 193, 214–15
psychodynamic therapy 34, 40–3,
46, 48, 49–53, 75, 101, 142,
143, 144, 198
psychopathology 38
psychopaths 107–8
psychoses 105–7, 243
causes 105–6
manic depression 106, 110, 226

schizophrenia 77, 106–7, 110, 226
psychotherapists 34, 35, 101
child psychotherapists 183, 198
psychoanalytic psychotherapists 50
psychotherapy 17, 32, 33
and counselling distinguished
33–4
NHS provision 75
public sector provision 72–7, 87, 171,
173
costs 87
integrated care 73
limitations 76–7
see also National Health Service
(NHS)

randomised controlled trials (RCTs)
140, 147, 230, 234, 236
rational emotive behavioural therapy
(REBT) 54–5, 144
recovered memory syndrome 167–8,
169
reference books and leaflets 258–60
referral 103, 166
GP referrals 88
for mental health assessment
174–5
self-referral 75, 201
registered mental nurses (RMNs)
100
rehabilitation centres 193, 202–3
RELATE 78, 206, 266
relationship difficulties 59, 243
couples therapy 67, 68, 70, 72, 85,
143, 179
interpersonal therapy (IPT) 55–6,
101, 143, 144
see also family therapy
relaxation therapy 19, 232, 235–6
repression 41, 42
research evidence 139–41, 208
complementary therapies 229
controlled trials 140

Department of Health review and recommendations 140, 141, 142, 144
'gold standard' approach 140
meta-analysis 141
randomised controlled trials (RCTs) 140, 147, 230, 234, 236
research difficulties 146–7
research paradigm 147
research reviews 141
untreated individuals 139
reservations about seeking treatment 112–31, 154
belief in efficacy of treatment 131, 136–7
childcare problems 121–2
choosing the time to begin therapy 117–23, 170
confiding in a stranger 124–5
costs 119–20
feeling your problems are petty 125–6, 154
group therapy 127–8
maintaining privacy 128–9
making life changes 135–6
personal resources and strengths 134
reasons given for not starting therapy 113–17
self-disclosure 130–1
taking work leave 122
therapist's emotional responses 126–7
time and commitment 120–1, 123
see also difficulties, dealing with
residential programmes 85–6
Resources section 257–76
Rogers, Carl 46, 57, 58, 153
role play 60, 227
Royal College of Psychiatrists 184, 271
Ryle, Anthony 55

safeguards 182–96
abuse of client's vulnerability 182, 194

practitioners 183–5
safety issues 190–1
see also boundaries; confidentiality
St John's Wort (hypericum) 233
Samaritans 19, 273
scapegoating 217
schema-focused therapy 56, 144
schizophrenia 77, 106–7, 110, 226, 275
school refusal 197
scripts 60–1
secondary gains 158–9
'sectioning' arrangements 109–10
selective serotonin re-uptake inhibitors (SSRIs) 223, 225
self-awareness 35–7, 43
self-disclosure 130–1, 179
self-help cassettes and CDs 14, 19, 260–1
self-help CD-ROMs 20, 261
self-help groups and organisations 18–19, 69, 70, 71, 72, 81–2, 89, 171, 263–7
self-help guides and manuals 14, 19, 259–60
self-reporting 53, 149, 245–55
session length 121, 162–3
sex, compulsive 76, 203, 266, 276
sex therapists 205
sexual abuse 167–8, 243
sexual problems 16, 205–6, 243
sexual relationships between clients and therapists 164, 194, 195
sexual therapy 205–6
sexually transmitted diseases 206–7
social exclusion 13
social phobia 143
social psychology 40
social services 72, 73
social workers 100, 183
socialising between client and therapist 192–3
sociology 39–40
sociopaths 107–8
somatic complaints 144

specialist areas *see* addictions; child/adolescent therapy; learning disabilities; sexual problems; sexually transmitted diseases
spiritual beliefs 27–8
stimulus-response analysis 43, 44, 45
stress 13, 14–17, 104, 106
  coping resources 14–16, 134, 153
  effects of 16–17
  environmental stress factors 240–1
  and life events 14, 16
  'normal' stress 14, 115
  stress-related problems 231
  see also support networks and strategies
stress inoculation 56
sublimation 42
suicide 29
superego 41–2
support networks and strategies 17–21
  community leaders and elders 18
  family and friends 15, 17–18
  Internet resources 20, 69, 90
  pastoral care 18
  self-help cassettes and CDs 14, 19, 260–1
  self-help CD-ROMs 20, 261
  self-help groups and organisations 18–19, 69, 70, 71, 72, 81–2, 89, 171, 263–7
  self-help guides and manuals 14, 19, 259–60
  telephone helplines 19, 199–200, 202, 272–6
systemic therapy 67–8, 70
  see also family therapy

taking a break from therapy 174
talking treatments 17, 30–2, 35
  costs 83–4, 87, 119–20, 173–4
  effectiveness 138–47, 242–3
  finding appropriate help 88–90
  formats 65–71
  history of 31–2
  reservations about 112–31, 154
  theoretical approaches 34, 38–64
  treatment providers 71–87
Tavistock Clinic 199, 205, 266
telephone counselling 68–9, 70, 72, 86
telephone directory listings 88–9
telephone helplines 19, 199–200, 202, 272–6
temazepam 225
tension headaches and migraine 16, 231, 232
Terrence Higgins Trust 207, 266, 275
therapeutic alliance 182
therapeutic communities 85–6
therapeutic relationship 126, 144–5, 182–3, 190, 192–3
  congruence 126
  countertransference 43, 172–3, 194
  cultural issues 212–20
  personal resources and strengths 134, 153
  primary relationship 194
  transference 42–3, 50, 172, 194
  see also boundaries
therapists
  term explained 33
  see also practitioners
therapy environment 57, 191, 192
therapy formats *see* formats
thinking about starting counselling or therapy 11, 90–1
  see also reservations about seeking treatment
third force thinking *see* humanistic therapies
time-limited therapies 66, 119, 123, 145, 154, 155, 171–2
transactional analysis (TA) 60–1
transcendental meditation (TM) 236
transference 42–3, 50, 172, 194
trauma 26–7, 28, 146, 159

treatment providers 65, 71–87
  locating 88–90
  private sector 82–7
  public sector 72–7, 87, 171, 173
  voluntary sector 77–82, 87, 171,
      173
tricyclics 223
troubleshooting *see* difficulties,
    dealing with
trust 154, 182
  breach of 194–6

UK Council for Psychotherapy
    184
uncomfortable issues 159–60, 176
unconditional positive regard 57
unconscious mind 40, 41, 49, 50, 52
United Kingdom Council for
    Psychotherapy 82, 268

Valium 222
video recordings of sessions 188
voluntary sector provision 77–82,
    171, 173
  child/adolescent therapy 199
  costs 87
  funding 78

government–voluntary
    partnerships 79
  information provision 81
  models of development 78–9
  project sizes 79–80
  self-help and social contact
      provision 81–2
  therapy and counselling 80–1
vulnerability, abuse of 182, 194

Watson, John B. 43, 44
Weissman, Myrna 56
Wells, Adrian 54
Winnicott, Donald 52
work
  company-sponsored counselling
      86–7
  maintaining privacy 129
  time off for appointments 122
  work-related problems 243
World Health Organisation (WHO)
    93

Yalom, Irvin 59
YoungMinds 200, 267

zopiclone 225